TEXAS
THE BEAUTIFUL
COOKBOOK

TEXAS
THE BEAUTIFUL
COOKBOOK

Edited by
ELIZABETH GERMAINE
with special contributions by
ANN CRISWELL
Food editor, *Houston Chronicle*

Contributing writer: KAREN HARAM,
Food editor, *San Antonio Express-News*

Food consultant: VIRGINIA T. ELVERSON,
consultant and freelance writer

NEWS AMERICA PUBLISHING CORPORATION INC.
AND INTERCONTINENTAL PUBLISHING CORPORATION LTD.

Published jointly by
News America Publishing Corporation Inc.
210 South Street, New York, N.Y. 10002
(A division of News Corporation)
and Intercontinental Publishing Corporation Ltd.
6/Fl. 69 Wyndham Street, Central, Hong Kong
(A member of the Weldon/Hardie Group of Companies)

(c) 1986 News American Publishing Corporation Inc. and
Intercontintental Publishing Corporation Ltd.

Library of Congress Catalog No 86-5044

ISBN 0-940672-39-1

Associate Publisher — John Owen
Editorial Director — Elaine Russell
Publishing Co-ordinator — Cecille Haycock
Managing Editor — Di Penney
Design — Warren Penney

Typeset by Phototext
Printed in Japan
by Dai Nippon Printing Co, Tokyo

A KEVIN WELDON PRODUCTION

PRINTED IN JAPAN

Captions to end sheets and pages 1 to 9

End sheets: *Blue bonnets, prolific Texas wildflowers, blanket the countryside.*

Page 1 *Tacos, Texas style*

Pages 2–3 *Rail fence and day primroses near Round Top*

Pages 4–5 From left to right: *Houston Club biscuits, country-fried chicken and country cream gravy (recipes page 27).*

Page 6 *A kitchen with the cooking paraphernalia common for an earlier era in Texas history.*

Page 7 *Resaca in the Rio Grande Valley*

Pages 8–9 *White Oak Creek Ridge, Southwest Gillespie County*

CONTENTS

Before it burned in 1981, the Country Kitchen Restaurant was a favorite for many Bryan-College Station residents.

INTRODUCTION

Texans are known throughout the world for devotion to their homeland, and it's no wonder. The huge state's variety of natural splendors is enough to cause the envy of others to burn hotter than a jalapeno.

But the pride Texans feel goes beyond the beauty of the state and its colorful history. It encompasses fierce loyalty to even the more mundane things. Nowhere else could a source of boastfulness be found in the prickly pear cactus, the tough-shelled armadillo or an ugly bovine named the longhorn.

As contagious as thirst on an August afternoon in the Pecos region, pride quickly instills itself in those who adopt the state as their own. Nor do those who move away forget. The pride lives on long after an expatriate's slow drawl becomes faster, if it ever does.

As much because of geography as choice, Texans are fiercely individualistic. Many natives almost consider the state an independent nation, and some even joke it should secede. Nowhere is that independence more apparent than in the foods.

Texas has its own cuisine, but the menu is an amalgamation concocted by the diversity of settlers, including Mexican, German, French, Indian, Spanish, Cajun, Asian and Southern.

Foods such as tacos, nachos, chili, fajitas and barbecue are uniquely Texan, yet all can trace their origins to a specific ethnic group.

But Texans added their own special twists. Inventive Lone Star cooks took corn tortillas one step further and developed flour tortillas, much as they took tough beef and an excess of chilies and made an American favorite, chili con carne.

With a deep sense of pride, we are pleased to share these recipes reflecting the flavors of Texas. We invite you to enjoy them and celebrate the magnificence of Texas cuisine.

Some serious dominoes at the Luckenbach General Store

Overleaf: *Cattle graze, oblivious to the deepening sunset.*

Captions to pages 16 to 19
Pages 16–17 *A barbecue spread in Fort Bend County*
Pages 18–19 *Fertile farmland in the Hill Country*

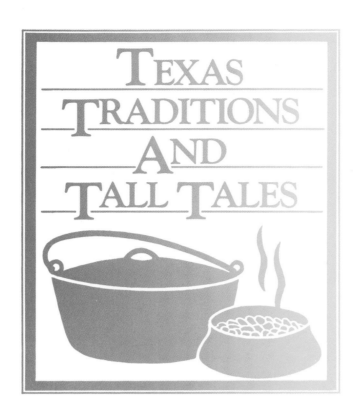

TEXAS TRADITIONS AND TALL TALES

It has been said there are two kinds of people in the world — Texans, and those who wish they were. It also has been said Texans have a tradition of telling "tall tales" and stretching the facts a bit. Perhaps that's true. But if it is, you'll never find any self-respecting Texan who will admit it.

Texans enjoy a unique life style built on a genuine pride in their state and all that makes it special. Part of that pride comes from a land varied in its geography and people. While the huge Lone Star State boasts rocky mountains, barren desert and wide plains, it also offers exceptional cities — romantic San Antonio, high-tech Houston, cosmopolitan Dallas, rugged El Paso, oil-rich Midland, Laredo with its Mexican flair, and so on.

The variety of cultures and geography makes Texas food particularly appealing. The northern part of the state has Mexican food, but it has more of a cowboy/pioneer influence. The eastern area of Texas has a hint of Cajun-Creole in its "Deep South" cuisine. In the west, including El Paso, the Indian influence is strong. And South Texas and San Antonio are where Tex and Mex really meet.

Many of the dishes that originated in Texas have gone on to national fame — Frito Pie, King Ranch Chicken, Chicken Fried Steak and Texas Chili, to name a few.

And don't forget barbecue, which comes from the Spanish "barbacoa". Texans will tell you commercial barbecuing started in the back rooms of Central Texas meat markets at the turn of the century. Today, you can scarcely find a Texas backyard, park or roadside table that doesn't boast a barbecue pit.

To do barbecuing right, do it as Texans do — in pits made from huge, 55-gallon oil drums sliced in half lengthwise, hinged and welded onto a metal frame. One bite of drum-smoked brisket, sausage or ribs will prove what Texans have always known — bigger truly is better!

Panhandle, near Perryeon on Wolf Creek

Texas barbecue

(photograph right)

In Texas, barbecue traditionally means beef, generally beef brisket. There are different regional ways of preparing it, but a common way is to rub the meat with a mixture of dry spices before cooking, cook the meat slowly at the opposite end of the barbecue from the fire (coals) and brush it occasionally with a mopping sauce as it cooks. Sometimes a red barbecue sauce is brushed on about a half hour before it is done. However, red sauces which contain tomatoes and sugar burn easily, so the red sauce is generally used as a condiment not a cooking sauce. Some cooks marinate the meat before cooking, but it is more traditional to rub the meat with dry spices and cook it very slowly.

Choose a 7-9 lb brisket; trim it but leave some fat. Rub the meat well with black pepper, salt and paprika and, if desired, garlic powder and lemon pepper marinade. At this point, some cooks like to let the meat sit at room temperature for about an hour. Build the fire with charcoal briquets in one end of the smoker or pit, adding hickory or mesquite chips which have been soaked in water. Let the fire burn down to a gray ash. Place meat on barbecue grill on end opposite the coals. Cover and cook very slowly, about 18 hours, turning a few times and brushing with Barbecue mop sauce. Serves 14-18.

Barbecue mop sauce

1 cup vinegar (can use apple cider or wine vinegar)
1/2 cup cooking oil
1/4 cup water and 1/4 cup lemon juice (or substitute 1/2 cup beef bouillon for both)
1 1/2 teaspoons salt
1 teaspoon garlic powder
1 teaspoon chili powder
1 1/2 teaspoons paprika
1 1/2 teaspoons hot pepper sauce
1/3 cup Worcestershire sauce
1/2 teaspoon ground bay leaf

Combine all ingredients in saucepan and bring to a boil. Keep warm on edge of barbecue while using. Makes about 2 1/3 cups.

Chef Harvey's barbecue sauce

Harvey Irvin, former chef of the Houston Club, made barbecued ribs a popular item on the Club's menu. He used this sauce on beef ribs, but it is equally good on pork or hamburgers. It is a full flavored, richly seasoned sauce, but not fiery.

3 medium onions, finely chopped
3/4 cup butter
4 cups tomato puree
Salt to taste
2 teaspoons paprika
2 cinnamon sticks
1 teaspoon freshly ground pepper
1 cup sugar
2 (12 oz) bottles chili sauce
1 cup pickle relish
2 teaspoons Worcestershire sauce
2 teaspoons hot pepper sauce
1/2 cup lemon juice
1 cup mixed pickling spice
2 cloves garlic sauteed in 2 tablespoons butter until golden brown
4 cups water
2 cups cider vinegar

Saute onion in butter until slightly golden. Add tomato puree and remaining ingredients except pickling spice, garlic, water and vinegar. Simmer tomato mixture, covered, for 2 hours, adding a small amount of water if needed. It should be thick. Meanwhile, boil pickling spice and garlic in water until reduced to half. Add cider vinegar and let stand 30 minutes. Strain and discard spices and garlic. Mix everything together. Makes about 8 cups.

Note: Sauce freezes well and will keep in refrigerator for 2 weeks. Recipe could be halved if desired.

LBJ barbecue sauce

1/4 cup butter
1/4 cup vinegar
1/4 cup ketchup
1/4 cup Worcestershire sauce
1/4 cup lemon juice
1/2 teaspoon hot pepper sauce
Lemon slices (optional)

Melt butter in saucepan. Stir in vinegar, ketchup, Worcestershire sauce, lemon juice, pepper sauce and lemon slices. Use as a basting sauce. Makes 1 1/4-1 1/2 cups.

Texas cornbread

1/4 cup bacon drippings or cooking oil
1 cup yellow cornmeal
1 cup flour
1/2 teaspoon salt
1 teaspoon baking powder
1 teaspoon baking soda
1 tablespoon sugar (optional)
1 cup buttermilk
2 eggs, lightly beaten

Heat bacon drippings in large, well-greased black iron skillet. Mix cornmeal, flour, salt, baking powder, baking soda and sugar. Add buttermilk, stir well. Add eggs and mix. Pour in hot bacon drippings, stirring rapidly. Have skillet sizzling hot—water should pop and sizzle when sprinkled in pan to test. Pour batter into skillet, cover, reduce heat and cook on top of stove until bread is browned and almost cooked through, about 3-4 minutes. Turn and brown other side, about 2 minutes. Cut in wedges to serve. Serves 6-8.

Tasty potato salad

12 cups (about 5 lb) sliced cooked potatoes
4 cups chopped celery
3/4 cup finely chopped parsley
1/2-3/4 cup finely chopped onion
2 1/2 cups salad dressing
1 teaspoon salt
1/4 teaspoon pepper
6-8 hard-boiled eggs, chopped (optional)
Salad greens

Toss potatoes, celery, parsley and onion together. Add salad dressing and season with salt and pepper. Add eggs and chill. Serve on salad greens. Serves 18 (3/4 cup).

Note: This recipe can easily be halved. The quantities are not critical.

Barbecued corn

(photograph below)

*There are two basic approaches
to roasting whole ears of corn.
We give them both.*

Corn in the husk: Make sure the corn is young and tender. (The time-honored test is to pierce a kernel with your fingernail—if milk spurts out, the corn is young. If the fingernail test strikes you and the supermarket proprietor as unhygienic, at least peel down the husk far enough to see that the kernels are smooth, small, plump and pale yellow — and not dried out.)

To prepare, gently pull down the husks without removing them, and peel away as much silk as possible. Smooth the husks back into shape, and tie into place at the pointed end with a strip of husk (use one of the outer ones). Soak the ears for 30 minutes in water, so they won't char too quickly, and drain. Arrange in a hinged, double-sided griller for easy turning, and grill directly on hot coals, or a little above them. Turn several times during cooking and allow about 10 minutes altogether. Allow to cool a little, then untie them, pull away the husks, and season corn generously with salt and pepper and melted butter.

Husked corn: Remove husks and silk from ears of corn and roll ears in melted butter. Arrange in a double-sided griller, and cook about 2 inches above glowing coals for 3-4 minutes each side. (If some of the kernels blacken a little, don't worry — the black ones seem extra sweet and delicious.) Season with salt and pepper and extra melted butter when cooked.

Note: Corn should be eaten in the hands so don't forget to provide plenty of paper napkins.

Coleslaw

*½ head cabbage, shredded
(about 1½ cups packed)*

1 medium onion, chopped

2 tablespoons vinegar

¼ cup evaporated milk

¼ cup salad dressing

¼ teaspoon salt

½ teaspoon dry mustard

Paprika

Combine cabbage and onion in a bowl. Beat together vinegar, milk, salad dressing, salt and dry mustard. Mix with cabbage. Cover and refrigerate several hours to let flavors blend. Sprinkle with paprika before serving. Serves 3.

Note: Can be multiplied many times over to feed a crowd.

Pot roast Texas style

4-5 lb beef blade pot roast	
2 tablespoons flour	
1 teaspoon chili powder	
1 tablespoon paprika	
2 teaspoons salt	
3 tablespoons lard or drippings	
2 medium onions	
16 cloves	
About 3-4 cups water or beef bouillon	
1 cinnamon stick	
Extra 2 tablespoons flour	
Extra ¼ cup water	

Trim meat if necessary. Combine flour, chili powder, paprika and salt. Dredge pot roast with seasoned flour. Brown pot roast in lard. Pour off drippings. Stud each onion with 8 cloves. Add enough water to come up about half way on the meat with onions and cinnamon stick. Cover and cook slowly 2½-3 hours or until tender. Remove meat to hot platter. Discard onions and cinnamon stick. Measure cooking liquid and discard fat from surface, add water to make 2 cups. Mix extra flour and extra ¼ cup water. Add to cooking liquid and cook, stirring constantly, until thickened. Serve pot roast with frijoles. Serves 8-10.

Frijoles

2 lb dried pinto beans	
½ cup bacon fat	
½ teaspoon pepper	
1 tablespoon sugar	
1 cup ketchup	
1 large onion, chopped	
1 tablespoon salt	
½ teaspoon ground cumin seed (cominos)	
1 tablespoon chili powder	
2 cloves garlic, chopped	
1 teaspoon vinegar	

Wash beans, cover well with cold water and soak overnight. Drain. Combine beans with remaining ingredients. Add water to cover. Bring to a boil, reduce heat and simmer 4-5 hours. Serves 8-10.

Hush puppies

Especially good with fried catfish, trout, shrimp, oysters, chicken or chicken-fried steak.

2½ cups yellow cornmeal	
1 teaspoon soda	
1 teaspoon salt	
2 tablespoons sugar	
2 tablespoons flour	
1 tablespoon baking powder	
1 egg, beaten	
2 cups buttermilk	
1½ cups cooking oil	

Mix dry ingredients, beat egg and buttermilk together and combine with dry ingredients; batter should hold its shape when picked up in spoon. If it is too soft, add more cornmeal. Drop by mounded tablespoonfuls into 350° oil and cook about 1½ minutes, turn and cook second side 1 minute. Allow oil to heat a few seconds after removing each batch. Delicious freshly cooked and hot; however, leftover hush puppies freeze well.

When ready to serve frozen hush puppies, place on oven rack in preheated 250° oven until very hot and crisp. Makes about 4 dozen.

Note: The batter is a little thin. It thickens somewhat if allowed to stand a few minutes after it is mixed. It produces a light, crusty hush puppy which is crunchy on the outside and light on the inside.

Fish fry

Fish filets may be fresh or frozen. Thaw frozen fish before preparing.

2 lb firm, white fish filets (catfish, yellow perch or similar fish)	
¼ cup milk	
1½ teaspoons salt	
Pinch pepper	
½ cup flour	
¼ cup yellow cornmeal	
1 teaspoon paprika	
Oil for frying	

Wipe fish filets with paper towels. Combine milk, salt and pepper. Combine flour, cornmeal and paprika. Dip fish in milk and roll in flour mixture. Pour oil in a heavy frying pan. Heat until oil is hot but not smoking. Add fish and fry 4 minutes. Turn and fry 3-4 minutes longer or until fish tests done. Drain on paper towels and serve as soon as possible.

Real Texas chili

If you like onion, it should be served at the table with the chili, but never in the chili. Beans should be fresh or dried, not canned, and also should be served as a side dish.

| 3 lb chuck or round steak |
| 6 oz beef suet, cut in pieces |
| 3-4 cloves garlic, crushed |
| 2 teaspoons salt |
| 1 teaspoon black pepper |
| 4-6 tablespoons chili powder |
| 8 tablespoons masa harina (Mexican corn flour) |
| 6 cups hot water |
| 2 tablespoons vinegar |
| 2 teaspoons or 2 cubes beef bouillon |
| Red chilies, dried and chopped or crushed (optional, add sparingly to taste) |

Remove gristle and most of the fat from meat, cut into ½-inch cubes. Place suet in a large skillet or heavy saucepan and render it. Discard the residue.

Saute meat in the hot fat until lightly browned. Add garlic, salt, pepper and chili powder. Mix well and allow seasonings to permeate meat for a few minutes.

Sprinkle in masa harina and mix thoroughly. Add hot water, vinegar, bouillon and chilies. Lower heat, cover pan and simmer until meat is very tender. In fact, some of the meat should virtually dissolve into the chili. If the chili becomes dry while cooking, add a little water from time to time. Correct seasonings, skim off some or all of the fat from the surface. Serves 6-8 chiliheads!

Pedernales River chili
(photograph left)

| 4 lb coarsely ground round steak or well-trimmed chuck |
| 1 large onion, chopped |
| 2 garlic cloves, crushed |
| 1 teaspoon oregano |
| 1 teaspoon ground cumin seed (cominos) |
| 6 teaspoons chili powder, or to taste |
| 1½ cups canned whole tomatoes |
| 2-6 generous dashes hot pepper sauce |

| Salt to taste |
| 2 cups hot water |

Saute meat, onion and garlic in large heavy pan or dutch oven until lightly browned. Add oregano, cumin, chili powder, tomatoes, hot pepper sauce, salt and hot water. Bring to a boil, lower heat and simmer about 1 hour. Skim off fat while cooking. Serves 8.

Country-fried chicken
(photograph page 4–5)

| 1 (2½-3 lb) chicken, washed and cut in pieces |
| 1 egg |
| 1 cup milk |
| 1½ cups flour seasoned with salt and pepper |
| Butter and cooking oil |

Wipe pieces of chicken with paper towels. Beat egg and milk together well. Roll chicken in seasoned flour, then in milk, then in flour again. Fry chicken pieces in a combination of butter and cooking oil (it should come half way up sides of chicken). Leave enough room in pan so chicken pieces do not touch. Cook until golden brown on first side, turn and cook on the other side, about 15-20 minutes in all. Remove from pan, drain and place in preheated 300° oven for 5-10 minutes. Serve with country cream gravy. Serves 2-3.

Note: Be sure oil is hot (about 350°) when you drop chicken in.

Country cream gravy
(photograph page 4–5)

| 2 cups milk |
| ¾ cup melted butter |
| ½ cup flour |
| Salt and pepper to taste |
| Extra 1 tablespoon butter |

Scald milk in saucepan (heat until bubbles form at edge). Melt butter in another saucepan until it begins to just barely form a haze (should not smoke). Add flour, stir until smooth and golden. Add salt and pepper to taste. Stir in scalded milk gradually and beat with a wire whisk until smooth. Reduce heat and simmer 5-10 minutes, stirring occasionally. Serves 4.

Note: Use a wire whisk for smoothest gravy. After removing from heat, finish off with a couple of pieces of butter on top.

Houston Club biscuits
(photograph page 4–5)

| 1 cup flour |
| 1 cup cake flour |
| 3 teaspoons baking powder |
| 2 tablespoons sugar |
| 1 teaspoon salt |
| ¼ cup shortening |
| ¾ cup cold milk |

Mix flour, cake flour, baking powder, sugar and salt (you don't have to sift). Cut in shortening until the size of peas. Add milk and mix well; the dough will be soft. Flour a board lightly and roll out the dough ½-inch thick. Cut into biscuits and place on greased cookie sheet barely touching. Bake in a preheated 450° oven about 10 minutes or until risen and golden brown. Makes 12-16 large biscuits.

Lemon barbecued chicken

| 2 (2½-3 lb) chickens |
| 1 cup salad oil |
| ½ cup lemon juice |
| 1 tablespoon salt |
| 1 teaspoon paprika |
| 2 teaspoons onion powder |
| 2 teaspoons basil |
| ½ teaspoon thyme |
| ½ teaspoon garlic powder |

Split chickens in half. Clean well. Place in a shallow glass dish. Combine oil, lemon juice, salt, paprika, onion powder, basil, thyme and garlic powder in a pint jar. Shake well to blend.

Pour over chicken. Cover tightly and marinate 6-8 hours or overnight, turning chicken occasionally. Bring to room temperature about 1 hour before ready to grill. Place chicken on grill, skin side up, brush with marinade often and grill 20-25 minutes. Turn chicken and brush with marinade often, until chicken is golden brown and cooked through, about 20 minutes longer. If desired, place chicken about 8-inches from broiler heat and broil in the oven. Serves 4.

Oven bag turkey

(photograph below)

Our favorite way to roast turkey, or for that matter, any meat is in oven roasting bags. The oven and pan stay clean and oven roasting bags cut about one-third off the cooking time, a real consideration when you're cooking a big stuffed turkey. Meats also stay very moist.

Put 1 tablespoon flour in oven bag and turn to coat inside; this is most important. Place bag in sturdy roasting pan large enough to contain bag when it puffs up during cooking.

Place stuffed turkey in bag. Close bag with twist tie. Make 5 (½-inch) slits in top of bag. Insert meat thermometer through bag into thickest part of turkey thigh or breast. Do not let it touch bone. Place in a preheated 350° oven and cook according to oven bag timetable. Start checking meat thermometer to see if cooked before end of suggested time. When meat thermometer registers 170° in the breast meat and 185° in the thigh meat, turkey is cooked.

Remove pan from oven and let cool slightly before handling. Open bag carefully, remove juices for gravy. Let turkey stand about 30 minutes before carving. A stuffed 8-12 lb turkey takes about 2½-3 hours in an oven roasting bag to cook. A 15 lb turkey, stuffed, about 3-3½ hours.

Perfect giblet gravy

(photograph below)

While turkey cooks (or the day before), cover the giblets, wing tips and neck bone with 8 cups cold water. Add 1 chopped onion, some chopped celery and parsley and simmer 2 hours. Strain the broth and put aside for gravy. Pick meat from neck and wing tips, chop giblets and meat fine.

Pour turkey drippings into bowl and let stand a few minutes until fat rises to top. Skim off all fat. Measure 3 tablespoons of fat into a saucepan for each 2 cups of gravy needed. Allow about ¼ cup per person. The meat juice under the fat should be used as part of the liquid for the gravy.

Set saucepan over low heat. Blend in 3 tablespoons flour for each 3 tablespoons of fat and cook until bubbly, stirring constantly. If desired, brown fat and flour slightly to give more color and flavor. Remove saucepan from heat. Stir in 2 cups liquid (meat juices, water from cooking vegetables, bouillon and/or water) and stir until completely blended with fat-flour mixture. Add chopped giblets. Simmer gently, stirring constantly, for about 5 minutes. Season to taste with salt and pepper and serve while hot.

Grandmother's favorite stuffing
(photograph left)

4 cups day-old bread cubes
4 cups crumbled cornbread
4 cups crumbled biscuits
1 cup chopped onion (including about 1/4 cup chopped green onions with tops)
1 cup chopped celery
1/4 cup finely chopped parsley
1 1/2 teaspoons sage, crushed
1 teaspoon salt
1/4 teaspoon pepper
1-4 cups turkey or chicken broth
1/2 cup melted butter
2 eggs, slightly beaten

Combine all ingredients except broth, butter and eggs. Toss well. Add broth, butter and eggs. Mix well, but lightly; it should be very moist. Use to stuff neck and body cavities of turkey, or for ease in preparation and serving, cook separately in a well greased baking dish or casserole during the last 45 minutes the turkey is in the oven. Makes 11-12 cups.

Cherry Coke salad

1 (16 oz) can Bing cherries, pitted and drained
1 (20 oz) can crushed pineapple, drained
2 cups fruit juice and water (combine cherry and pineapple juice plus water)
1 (4 serving-size) package black cherry gelatin
1 (4 serving-size) package raspberry, cherry or strawberry gelatin
1 (12 oz) can Coca-Cola, cold
2 (3 oz) packages cream cheese, at room temperature
1 cup celery, finely diced
1 cup coarsely chopped pecans
1/2 cup flaked coconut (optional)

Place drained fruit in a bowl. Heat fruit juice to boiling point. Pour over combined gelatins. Stir until dissolved. Add Coke, chill until slightly thickened. Beat cream cheese and add to fruits in bowl; add celery, nuts and coconut, mix and fold into gelatin. Chill until firm. Serves 12.

Note: Amounts of fruit, cream cheese and nuts may be varied to taste.

Cranberry-apple gelatin salad
(photograph left)

1 (4 serving-size) package mixed fruit or raspberry gelatin
3/4 cup boiling water
1 tart medium apple, finely chopped (about 1 cup)
1 cup whole-berry cranberry sauce
1 tablespoon grated orange rind
1/8 teaspoon salt
1/8 teaspoon cinnamon
Pinch cloves

Dissolve gelatin in boiling water. Add remaining ingredients. Stir to blend. Pour into a 3-cup mold. Chill at least 5 hours. Serve as a relish with meat or poultry. Serves 6-8.

One-hour rolls

2 cakes compressed yeast or 2 envelopes dry yeast
1/4 cup warm water (85° for compressed yeast, 110° for dry yeast)
1 1/2 cups buttermilk, heated to lukewarm
1/4 cup sugar
1/2 cup melted shortening or cooking oil
1 teaspoon salt
4 1/2 cups flour
1/2 teaspoon baking soda
Butter

Dissolve yeast in warm water. Combine buttermilk, sugar, melted shortening and salt. Sift flour and soda into a large bowl. Mix yeast with buttermilk and add to flour mixture. Mix well. Allow to stand 10 minutes. Roll out 1/2-inch thick and cut in desired shapes.

Melt some butter in a baking pan, place rolls in pan, turning each over to allow butter to coat tops. Allow rolls to stand 30 minutes and bake in a preheated 425° oven for 10-12 minutes. Makes 4-5 dozen, depending on size of rolls.

King Ranch chicken

The King Ranch, which sprawls over half of South Texas, is one of the living Texas legends. It was here that Santa Gertrudis cattle were developed, but for some reason this chicken recipe has become associated with the famous ranch.

This is an easy, good casserole for a buffet supper.

1 (3½-4 lb) chicken, poached, boned and cut into bite-size pieces
1 large onion, chopped
1 large green pepper, chopped
1 (8 oz) package tortillas
Broth (from cooking chicken) or canned chicken broth
8 oz Cheddar cheese, grated
1½ teaspoons chili powder
Garlic salt to taste
1 (10¾ oz) can condensed cream of chicken soup
1 (10¾ oz) can condensed cream of mushroom soup
1 (10 oz) can tomatoes with green chilies

Combine chicken, onion and pepper. Layer alternately with tortillas, which have been dipped into hot chicken broth just long enough to soften, in a shallow 3-quart greased casserole. Top with grated cheese and sprinkle with chili powder and garlic salt. Spoon over chicken soup, mushroom soup and tomatoes which have been broken up into smaller pieces. Bake in a preheated 350° oven for 30-45 minutes or until hot. Serves 8-10.

Chicken and andouille gumbo

1 (6-7 lb) hen or 2 (3 lb) chickens, cut in pieces
Salt, pepper and cayenne pepper to taste
½ cup cooking oil
⅔ cup flour
2 large onions, chopped
4 green onions, chopped
2 ribs celery, chopped
2 lb andouille sausage, sliced
5 cloves garlic, crushed
2 teaspoons Worcestershire sauce
4 quarts boiling water
3 tablespoons chopped parsley
2-3 tablespoons gumbo file (ground sassafras leaves)
2 dozen oysters (optional)
Cooked white rice

Wipe chicken pieces and season with salt, pepper and cayenne pepper. Heat oil and flour together in a large (4-gallon) pot and cook roux, stirring constantly, until it is golden brown.

Add chicken and cook about 10 minutes. Add onion and celery, cook until onion is clear, about 5 minutes. Add andouille sausage and garlic and cook for a few minutes, season with salt, pepper and cayenne pepper. Add Worcestershire sauce and boiling water, simmer gumbo about 2 hours or until meat is tender. While gumbo is cooking, continue to add boiling water so you still have 4 quarts of liquid when the gumbo is cooked.

Add parsley and let gumbo stand for at least an hour before serving. Add file as desired. Add oysters 20 minutes before resting period is over. Before serving, heat gumbo to boiling point and serve over rice. Serves 8 or more.

Note: Firm Polish-type sausage or chunks of smoked ham may be substituted for andouille sausage.

Smoky country-style ribs

(photograph right)

4 lb Texas country-style pork ribs
Garlic salt
Freshly ground pepper
1¼ cups ketchup
¾ cup brown sugar, firmly packed
½ cup chili sauce
2 tablespoons cider vinegar
2 tablespoons liquid smoke
1 tablespoon lemon juice

Sprinkle ribs with garlic salt and pepper. Combine remaining ingredients in a saucepan. Cook over medium heat for about 10 minutes, stirring occasionally, keep warm. Place ribs, rib bones down, on rack of a shallow roasting pan. Baste with sauce. Bake in a preheated 325° oven for 1½-2½ hours, turning and basting with sauce every 30 minutes. Cut into serving-size portions. Heat remaining sauce and serve with ribs. Serves 4-6.

Chicken-fried steak with cracker crumb batter

1½ lb top round steak, ½-inch thick
1 beaten egg
1 tablespoon milk
1 cup fine cracker crumbs
¼ cup cooking oil
Salt and freshly ground pepper

Pound steak ¼-inch thick and cut in serving pieces. Blend egg and milk. Dip meat in egg mixture, then in crumbs. Slowly brown meat in hot oil, turning once. Cover, cook over low heat 45 minutes-1 hour until tender. Season to taste. Serve with Country cream gravy. Serves 6.

Note: Flour seasoned with salt and pepper may be substituted for cracker crumbs.

Texas hash

| 2 large onions, chopped |
| 2 green peppers, chopped |
| 2 tablespoons oil |
| 1½ lb ground beef |
| 1 (16 oz) can tomatoes |
| ½ cup rice |
| 1 teaspoon chili powder |
| 2 teaspoons salt |
| ¼ teaspoon pepper |

Brown onion and pepper slowly in oil. Add ground beef and cook until mixture is crumbly. Pour off any fat. Add tomatoes, rice and seasonings. Mix thoroughly.

Turn into a 1½-quart casserole, cover and cook in a preheated 350° oven for 45 minutes or until cooked. Serves 4-6.

Venison ham

| 1 fresh venison ham |
| Marinade for game (page 32) |
| Salt |
| Bacon drippings |
| 1-1½ tablespoons cornstarch |

Marinate venison in an enamelware or glass dish in refrigerator about 2 days, turning every 12 hours. Remove from marinade, wipe dry, season with salt and brown well on all sides in bacon drippings. Remove venison from pan. Pour off excess fat and deglaze pan with ½ cup of the marinade which has been strained. Return venison to pan, cover tightly and bake in a preheated 350° oven for several hours until well done. Time varies according to size and age of animal. If necessary, add more marinade with an equal amount of water during cooking, maintaining 1½ inches of liquid in bottom of pan.

When done, remove meat to a hot platter. Thicken pan juices with cornstarch to serve with meat.

Chile con queso

| 1 lb pasteurized processed cheese spread loaf |
| 1 (10 oz) can tomatoes with green chilies or 6 tablespoons bottled picante sauce |

Cut cheese in chunks and melt in the top of a double boiler or in microwave oven. Blend in tomatoes. Keep hot in a chafing dish. May be thinned with a little milk if necessary. Serve with tortillas, corn chips or pieces of crisp vegetables. Enough for 20 as an appetizer.

Marinade for game

Venison backstrap roast is especially delicious when marinated in this mixture for 24 hours, then cooked over charcoal until just pink in the center. Marinade is also good for beef, pork, duck, goose and dove.

| 1 onion, sliced |
| 2 carrots, sliced |
| 4 green onions, chopped |
| ¼ cup chopped parsley |
| 1 teaspoon salt |
| 10-12 peppercorns |
| 4 juniper berries, crushed |
| ¼ teaspoon thyme |
| 1 cup red wine |
| 1 cup olive oil |

Mix all ingredients to make the marinade. Marinate game in refrigerator at least 12 hours, turning several times. Wipe game and proceed to cook as desired. Makes about 4 cups.

Note: Check food import shops or specialty stores for juniper berries.

Barley

This often neglected grain is a delicious accompaniment to game birds or roast beef.

Pearl barley: Rinse in a colander, then cover with cold water and add 1 teaspoon salt for each 1 cup barley. Bring to a boil, reduce heat to a simmer and cook 1 hour or until tender. You may need to skim off the top occasionally as the barley cooks. Stir now and then to keep from sticking.

Season with salt, pepper and butter. Sliced mushrooms and chopped green onions browned in butter make a delicious addition mixed with the cooked barley, which is bland.

Scotch barley: Soak in cold water to cover overnight. Drain, cover with fresh cold water, then proceed as with pearl barley.

Treebeard's red beans and rice

Cajun fare is tops at Treebeard's restaurant downtown Houston on Old Market Square. Owner Dan Tidwell passes along the secrets of Treebeard's soul-satisfying red beans, rice and sausage.

| 1 lb dried red kidney beans |
| 6 cups water |
| 2 medium onions, chopped |
| 2 ribs celery with leaves, chopped |
| ½ green pepper, chopped |
| 2 cloves garlic, crushed |
| Ham bone or bacon drippings if available |
| 1 lb or more large smoked link sausage, sliced |
| Optional seasonings: salt, freshly ground pepper, fresh garlic, cayenne pepper (for a hot, spicy flavor), bay leaves, thyme and/or oregano |

Soak beans in water overnight, or bring to a boil, reduce heat and simmer 2 minutes, turn off heat, cover and let stand 1 hour.

When ready to cook, add onion, celery, green pepper, garlic, and ham or drippings. Bring to a boil and simmer about 2 hours until beans are soft and start to thicken at the bottom of the pan. Add sausage and desired seasonings during the last 30 minutes. Serve with hot fluffy rice and a green salad and enjoy a great meal. Serves 6.

Note: If desired, serve with grated sharp Cheddar cheese, chopped green onions and jalapeno cornbread or French bread, as they do at Treebeard's, or with Tabasco sauce, Tabasco peppers in vinegar or Louisiana hot sauce, but watch that cayenne pepper!

Old-fashioned mustard greens

Slash a piece of salt pork in several places. Boil in a large saucepan in water to cover, about 20-30 minutes. Meanwhile, wash 2 bunches mustard greens or other greens thoroughly. Cut off roots and any tough stems. Rinse until no grit clings to greens. Add greens to salt pork water, add pepper to taste. Cook, covered, until tender, about 25-30 minutes. Most old-time Texas cooks add a pinch of sugar to the cooking water too. No extra salt is needed when salt pork is used.

If salt pork is not used, 4 slices bacon may first be cooked in saucepan, then water and greens added.

Drain and save the liquid—this is pot "likker". Chop greens and season to taste. Slice pork and place on top of chopped greens; pour pot "likker" over all. Serves 4.

Frito pie

This is an instant dish and quite inexpensive.

Cover the base of a casserole dish with small size Fritos—don't skimp on the corn chips. Cover with a thick layer of homemade or canned chili. Sprinkle chili generously with grated sharp American cheese, mild Cheddar or Longhorn cheese. Top with chopped white onion (not too finely chopped). Can make more than one layer, depending on quantity required. Place in a preheated 350° oven and cook until hot and bubbly!

Baked beans

| ½-1 lb sliced lean bacon |
| 1 medium onion, chopped |
| 1 (3 lb 7 oz) can pork and beans |
| ¼ cup dark molasses |
| ½ cup ketchup |
| ½ teaspoon dry mustard |
| ¼ cup brown sugar, firmly packed |

Fry bacon until crisp, remove from pan and cut into pieces. In bacon fat, cook onion until soft. Combine all ingredients, including bacon fat, in a large casserole, cover and cook in a preheated 350° oven for at least 1 hour. Serves 10-12.

Hopping John

| 1 lb (2 cups) dried black-eyed peas |
| 6 cups cold water |
| 1 medium onion, sliced |
| 2 teaspoons salt |
| ¼ lb lean salt pork, sliced |
| 2 cups hot cooked rice |

Wash peas, add water and boil for 2 minutes. Remove from heat and let stand 1 hour. Boil peas gently in the same water with onion, salt and salt pork until peas are soft, about 1 hour. Add rice and cook 10 minutes more to blend flavors. Serves 8-10.

Ice cream pecan balls and hot fudge sauce (page 36)

Mexican rice

½ cup cooking oil

1 cup rice

4 cloves garlic, crushed

12 black peppercorns, ground

¼ teaspoon ground cumin seed (cominos)

1 onion, chopped

2 tomatoes, peeled and chopped or 1 cup canned tomatoes

½ green pepper, coarsely chopped

2 cups water

Heat oil until hot in an iron skillet or saucepan. Add rice and stir constantly until it is nice and brown. Remove from heat and drain off all the oil. Add spices and stir briefly. Add onion, tomatoes, pepper and water. Stir well and bring to a boil. Cover pot, lower heat and allow to simmer. Do not stir. Cook until it has absorbed all the liquid, being careful not to allow it to burn. Serves 4.

Cheese grits casserole

2 cups hominy grits

6 cups water

1 teaspoon salt

½ cup butter

½ cup milk

4 eggs, beaten

2 (6 oz) rolls garlic cheese

Stirring constantly, pour grits into boiling salted water in a large saucepan. Cook until thick. Add butter, milk, eggs and cheese (cut in small pieces). Stir thoroughly until cheese melts.

Place in a large, greased casserole. Bake in a preheated 350° oven about 30 minutes. Serves 10.

Fried green tomatoes

The pioneers used green tomatoes in relish, and in West Texas in pie when other pie-makings were scarce. We like them fried like this.

Select firm green tomatoes. Slice about ¼ to ½-inch thick. Dip each slice in cornmeal and sprinkle with salt and pepper and a pinch of sugar. Fry in bacon fat or oil until brown, turn once. One tomato makes 3-4 slices. Serve 1 tomato per person.

Mother Malone's heavenly hash

3 (16 oz) cans pear halves

1 (16 oz) can light pitted cherries

2 (20 oz) cans pineapple tidbits

1 egg yolk

2 teaspoons prepared mustard

½ cup milk

2 cups miniature marshmallows

1 cup whipping cream

Slice pear halves and cherries. Drain all fruit overnight, then chill in refrigerator. Make a dressing by blending the egg yolk with mustard and milk. Place pan over low heat and stir until thick. Do not allow to boil. Refrigerate. Add marshmallows to chilled fruit mixture, pour dressing over and add cream, which has been whipped until stiff. Fold carefully together. Chill and serve.

Texas prune cake

(photograph left)

½ cup shortening

1 cup sugar

2 eggs

1⅓ cups flour

½ teaspoon soda

½ teaspoon salt

½ teaspoon cinnamon

½ teaspoon nutmeg

½ teaspoon allspice

½ teaspoon baking powder

⅔ cup buttermilk or sour milk

⅔ cup chopped pitted prunes

Prune frosting:

2 tablespoons butter

2 tablespoons prune juice

1 tablespoon lemon juice

½ teaspoon cinnamon

½ teaspoon salt

1½ cups powdered sugar

½ cup chopped pecans

½ cup chopped prunes

Cream shortening, add sugar and eggs. Beat well and mix in combined dry ingredients alternately with buttermilk. Add chopped prunes and mix thoroughly. Bake in 2 (9-inch) round cake pans lined with waxed paper, in a preheated 350° oven for about 25 minutes or until layers test done. When cool, frost cake with prune frosting.
Prune frosting: Cream butter with juices, cinnamon and salt. Add chopped pecans and prunes. Add sugar last, beating in gradually.

Coke cake

2 cups flour
2 cups sugar
1½ cups chopped marshmallows or miniature marshmallows
½ cup shortening
½ cup margarine
3 tablespoons cocoa
1 cup Coca-Cola
½ cup buttermilk
1 teaspoon baking soda
2 eggs, beaten

Coke cake frosting:

½ cup margarine
3 tablespoons cocoa
6 tablespoons Coca-Cola
1 lb powdered sugar
1 cup chopped pecans

Sift together flour and sugar, stir in marshmallows and set aside.

Bring to a boil, shortening, margarine, cocoa and Coke. Remove from heat and pour over dry ingredients. Stir in buttermilk, baking soda and eggs. Do not beat this cake mixture.

Pour into a greased 13x9x2-inch pan and bake in a preheated 350° oven for 45 minutes or until done. Cool about 30 minutes before frosting cake.

Coke cake frosting: Bring margarine, cocoa and Coke to a boil. Boil a minute, remove from heat and gradually add sugar. Stir in pecans.

Ice cream pecan balls

(photograph page 33)

For each serving:

1 scoop vanilla ice cream
Chopped toasted pecans, salted or plain
Hot fudge sauce

Roll round scoop of ice cream in chopped nuts until well coated. Place in dessert dish. Top with Hot fudge sauce.

Note: For convenience, you may want to freeze the nut-coated ice cream balls until ready to serve.

Hot fudge sauce

(photograph page 33)

½ cup unsalted butter, at room temperature
1⅔ cups powdered sugar
⅔ cup evaporated milk
6 squares (6 oz) semi-sweet chocolate
¼ teaspoon salt

Cream butter and sugar together in the top of a double boiler until smooth. Add milk and chocolate and allow to cook over simmering water, without stirring, for 30 minutes. Remove from heat and stir in salt. Stir until smooth. Do not add salt before removing sauce from heat. Makes about 2 cups of thick fudgy sauce.

Note: This sauce can be successfully reheated in a double boiler or microwave oven.

Sweet potato pie

1½ cups hot, mashed sweet potatoes (about 3 medium potatoes)
3 eggs, slightly beaten
⅓ cup brown sugar, firmly packed
Pinch salt
¼ teaspoon cinnamon
¼ cup half and half or cream
2 tablespoons melted butter or margarine
¼ cup brandy or sherry or 1 teaspoon vanilla
1 (9-inch) unbaked pastry pie crust

Bake potatoes until tender. Peel, slice and mash. Beat eggs, sugar, salt, spices, half and half, butter and brandy into potatoes. Pour into unbaked pie crust. Bake in a preheated 450° oven for 10 minutes. Reduce heat to 350° and bake for an additional 30 minutes or until filling is set and crust brown.

Note: 1½ cups of mashed canned sweet potato may be substituted for fresh sweet potato.

Fudgy Texas brownies

½ cup margarine, softened
1-1½ cups sugar
1 (16 oz) can chocolate syrup
4 eggs
1 cup flour
1 cup chopped nuts

Frosting:

1 cup margarine
1-1½ cups sugar
⅓ cup evaporated milk
½ cup chocolate chips

Cream margarine and sugar together. Slowly add syrup, beating well. Add eggs, one at a time, beating well after each addition. Stir in flour and nuts. Pour into a greased 13x9x2-inch baking pan and bake in preheated 350° oven for 25 minutes or until brownies test done. When cool, frost and cut into bars. Makes 2 dozen.

Frosting: Combine margarine, sugar and milk in a saucepan and bring to a boil. Boil 2 minutes. Remove from heat and add chocolate chips. Stir until they are dissolved.

Texas plantation pecan pie

This is our most popular pecan pie and one of the best we've ever tasted. The recipe is from a former "Mrs. Texas".

⅓ cup melted butter
1 cup sugar
1 cup light corn syrup
1 teaspoon salt
1½ teaspoons vanilla
4 eggs
1 (8 oz) package pecans or mixed walnuts and pecans
1 (9-inch) unbaked pastry pie crust

Thoroughly beat butter, sugar, syrup, salt and vanilla together. Add eggs and beat gently until blended. Fold in nuts. Pour into unbaked pie crust. Bake in a preheated 375° oven for 40-50 minutes.

Note: More pecans can be added to the pie if desired.

Texas pecan cake

2 cups butter or margarine
3 cups sugar
7 eggs, separated
5 cups flour, sifted
1 teaspoon baking soda dissolved in 4 tablespoons warm water
1 (2 oz) bottle pure lemon extract
4 cups pecan pieces
2 cups candied pineapple pieces
2 cups candied cherries, halved

Cream butter and sugar well. Add well beaten egg yolks. Add a little flour, the soda dissolved in water, lemon extract and a little more flour. Dredge pecans and candied fruit with some of the flour. Stir into batter with remaining flour. Beat egg whites stiff and fold in well. Bake in a large lined tube pan in a preheated 300° oven for 2½ hours. Place foil over and under cake while baking.

Note: This makes an extra large cake—bake in 2 loaf pans if desired and adjust cooking time accordingly.

Son-of-a-bitch stew

In his book, "A Bowl of Red," Frank X. Tolbert recounts the story of Son-of-a-Bitch Stew (or Son-of-a-Gun or Gentle-man-From-Odessa Stew as it is more politely called).

Legend has it that S.O.B. acquired its name when an Eastern visitor at a Texas ranch asked one of the cowboys what was in the delicious stew the cook had just served him.

"I'll be a son-of-a-bitch if I know all that goes in it. Different cooks put in different things, but it's sure good," replied the cowboy.

The range cook did put into it an unweaned calf, all the marrow gut, brains, sweetbreads, liver, tongue and various other glands and unmentionables.

Tolbert says his grand-uncle, a trail driver, was once introduced at a stock show as "the gentleman from Odessa."

Asked to explain this, his uncle said that when Odessa first became a town it was considered rough and uncivilized. The surrounding towns had a joke. They said a gentleman from Odessa would be a son-of-a-bitch anyplace else.

Eventually, many cafes in West Texas sometimes had the entree printed as Gentleman From Odessa Stew.

Texas caviar (Pickled black-eyed peas)

2 (15 oz) cans or 4 cups cooked black-eyed peas, well drained
1 cup salad oil
¼ cup wine vinegar
1 clove garlic or garlic powder
¼ cup thinly sliced onion
⅓ teaspoon salt

Place peas in a bowl, add remaining ingredients and mix thoroughly. Place in a covered container in refrigerator and remove garlic after 1 day. Keep at least 2 days or as long as 2 weeks before eating. May be served as an accompaniment to a buffet meal or on crackers or corn chips.

Rattlesnake steak

2 lb rattlesnake meat
Salt and pepper to taste
Paprika to taste
¾ cup flour
½ cup cooking oil

Cut meat into 1-inch thick steaks. Dredge meat in a combination of salt, pepper, paprika and flour. Fry in oil until cooked and nicely browned, about 10 minutes. Serves 4.

Alligator chili

1 large onion, finely chopped
2 tablespoons bacon drippings
1 lb ground alligator meat
1 (15 oz) can New Orleans-style red beans or ranch-style beans
1 (8 oz) can tomato sauce
2-3 cups water
3-4 tablespoons chili powder
Salt to taste

Brown onion in drippings until wilted, add ground alligator meat and saute 4-5 minutes. Add beans, tomato sauce, water, and chili powder. Stir well and add salt. Cover and simmer 45 minutes-1 hour, stirring occasionally. Serves 4-6.

Fricassee of armadillo

1 armadillo (about 4 lb dressed)
¾ cup flour
Salt and pepper to taste
¾ cup oil
¾ cup milk

Disjoint armadillo as you would a chicken. Dredge in flour, salt and pepper. Brown in oil. Remove from pan and pour off oil. Return meat to pan, add milk, cover and simmer over low heat for 1½ hours or until tender. Serves 4-6.

Overleaf: Holding stock at the tank in King Country

BEEF IS KING

Texans love beef in any form — from thick, juicy hamburgers to tender T-bones cooked over native mesquite.

From the days of the early pioneers, Texans have been cattlemen and ranchers. The legendary Texas Longhorn has given way to more modern breeds, including the Santa Gertrudis, which was developed on the famous King Ranch. Founded by Captain Richard King, this South Texas ranch, long famous for its beef, is still one of the largest in the country.

Beef has been consumed in generous quantities since the days of the cattle drives, when necessity invented one of Texas' most popular dishes — Chicken Fried Steak. When cowboys got hungry, the trail cook (called Cookie) would slice a piece of beef off the hindquarter, tenderize it by pounding it again and again to break up the tough connective tissue, roll it in seasoned flour, and fry it in hot oil. Some inventive cook then took the operation one step further and topped the meat with a milk gravy, much as it is still served today.

The annual roundup of cattle was a custom in Texas for nearly 100 years. Even today, that grand tradition is honored each year in San Antonio, Houston and other Texas cities. In February, groups of trail riders set out from various points and converge on these cities, where festivities culminate in huge livestock shows and rodeos. The thousands of people who take part in these trail rides include doctors, lawyers and executives as well as ranchers and cowhands. Their enthusiasm for the sacrifices of these hard drives is reminiscent of the spirit associated with the state's frontier past.

But one area in which the riders don't sacrifice is good food. You can bet that, true to their heritage, riders still enjoy their beef. Served on the trail as it was 100 years ago, steak, chili and barbecue never tasted better.

Making biscuits out on the range near Abilene

Beef salad platter

(photograph left)

| 1 small lettuce |
| 2 medium carrots, cut in julienne |
| 8 slices rare roast beef |
| 1 cucumber, cut in julienne |
| 2 medium tomatoes, sliced |
| 2 teaspoons chopped parsley |
| ½ honeydew melon, cut into crescents or wedges |
| 1 bunch radishes |
| **For dressing:** |
| ⅓ cup plain yogurt |
| ⅓ cup sour cream |
| 1 teaspoon Worcestershire sauce |
| 4 tablespoons grated Parmesan cheese |

Shred lettuce and arrange on a platter with carrot sticks on top. Arrange beef slices and cucumber sticks on the sides of the platter. Add tomato slices and sprinkle with parsley, then add honeydew and radishes. Prepare the dressing by mixing all ingredients together thoroughly, and serve separately or spoon over the salad. Serves 4.

Herbed beef salad

Leftover roast beef makes a very special salad.

| 6-8 slices rare roast beef, cut in julienne (there should be about 2 cups) |
| 2 medium onions, thinly sliced |
| ¼ cup white wine vinegar |
| ½ cup olive oil |
| 3 tablespoons drained capers |
| 3 tablespoons chopped parsley |
| 4 green onions, finely chopped |
| 2 teaspoons chopped fresh marjoram or ½ teaspoon dried |
| 2 teaspoons chopped fresh tarragon or ½ teaspoon dried |
| ½ teaspoon dry mustard |
| Salt and freshly ground pepper |
| Lettuce leaves to serve |

Place beef in a bowl and add onion slices separated into rings. Toss with remaining ingredients, cover, and stand at room temperature for 2-3 hours, stirring occasionally. Serve in a bowl lined with lettuce leaves. Serves 4.

Texas beef nuggets

A former state beef cook-off winner for Houstonian Helen Worden.

| 2 lb beef tenderloin, cut in 2-inch slices |
| ⅔ cup flour seasoned with salt and pepper |
| 2 cups cornflake crumbs |
| 1 cup finely chopped pecans |
| ½ cup grated Parmesan cheese |
| 1 teaspoon paprika |
| ½ teaspoon nutmeg |
| 4 tablespoons butter |
| Extra 4 tablespoons flour |
| 2 cups milk |
| 2 teaspoons Worcestershire sauce |
| 1 (10 oz) package sharp cheese, grated |

Cut beef tenderloin in bite-size squares. Shake pieces in bag with seasoned flour until each piece is individually coated. Refrigerate while continuing preparation.

Thoroughly blend cornflake crumbs, chopped pecans, Parmesan cheese, paprika and nutmeg in a bowl.

In a saucepan melt butter, add flour and stir to blend. Add milk, heat and stir until mixture boils. Lower heat to simmer, add Worcestershire sauce and grated cheese and continue stirring and cooking until cheese melts. Keep warm.

Dip each floured beef cube in cheese sauce, let drain a little, then roll in crumb mixture so all sides are well coated. Place on well buttered or Teflon-coated cookie sheets, leaving space between each. If you prefer to prepare ahead of time, at this stage, they may be chilled until needed.

Bake in a preheated 350° oven for 15-20 minutes until cubes are a deep golden brown. Cool slightly before removing from pan with spatula. Delicious served warm or at room temperature. Serves 10.

Hamburger hors d'oeuvre

| 1 lb ground beef |
| 4 tablespoons dark soy sauce, imported |
| 1 teaspoon sugar |
| 3 green onions, finely chopped |
| 4 slices sandwich bread |

Mix all ingredients, except bread, together. Spread evenly over each slice of bread. Bake in a preheated 450° oven for 8-10 minutes, then broil until meat is brown, about 2-3 minutes. Cut each slice diagonally twice into triangular pieces or lengthways into 3 strips. Serve immediately.

Beef tartare

Piquant raw ground beef served with garnishes makes a superb appetizer. Here's an unusual way of presenting it.

8 oz beef tenderloin

2 egg yolks

1 tablespoon Dijon mustard

1 tablespoon ketchup

1 tablespoon grated onion

1 clove garlic, crushed

Salt and freshly ground pepper

¼ cup finely chopped parsley

1 medium onion, sliced and separated into rings

Extra Dijon mustard

Slivered sweet gherkins or dill pickles

Remove any fat and gristle from beef, grind meat finely or chop very finely by hand. Combine with egg yolks, mustard, ketchup, onion, garlic, and salt and pepper to taste. Shape into 2 thick patties, and roll edges in chopped parsley. Arrange on a platter with onion rings, extra mustard, and sweet gherkins or dill pickles, and serve with crusty bread. Serves 6-8 as an appetizer.

Pan-fried steak with peppercorn mustard sauce

The sauce adds flavor and piquancy.

4 thick slices beef tenderloin

Salt and freshly ground pepper

1 clove garlic, crushed

4 tablespoons butter

1 tablespoon olive oil

⅔ cup whipping cream

1 tablespoon Dijon mustard

1 tablespoon drained green or pink peppercorns

Trim any fat from steaks, and season with salt, pepper and crushed garlic, rubbing it in.

Heat butter and oil in a heavy frying pan, and saute steaks on both sides for 3 to 5 minutes, or until cooked to your liking.

Remove steaks to a heated platter. Add cream to pan, stirring to get up crusty bits from the bottom. Add mustard and peppercorns and continue stirring over low heat until sauce thickens a little. Taste for seasoning, spoon over steaks, and serve at once. Serves 4.

Mushroom-wine steak sauce

When you're in the mood for a thick piece of tender steak, do it justice with this superb sauce.

4 tablespoons butter

1 tablespoon cooking oil

¼ lb mushrooms, finely chopped

1 clove garlic, crushed

1 small onion, finely chopped

2 tablespoons flour

Dash of cayenne pepper

1 cup beef bouillon or stock

¾ cup red wine

Salt and freshly ground pepper, to taste

Heat butter and oil and fry mushrooms, garlic and onion over moderate heat until softened. Sprinkle flour and cayenne over and stir until flour is brown, about 3 minutes.

Slowly stir in bouillon and wine, and bring to a boil. Simmer very gently 20 minutes, stirring often. Season with salt and pepper to taste and serve over freshly grilled or pan-fried thick pieces of sirloin or filet steak. Makes enough for 4 servings.

Brandied pepper steaks

(photograph left)

There are many versions of pepper steak — this one is easy, with a simple but delicious sauce of brandy and creamy pan juices.

| 4 thick slices beef tenderloin |
| 2 tablespoons black peppercorns, coarsely crushed |
| 6 tablespoons butter |
| Salt |
| 3 tablespoons brandy |
| ½ cup whipping cream |

Trim excess fat from steaks. Press peppercorns into both sides, allow to stand at room temperature for 30 minutes.

Heat the butter in a large, heavy frying pan. Add steaks and cook over moderately high heat for 2 minutes each side, or until well browned. Season with salt.

Lower heat to moderate and cook for another 2 minutes each side, or until done to your liking.

Remove steaks to a heated platter. Add brandy and cream to juices in pan, stir until slightly thickened, and taste for seasoning. Spoon over steaks and serve at once. Serves 4.

Carpetbag steak

For each person, allow a piece of sirloin steak cut at least 1-inch thick, and 2-3 oysters. You will also need salt and freshly ground black pepper, a little oil, and pats of butter for garnish.

Trim excess fat from steak, and snip remaining fat at intervals so steak will remain flat while grilling. Cut a pocket in each steak, stuff with oysters, and fasten opening with small skewers.

Season steak on both sides with freshly ground pepper, and allow to stand 5 minutes.

Preheat barbecue to very hot, and brush grill bars and steak with oil. Grill at high heat until brown and crusty both sides, turning once. Then lower heat to moderate, or move steaks away from intense heat if you can't adjust barbecue heat.

Allow about 4 to 5 minutes each side for rare steak, 6 to 7 minutes for medium rare.

When steak is cooked, remove skewers and season each side lightly with salt. Serve with a generous pat of butter on top.

Grilled T-bones

A big, juicy steak on a grill should appear on the Texas coat of arms.

Place steaks, cut 1 to 2-inches thick, on grill 2 to 3-inches from moderate heat. When first side is brown, turn, season and finish cooking. When done, season with salt and pepper. A 1-inch steak takes about 15-20 minutes for rare, a 2-inch steak, 30-35 minutes.

Beef ribs with onion gravy

Beef ribs make a hearty meal for winter appetites.
This gravy is especially nice, with sugar adding richness and flavor to the onions.

| 3 lb beef ribs |
| Flour |
| 4 tablespoons cooking oil |
| Salt and freshly ground pepper |
| 1 medium onion, finely chopped |
| ½ cup water or beef bouillon |
| **Gravy:** |
| 2 medium onions, finely chopped |
| 3 tablespoons sugar |
| 2 tablespoons flour |
| 2 cups beef bouillon |
| 1 tablespoon vinegar |
| Salt and freshly ground pepper |

Trim as much fat as possible from ribs. Roll ribs in flour and shake off excess.

Heat oil in a large frying pan and brown ribs over high heat on all sides. Season generously with salt and pepper and transfer to a shallow casserole dish. Sprinkle with onion, pour water over and cover tightly with a lid or foil. Bake in a preheated 350° oven for 2 hours, or until tender. Turn several times during cooking, and add more water if needed to prevent sticking.

Gravy: Add onion to same pan used for browning beef, stir to get up brown bits from the bottom. Cook over moderate heat until soft, sprinkle with sugar, and stir for a minute. Sprinkle with flour and stir in, then add beef bouillon and vinegar and stir until gravy is smooth and thickened. Taste for seasoning, adding salt and pepper if necessary.

To serve, arrange ribs on a heated platter. Spoon some of the gravy over, and serve the rest separately. Serves 6.

Sharp steak

Spicy and very easy to prepare — a good dish for beginner cooks.

| 2 lb round steak |
| 1 large onion, finely chopped |
| Salt and freshly ground pepper |
| Dash cayenne pepper or Tabasco sauce |
| 1 teaspoon mixed dried herbs |
| 3 tablespoons ketchup |
| 3 tablespoons brown sugar |
| 1 tablespoon Worcestershire sauce |
| 3 tablespoons vinegar |
| 1 cup beef bouillon or water |
| Chopped capers or sweet gherkins to garnish |

Trim fat and gristle from steak and cut into bite-size cubes. Arrange in a shallow casserole and sprinkle with onion.

Mix remaining ingredients except capers together and spoon over the meat. Allow to marinate for several hours or overnight, turning meat now and again.

Cover dish tightly with a lid or aluminum foil, and cook in a preheated 350° oven for 1 hour, or until meat is tender. Taste for seasoning, and serve from casserole sprinkled with capers. Serves 6.

Steak and cheese

Something that's a little bit different — good served with hot fluffy rice.

| 2 lb top round steak, cut in thin slices |
| 1/4 cup flour |
| 1/2 teaspoon salt |
| 1/4 teaspoon pepper |
| 1/4 teaspoon garlic or celery salt |
| 6 tablespoons butter |
| 1 large onion, finely chopped |
| 1 cup beef bouillon |
| 1 cup grated, sharp Cheddar cheese |
| 2 tablespoons finely chopped parsley |

Pound steak out until it is about 1/4-inch thick.

Combine flour, salt, pepper and garlic salt and rub well into steak on both sides. Allow to stand for 5 minutes, then cut into 8-10 serving pieces.

Heat butter in a large, heavy frying pan and brown steak on both sides over moderate heat. Sprinkle with chopped onion and add bouillon. Bring to a boil, cover pan, and simmer for 1 hour or until steak is tender.

Sprinkle cheese and parsley over top, cover again, and cook another minute or so to melt the cheese. Serves 6-8.

Roquefort steak

| 2-3 lb strip sirloin or other good grilling steak, 2 1/2-inches thick |
| 1 oz blue or Roquefort cheese |
| 1 large clove garlic, crushed |
| 1/2 teaspoon coarse black pepper |
| 1 teaspoon salt |
| 1 tablespoon soy sauce |
| 2 tablespoons powdered coffee |
| 1 tablespoon Worcestershire sauce |
| 1/2 cup olive or cooking oil |

Wipe meat with paper towels. Mix cheese, garlic, pepper, salt, soy sauce, coffee, Worcestershire sauce and oil in a blender. Pour over steak, rubbing marinade in with hands. Marinate several hours or overnight.

Grill steak 4-inches above white coals. Cook 20 minutes each side. Steak will be medium rare. Adjust time accordingly if you like your meat rare or well done.

Steak and mushroom casserole

You can cook this on top of the stove, or in a covered casserole in the oven.

| 2 lb lean stewing beef |
| Flour seasoned with salt and pepper |
| 4 tablespoons butter or margarine |
| 1 tablespoon cooking oil |
| 1 large onion, finely chopped |
| 1/2 lb mushrooms |
| 2 tablespoons chopped parsley |
| 1 teaspoon mixed dried herbs |
| 3 cups beef bouillon or water |
| Salt and freshly ground pepper |

Cut meat in 1-inch cubes, after removing any fat or gristle. Roll in seasoned flour and shake off excess.

Heat butter and oil in a saucepan or flameproof casserole and fry onion until soft and golden. Add meat and stir over medium heat until meat is brown.

Wipe mushrooms with a damp cloth, cut into slices if large. Add to pan with herbs and bouillon and bring to a boil, stirring. Taste for seasoning and cover tightly. Simmer on top of the stove, or place in a preheated 350° oven. Cook for 1 1/2-2 hours, or until meat is very tender. Serves 6.

Beef stew with rice, cheese

| 1/2 lb bacon, cut in thick slices |
| 3 lb lean stewing beef, cut into 2 1/2-inch pieces |
| 1 cup thinly sliced onion |
| 1 teaspoon salt |
| 1/4 teaspoon pepper |
| 1 clove garlic, crushed |
| 1 bay leaf, crushed |
| 2 cups beef bouillon |
| 1 cup vermouth |
| 1 (16 oz) can tomatoes |
| 4 cups cooked rice (1 1/2 cups uncooked) |
| 3/4 cup grated Cheddar cheese |

Cut the bacon into cubes and fry until fat is clear but not brown; place bacon in Dutch oven. Brown meat quickly on all sides in the bacon drippings. Transfer pieces of meat to the Dutch oven as they brown. Saute onion for 2 minutes in the same skillet and add to the meat. Add salt, pepper, garlic and bay leaf. Cover with beef bouillon and vermouth and simmer, covered, for 1 hour or until meat is almost tender. Add tomatoes and cook 30 minutes more. Serve over steaming rice and sprinkle with grated Cheddar cheese. Serves 6-8.

Beef olives

(photograph right)

These olives have an interesting stuffing of ground pork and mushrooms.

| 1 1/2 lb round steak, thinly sliced |
| 1/4 lb ground pork |
| 1/2 cup soft breadcrumbs |
| 1/4 lb mushrooms, finely chopped |
| 3 tablespoons grated Parmesan cheese |
| 3 tablespoons finely chopped parsley |
| 1 teaspoon sage |
| Salt and freshly ground pepper |
| 3 tablespoons cooking oil |
| 1 small carrot, chopped |
| 1 medium onion, chopped |
| 1 1/2 cups beef bouillon |
| 1 tablespoon tomato paste |
| 2 teaspoons cornstarch mixed to a smooth paste with a little water |

Pound the steaks between two sheets of plastic wrap to flatten them, and cut into pieces about 5 x 3-inches. Mix together ground pork, breadcrumbs, mushrooms, cheese, parsley and sage and season to taste with salt and pepper. Spread stuffing over steaks, and roll up firmly, tucking in the ends.

Tie with white string, or secure with small skewers. Heat oil in a large, heavy frying pan and brown the rolls on all sides. Sprinkle carrot and onion over and add bouillon mixed with tomato paste. Bring to a boil, then cover pan and simmer for 45 minutes, or until meat is tender. Remove rolls from pan and keep warm, and strain the gravy. Return gravy to pan, bring to a boil, and stir a little hot liquid into the cornstarch paste. Tip this back into pan, stir until gravy is smooth and thickened, and taste for seasoning.

Meanwhile, remove string or skewers from rolls and arrange on a heated platter. Spoon gravy over and serve at once.

Rich beef stew
(photograph left)

2 lb stewing beef
Flour seasoned with salt and pepper
¼ lb salt pork
4 tablespoons cooking oil
1 large carrot, sliced
12 small onions, peeled
2 cloves garlic, crushed
2 large tomatoes, peeled and chopped
About 2 cups beef bouillon
2 teaspoons sugar
1 teaspoon thyme
Salt and freshly ground pepper
1 cup pitted Greek black olives

Remove any fat or gristle from beef, and cut meat into 2-inch squares. Roll in seasoned flour and shake off excess. Cut the salt pork into small cubes.

Heat oil in a heavy saucepan or Dutch oven and fry pork until the fat starts to run. Add beef, and toss over moderately high heat until brown. Add remaining ingredients except olives, using just enough bouillon to cover the beef and vegetables. Stir to get up the brown bits from the bottom, cover tightly, and simmer 2 hours or until beef is tender. Add olives and cook for a further 10 minutes. Taste for seasoning, and serve piping hot. Serves 6.

Homestead beef and vegetable stew

1½ lb lean stewing beef
Flour seasoned with salt and pepper
4 tablespoons butter or margarine
1 tablespoon cooking oil
2 cloves garlic, crushed
4 medium onions, cut in quarters
8 small carrots
4 ribs celery, cut in finger lengths
1 large turnip, thickly sliced
1 bay leaf
2 teaspoons chopped fresh thyme or ½ teaspoon dried
3 cups beef bouillon or water
Salt and freshly ground pepper
4 small potatoes (optional)
Finely chopped parsley to garnish

Trim excess fat from beef, and cut meat into bite-size cubes. Toss in seasoned flour and shake off excess.

Heat butter and oil in a heavy saucepan or Dutch oven and brown meat on all sides. Remove with a slotted spoon. Add garlic and vegetables to pan, and toss for a few minutes. Return meat and add bay leaf, thyme and bouillon. Bring to a boil, taste for seasoning, reduce heat and simmer covered for 2 hours, or until beef is tender. During last half hour, add potatoes if desired. Sprinkle stew generously with parsley to serve. Serves 4.

Jessie's pot roast

This is best with cheap cuts of chuck roast. Occasionally we have used shoulder roast and it's good, but we prefer the chuck flavor. Buy a roast that will fit nicely in your electric skillet (about 4-5 lb).

Sprinkle liberally with salt, coarse ground pepper and whatever strikes your fancy on the spice shelf. Paprika browns the meat nicely. If you use meat tenderizer as we sometimes do, omit salt.

Cut slits in the roast here and there, both sides, and tuck in slivers of garlic. Dredge the meat with flour. Heat a little cooking oil in the electric skillet and sear the meat quickly on both sides. Pour in about 1-inch of hot water and add 2 teaspoons instant beef bouillon.

Turn the heat down to 200° (250° at the most). Place a couple of ribs of celery, leaves and all, and 1 sliced onion on top of the meat. Cover and cook until the meat is tender enough to separate from the bones (about 3-4 hours).

If you like, about 30 minutes before the meat is done, add some halved, peeled potatoes and scrubbed carrots (halve them too, if too thick).

Check the liquid in the pan from time to time and add more hot beef bouillon if needed.

Herbed patties

3 slices homemade style white bread,
crusts removed

½ cup milk

2 tablespoons butter or margarine

1 medium onion, finely chopped

2 lb lean ground beef

½ cup finely chopped parsley

1 tablespoon each chopped fresh
oregano and thyme, or 1 teaspoon
each dried

2 eggs, beaten

2 teaspoons salt

¼ teaspoon pepper

3 tablespoons cooking oil

For gravy:

2 tablespoons flour

1½ cups beef bouillon

Crumble bread and soak in milk for 5
minutes. Meanwhile, heat butter in a
small frying pan and fry onion until soft
and golden. Combine bread, onion, beef,
herbs, eggs and salt and pepper in a large
mixing bowl — easiest way is to use your
hands.

Shape mixture into 12 patties about
3-inches across.

Heat oil in a large frying pan, and add
patties (you will probably need to cook
them in two batches). Cook over moderate heat for 4-5 minutes each side, or
until they are well browned and cooked
through.

Keep patties hot on a serving plate
while making gravy: Pour off all but 2
tablespoons of fat from pan, and stir in
flour over low heat. Gradually stir in
bouillon, and keep stirring until gravy is
smooth and thickened. Taste for seasoning, and spoon over patties or serve separately. Serves 6.

Fast and easy meat loaf

(photograph above)

Twin loaves bake quickly, and there's
a savory tomato mixture in the
middle, so no sauce is needed.

1½ lb lean ground beef

2 slices white bread, crust removed

¼ cup milk

1 egg

1 small onion, grated

1 teaspoon mixed dried herbs

Salt and freshly ground pepper

1 tablespoon soy sauce

1 (16 oz) can peeled tomatoes

2 cloves garlic, crushed

1 teaspoon sugar

¾ cup breadcrumbs

3 tablespoons butter or margarine

¼ cup finely chopped parsley

Place ground beef in a bowl. Soak bread
in milk until soft, and add to beef with
egg, onion, herbs and salt and pepper to
taste. Combine lightly. Shape into 2
long rolls, and arrange in a greased baking
dish, leaving a space in the middle.

Brush tops of meat with soy sauce and
bake in a preheated 350° oven for 45
minutes. Meanwhile, chop tomatoes
finely and combine tomatoes and their
juice with garlic, sugar, and salt and
pepper to taste.

Fry the breadcrumbs in butter until
golden, toss with parsley, and season
with salt and pepper.

When meat has cooked for 45 minutes,
spoon tomato mixture in the middle and
sprinkle breadcrumbs on the top. Bake
for a further 15 minutes, until loaves are
cooked through and breadcrumbs crisp
and golden. Serves 6.

Texas roast beef hash

2 cups chopped, cooked roast beef

2 large raw potatoes, diced

2 cups finely chopped onion

1 clove garlic, crushed

2 cups beef stock or bouillon

1 teaspoon salt

¼ teaspoon freshly ground black pepper

Combine roast beef, potatoes, onion, garlic, stock, salt and pepper in a large heavy
skillet. Simmer over medium heat until
potatoes are tender and all liquid is
absorbed. Serves 4.

Note: One chopped rib of celery and
half a chopped green pepper can be added
to hash.

Ground beef patties Diane

2 lb lean ground beef
1 teaspoon salt
½ teaspoon freshly ground pepper
1 tablespoon grated onion
1 teaspoon grated lemon rind
3 tablespoons cooking oil
4 tablespoons butter
2 cloves garlic, crushed
3 tablespoons lemon juice
1 tablespoon Worcestershire sauce
¼ cup finely chopped parsley

Lightly mix together ground beef, salt, pepper, onion and lemon rind, gently shape into 6 patties. Heat the oil, add patties and cook over medium heat for 3-5 minutes on each side, or until done to your liking.

Remove to a heated platter and keep warm. Pour oil from pan, add butter and garlic, heat until butter has melted. Add lemon juice, Worcestershire sauce and parsley and stir over low heat until well blended. Spoon over patties and serve at once. Serves 6.

Spicy pot-roasted beef

Here's a German-inspired way with beef, which makes an economical cut tender and full of flavor.

4 lb beef brisket or shoulder
1 cup red wine
½ cup wine vinegar
½ cup water
2 medium onions, roughly chopped
2 bay leaves
12 peppercorns
10 cloves
3 tablespoons sugar
2 teaspoons dry mustard
½ teaspoon ginger
1 teaspoon salt
4 tablespoons bacon fat or cooking oil

Trim excess fat from beef and place meat in a deep bowl. Combine remaining ingredients except bacon fat and pour over meat. Cover, and refrigerate 3-4 days, turning meat over several times. Remove meat from marinade and dry well with paper towels. Strain marinade. Heat bacon fat in a large heavy saucepan or Dutch oven, and brown meat slowly on all sides. Pour marinade over, cover tightly, and simmer 3 hours or until beef is very tender, turning beef occasionally.

Place beef on a platter and keep warm. Blot fat from surface of liquid in pan and if necessary reduce by boiling to gravy consistency. Serve beef in fairly thick slices, with gravy. Serves 8.

Spicy meatballs
(photograph below left)

The meatballs are browned first, then simmered in sauce, so they absorb the spicy flavoring.

For meatballs:

1 lb lean ground beef
½ cup soft breadcrumbs
3 tablespoons finely chopped parsley
1 egg
1 small onion, grated
2 teaspoons grated lemon rind
Salt and freshly ground pepper
3 tablespoons cooking oil

For sauce:

1 medium onion, finely chopped
½ teaspoon curry powder
1 teaspoon cinnamon
1 teaspoon ground cumin seed
1 teaspoon ground coriander seed
2 cups beef bouillon
¼ cup coarsely chopped seedless raisins
Salt to taste
A little sugar (optional)

Mix together all ingredients for meatballs except oil. Heat the oil in a heavy frying pan and brown meatballs over moderate heat. Remove from the pan and set aside while you make the sauce.

Add onion to the same pan (you may need a little extra oil) and stir until starting to soften. Add curry powder, cinnamon, cumin and coriander, and stir for 1 minute. Add bouillon, raisins, and salt to taste and bring to a boil.

Return meatballs to the pan, cover, and simmer 30 minutes.

Taste sauce and adjust seasoning, adding a little sugar if desired. Serve meatballs and sauce in a heated dish, with rice, chutney and sliced cucumbers. Serves 4.

ten, separate with chopsticks, or a fork. Cook until just tender and drain thoroughly.

Return meat to the pan, lightly mix in the mushrooms and noodles, and cook for another 2-3 minutes. Serves 6.

Salisbury steak

| 1 lb chopped round steak |
| 1 teaspoon salt |
| Freshly ground pepper |
| ½ cup coffee cream |
| Fine soft breadcrumbs |
| 1 tablespoon cooking oil |
| ½ cup water |
| 2 tablespoons butter |

Mix chopped steak with seasonings and cream and form lightly into individual patties. Coat with crumbs and "pan broil" in a heavy, oiled skillet, turning frequently. Remove to a heated platter. Add water to fat in pan. Season with salt and pepper. Bring to a boil, scrape up drippings, add butter and pour over steaks.

No peek casserole

| 2 lb lean stewing beef, cut into 1-inch pieces |
| 1 envelope onion soup mix |
| 1 (10¾ oz) can condensed cream of mushroom soup |
| 1 (4 oz) can whole mushrooms, drained |
| ½ cup red wine |

Combine ingredients well in a 2-quart casserole. Cover. Bake in a preheated 300° oven for 3 hours. Don't peek until it's done. Serve over noodles or rice. Serves 4-6.

Beef teriyaki

Crisp vegetables, subtle flavorings and thin egg noodles combine with sliced beef in this Japanese favorite.

| 1½ lb sirloin or tenderloin steak |
| 4 tablespoons cooking oil |
| 1 clove garlic, halved |
| 1 large onion, sliced and separated into rings |
| 1 large green pepper, halved and sliced |
| 1 large red pepper, halved and sliced |
| 4 small zucchini, sliced |
| 2 medium carrots, cut into thin sticks |
| ½ cup light soy sauce |
| 1 tablespoon sugar |
| ¼ cup Mirin or sweet sherry |
| ½ lb thin egg noodles |
| ½ lb small mushrooms, thinly sliced |

Cut steak into paper-thin slices (if meat is placed in freezer until well chilled, slicing will be easier). Heat oil with garlic. Remove garlic, add meat a few pieces at a time, and quickly brown on both sides. Remove from pan. Add onion rings, fry for 2 minutes, then add peppers, zucchini and carrots. Cook for 2 minutes, stirring constantly. Add soy sauce, sugar and Mirin or sherry. Stir for another minute, or until vegetables are just tender-crisp.

Meanwhile, drop noodles into boiling salted water, and when they begin to sof-

Stir-fried beef with broccoli

(photograph right)

| 1-1¼ lb round steak, sliced about ⅛ to ¼-inch thick and 2-inches long |
| 1 lb fresh broccoli |
| 1 teaspoon sugar |
| 1 tablespoon cornstarch |
| 1 tablespoon dark soy sauce |
| 2 tablespoons oyster sauce |
| Dry sherry |
| ¼ cup peanut or safflower oil |
| ⅛ teaspoon salt |
| 1 clove garlic, crushed |
| 2 green onions, cut in 1½-inch lengths |
| 6 fresh mushrooms, sliced |
| ½ cup chicken broth |
| Finely chopped parsley to garnish |

Prepare steak (easier to cut if partially frozen). Trim and discard toughest portion of broccoli stem. Cut off remaining stem just under flower head and slice paper thin. Cut broccoli florets into even pieces. Set aside. Combine sugar, cornstarch, soy and oyster sauces and pour over meat in a flat dish. Sprinkle with sherry. Let marinate 10-30 minutes.

Heat wok or frying pan hot and dry over high heat. Add half the oil. Add salt and garlic; stir and brown quickly. Add beef and brown on outside, about 1 minute. Turn off heat, remove meat and juices to a bowl or dish. Set aside.

Reheat wok. Add rest of oil. Add broccoli, green onions and mushrooms. Saute 2 minutes over high heat stirring constantly. (Broccoli should remain crisp.) Sprinkle in 2 tablespoons sherry, cover and cook 1 minute. Remove cover. Return beef to pan. Add broth, stir while cooking until gravy thickens. Turn off heat, serve at once over cooked rice and garnish with chopped parsley. Serves 6.

Beef stew with horseradish

2 lb lean stewing beef, cut into bite-size pieces

2 medium onions, chopped

2 tablespoons margarine

1 (1⁵⁄₈ oz) package beef stew mix

½ cup water or as needed

1 (8 oz) can tomato sauce

½ teaspoon Worcestershire sauce

1 tablespoon prepared horseradish, or to taste

Salt, pepper, onion salt, garlic powder, celery salt and paprika to taste

Brown beef and onion in margarine in a large skillet. Add beef stew mix and water, stirring until well blended. Add tomato sauce, Worcestershire sauce and horseradish. Add spices to taste. Let simmer, covered, for about 45 minutes or until tender, stirring occasionally. Serve over noodles. Serves 6.

Swiss steak

6 beef cutlets or chopped round steak patties

Flour

Cooking oil

1 onion, chopped

1 (16 oz) can tomatoes, chopped

½ green pepper, chopped

1 teaspoon salt

¼ teaspoon pepper

1½ teaspoons Worcestershire sauce

Coat cutlets with flour, shake off excess. Brown cutlets in hot oil in a skillet. Remove cutlets and pour off most of the oil, leaving enough to saute onion until tender. Add tomatoes, green pepper, salt, pepper and Worcestershire sauce. Return cutlets to mixture in skillet and simmer, covered, for 1 hour or until tender. Serve cutlets on a bed of boiled rice covered with sauce. Also good served with spinach noodles. Serves 6.

Beef tips and noodles

1½ lb round or sirloin steak, cut into bite-size pieces

Flour seasoned with salt and pepper

6 tablespoons shortening or oil

Extra ¼ cup flour

2 cups beef stock or bouillon, heated

Salt and pepper

1 teaspoon Worcestershire sauce

Dredge meat cubes in seasoned flour and brown quickly in shortening. Set aside. Pour off excess drippings. Heat ¼ cup drippings, stir in extra flour and add hot stock. Stirring constantly, add salt, pepper and Worcestershire sauce and simmer over medium heat until thickened.

Return meat to skillet, cover and simmer in gravy until fork tender, about 2 hours. (Can be cooked in a covered casserole in a preheated 300° oven until tender.) Serve with noodles or rice. Serves 6.

Texas beef spaghetti sauce

2 tablespoons butter

3 tablespoons olive oil

4 slices lean bacon, chopped

1 onion, finely chopped

1 carrot, finely chopped

1 lb ground beef

1 strip lemon rind

½ cup tomato paste

1¼ cups beef stock or water and beef bouillon cube

⅔ cup dry red or white wine

1 bay leaf

Pinch nutmeg

½ teaspoon salt

Freshly ground pepper

1 lb spaghetti

Extra olive oil

Parmesan cheese to serve

Heat the butter and oil in a saucepan and saute the bacon, onion, and carrot for 5 minutes. Stir in ground beef and cook until browned. Add the lemon rind, tomato paste, beef stock, wine, bay leaf, nutmeg, salt and pepper. Bring to a boil and simmer, covered, for 30 minutes, stirring occasionally. Remove the lemon peel and bay leaf, and simmer, uncovered, for a further 30 minutes.

Cook spaghetti in boiling, salted water. Drain and swirl with about 2 tablespoons extra oil. Serve with the sauce spooned into the center and sprinkle with Parmesan cheese. Serves 6-8.

Brandied pepperburgers

(photograph right)

¼ cup finely chopped onion

¼ teaspoon thyme

2 tablespoons butter

¼ cup brandy

½ cup fine soft breadcrumbs

2 tablespoons water

1 teaspoon salt

1 lb ground chuck steak

2 teaspoons coarsely ground pepper

4 slices French bread

2 teaspoons finely chopped parsley

Brandy-sauteed mushrooms

Saute onion and thyme lightly in 1 teaspoon of the butter in a small pan, remove from heat. Add brandy. Return pan to heat and simmer a minute. Pour over breadcrumbs, water, salt and ground chuck. Mix well. Shape into 4 oval patties about 1-inch thick. Sprinkle each side of each patty with ¼ teaspoon pepper. Broil 6-inches from heat, about 5 minutes each side, until cooked to desired degree of doneness. While meat broils, toast bread under broiler. Mix parsley with remaining butter and spread on toast. Serve patties on the toast, with Brandy-sauteed mushrooms. Serves 4.

Brandy-sauteed mushrooms

(photograph right)

1 lb fresh mushrooms, sliced

2 tablespoons butter

1 tablespoon lemon juice

¼ cup brandy

½ teaspoon salt

½ teaspoon basil

1½ teaspoons cornstarch

2 teaspoons water

⅓ cup sliced green onion

2 tablespoons chopped parsley

Saute mushrooms in butter with lemon juice over high heat for 1 minute. Add brandy, salt and basil. Cook 2-3 minutes longer, stirring occasionally. Mix cornstarch with cold water and stir into mushrooms. Cook, stirring until mixture boils and thickens slightly. Stir in green onion and parsley. Makes about 2 cups.

Beef stroganoff

2 lb beef tenderloin
Salt and pepper
¼ cup butter
¼ cup tomato paste
⅔ cup sour cream
2 tablespoons grated onion

Cut the beef into thin strips, 1½-inches long and ¼-inch wide. Sprinkle well with salt and pepper and let stand for 2 hours in a cool place or in the refrigerator.

Heat a skillet, add the butter, and fry the pieces of beef until just colored. Add the tomato paste and sour cream, heat gently or cook in a double boiler over hot water for 10-15 minutes. Taste for seasoning and just before serving add the grated onion. Serve at once with boiled rice. Serves 6.

Beef bourguignonne

¼ cup plus 1 tablespoon butter
2 lb lean stewing beef, cut in 1½-inch cubes
2 tablespoons brandy
2 tablespoons flour
1 teaspoon salt
¼ teaspoon pepper
1½ cups dry red wine (Burgundy-type)
2 medium onions, coarsely chopped
1 medium carrot, cut in pieces
1 clove garlic, crushed
1 bouquet garni
Beef bouillon
½ lb mushrooms, sliced

Heat ¼ cup butter in a heavy skillet and brown beef, transfer to a 3-quart casserole. Heat brandy, pour over meat and carefully flame with a match. Stir flour into meat. Season with salt and pepper. Add wine. Add remaining butter to skillet and brown onion. Add onion, carrot, garlic and bouquet garni to casserole with enough bouillon to cover. Cook in a preheated 350° oven for 3 hours or until meat is tender. Add mushrooms for the last 30 minutes of cooking time. Remove bouquet garni before serving. Serves 6.

Note: To make a bouquet garni, (1) tie 1 bay leaf, fresh thyme and parsley in a bouquet to drop in the pot, or (2) wrap and tie dried herbs (about ½ teaspoon each and 1 small bay leaf) in a 4-inch square of cheesecloth.

Chinese-style beef with Romaine

1 lb flank steak
1 cup water
2 tablespoons cornstarch
1 tablespoon sugar
1 tablespoon lemon juice
1 tablespoon soy sauce
1 teaspoon salt
1 beef bouillon cube, crumbled
3 tablespoons cooking oil
1 cup sliced mushrooms
1 (8 oz) can water chestnuts, drained and sliced
½ cup sliced green onions, 1-inch lengths
4 cups sliced Romaine lettuce, 1-inch pieces

Partially freeze meat, if desired, to make slicing easier. Cut meat diagonally across the grain into very thin slices. Combine water, cornstarch, sugar, lemon juice, soy sauce, salt and bouillon cube in a bowl, mix well. Heat oil in Chinese wok or heavy skillet over high heat until moderately hot. Add meat, stir-fry over high heat 2 minutes or until meat has lost its pink color. Add mushrooms, water chestnuts and green onion. Stir-fry 2 minutes.

Add Romaine lettuce and stir well. Add liquid, stir and cook until sauce is thickened and clear. Serve with hot fluffy rice. Serves 4-6.

Company best casserole

4 cups (½ lb) noodles
1 lb lean ground beef
1 tablespoon peanut oil
2 (8 oz) cans tomato sauce (plain or with onion)
1 cup cottage cheese
1 (8 oz) package cream cheese, softened
¼ cup sour cream
⅓ cup finely chopped green onion
1 tablespoon finely chopped green pepper
1½ teaspoons oregano leaves
¼ teaspoon basil
Salt and pepper or garlic salt and lemon pepper marinade to taste
2 tablespoons melted butter or margarine

Early in the day, cook noodles until tender as package directs. Drain. Meanwhile, saute meat until browned in oil. Stir in tomato sauce. Remove from heat. Combine cheeses, sour cream, green onion, pepper and seasonings.

Spread half the noodles in a 2-quart casserole. Cover with cheese mixture. Cover with rest of noodles. Pour melted butter over noodles, then tomato meat sauce. Refrigerate.

About 1 hour before serving, cook casserole in a preheated 375° oven for 45 minutes or until hot. Serves 6.

Oven bag brisket

4-5 lb boneless beef brisket
1 tablespoon flour
1 envelope onion soup mix
Garlic powder
Freshly ground pepper
1-2 tablespoons Worcestershire sauce
2 cups beef bouillon

Wipe meat with paper towels. Place flour in oven cooking bag, add soup mix. Rub both sides of meat with garlic powder, pepper and Worcestershire sauce. Place meat in bag in a roasting pan. Pour bouillon on both sides of beef. Seal bag with twist tie and cut 6 slits in top of bag. Roast brisket in a preheated 300° oven for about 4 hours or until tender. Serves 12-15.

Peppered beef

1/8 cup coarsely ground pepper
1/2 teaspoon ground cardamon (optional, but good)
1-2 lb flank steak
Marinade:
2/3 cup soy sauce
1/2 cup vinegar
1 tablespoon tomato paste or ketchup
1 teaspoon paprika
1 clove garlic, crushed
Horseradish sauce:
1/4 cup prepared horseradish, drained
1/2 teaspoon salt
1 cup sour cream

Combine pepper and cardamon and spread evenly on a sheet of waxed paper. Place steak firmly over the mixture, press down, turn steak over. With heel of hand, press pepper mixture firmly down into the steak, covering both sides evenly and thoroughly.

Combine marinade ingredients. Place meat in shallow dish and pour marinade over. Cover and refrigerate overnight, turning meat occasionally. If desired, marinate in a heavy plastic bag, turning occasionally.

When ready to cook, place meat with marinade in a covered baking dish and cook in a preheated 300° oven for 30-40 minutes. May be served hot or cold with horseradish sauce. Serves 4-6.

Horseradish sauce: Combine horseradish, salt and sour cream. Cover and chill until ready to serve.

Beef medallions Paramount

Helen Worden of Houston represented Texas in the National Beef Cook-Off with this recipe.

1 cup beef bouillon
3/4 cup dried apricot halves, sliced thin
2 teaspoons brown sugar
2-2 1/2 lb eye of round steak
3 tablespoons flour
1/2 teaspoon paprika
1/2 teaspoon cinnamon
1/2 teaspoon onion powder
Salt and pepper to taste
4 tablespoons butter or margarine
1/2 cup sliced small onions
1/4 lb sliced mushrooms (discard stems)
1 tablespoon Worcestershire sauce
1/2 cup rose wine or water

Bring beef bouillon to a boil in a saucepan. Add apricots and brown sugar, cover and set aside. Trim fat from meat, cut in 1/4-inch slices. Mix flour, paprika, cinnamon, onion powder, salt and pepper in a plastic bag. Shake meat slices in bag to

Roast tenderloin of beef
(photograph left)

2½-3 lb beef tenderloin
2 tablespoons Cognac or brandy
Salt
Cayenne pepper
Soft butter
Marchand de vin sauce

Rub beef with Cognac, then sprinkle with salt and cayenne pepper. Rub generously with soft butter. Insert meat thermometer and roast about 40 minutes to 1 hour, to desired doneness, 140° for rare, 150° for medium rare. Serve with Marchand de vin sauce. Serves 6.

Marchand de vin sauce
(photograph left)

½ cup butter
⅓ cup finely chopped mushrooms
½ cup minced ham
⅓ cup finely chopped shallots
½ cup finely chopped onion
5 cloves garlic, crushed
2 tablespoons flour
½ teaspoon salt
⅛ teaspoon pepper
Pinch cayenne pepper
¾ cup beef stock or bouillon
½ cup dry red wine

In a small, heavy saucepan melt butter and saute mushrooms, ham, shallots, onion and garlic. When onion is golden, add flour, salt, pepper and cayenne pepper. Stir thoroughly and brown well, about 7-10 minutes. Blend in the stock and wine, cover and simmer over very low heat 35-45 minutes. Makes 2 cups.

lightly coat them. Heat butter in large skillet and brown beef slices.

Remove meat and add onions and mushrooms. Stir over heat until soft. Add beef, apricots, bouillon, Worcestershire sauce and wine. Cover tightly and simmer about 30-45 minutes or until beef is tender. Check periodically for dryness and add more bouillon if needed.

Arrange meat on a platter and spoon apricot-mushroom sauce over. Serves 6-8.

Roast prime rib

Whether you call it a standing rib roast or prime rib of beef, it's important to judge the cut by the color and amount of marbling. The color of good aged beef is dark red, which means it has at least two to three weeks aging to it. Marbling through the eye should be heavy. When most people see the heavy marbling, they tend to think it is fatty and tough. This is not true. The marbling, when the roast is cooked properly, dissolves and makes the beef very juicy and tender. Allow about 1 lb beef per dinner guest.

Place roast on a wire rack in a pan to keep it out of the drippings. Place meat in a preheated 500° oven for 25 minutes (to seal in juices), then reduce temperature to 300° and roast to desired doneness. Using a meat thermometer, internal temperature should register 130° for rare, 140° for medium and 160° for well done. Remove from oven when thermometer registers 5° below desired temperature as roast will continue to cook after it is removed from the oven. For easier carving, let roast stand covered with foil in a warm place 15-20 minutes.

Overleaf: East Texas's many lakes hold sport for the fisherman and food for the table.

OTHER TOP CHOICES

From rugged mountains to golden beaches, tall skyscrapers to dusty plains, haute cuisine to down-home cooking, Texas is a state of great diversity. But one thing all Texans seem to have in common is a love of meat, including game, pork, veal, lamb and poultry.

Recipes for these Texas favorites are as varied as the state itself. Chicken might be fried, old-fashioned style, cooked in pastry, Wellington-style, or served Mexican-style with flour tortilla dumplings. Chicken has become more popular in Texas in the last few years because of its high nutritional value and low cost. It also contains less fat than beef and pork and combines well with fruits, vegetables and grains.

Dove and quail are other Texas classics. Hunting these game birds on Texas ranches is a favorite sport. Because they are so plentiful, cooks have devised myriad ways to prepare them. Dove might be smothered in a garlic-wine sauce or seasoned with hot pepper sauce, dipped in flour and fried. Quail might be roasted in the oven or on the grill, or fried, perhaps Mexican-style.

Venison is another favorite. Hunting season is greatly anticipated because deer are both close at hand and abundant. With the arrival of deer season, hunters bring home venison, which goes into sumptuous sausage, a spicy chili, a filling stew or a tasty casserole. The remainder fills freezers to overflowing.

Pork and lamb also are popular. Texas is a large lamb-producing state and cooks often use the meat as the basis for gourmet dishes. Pork is used in a variety of ways, but most popularly as ribs, barbecued Texas-style.

Whichever way it is served, meat provides a substance to a meal no other food can replace.

Triple decker pork (page 74)

Fireside chicken soup

(photograph right)

1 lb chicken pieces
8 cups water
Salt and freshly ground pepper
2 ribs celery, sliced
2 carrots, sliced
1 turnip, sliced
3 tablespoons chopped parsley
½ teaspoon thyme
1 teaspoon grated lemon rind
1 clove garlic, crushed
Extra tablespoon chopped parsley

Place chicken pieces, water, salt and pepper in a large saucepan. Cover and simmer 1 hour. Add vegetables, parsley and thyme and simmer 25 minutes more. Remove chicken from soup and pick meat from bones. Return meat to pan and taste soup for seasoning. Mix together lemon rind, garlic and extra parsley. Ladle soup into heated bowls and sprinkle with parsley mixture. Serves 6.

Chicken pot-au-feu

1 chicken, quartered
Giblets from chicken
4 cups water
1 onion
2 ribs celery
1 carrot, sliced
2 chicken bouillon cubes
3 sprigs parsley
1 teaspoon salt
1 small cabbage, cut in eighths
8 small onions
Extra 4 carrots, sliced
Extra 2 ribs celery, sliced
1 cup frozen peas
1 tablespoon margarine

Put chicken and giblets in 5-quart Dutch oven. Add water, onion, celery, carrot, bouillon cubes, parsley, and salt. Bring to a boil, cover tightly. Reduce heat and simmer 40 minutes or until tender. Remove from heat, strain broth. Discard vegetables and refrigerate chicken and broth. When chicken is cool, remove meat from bones, cut into bite-size pieces. Skim fat from broth.

Heat reserved broth in saucepan. Add cabbage and onions and simmer 20 minutes. Add carrots and celery and simmer 10 minutes longer. Add peas, cut-up chicken and margarine. Cook 5 minutes longer. Serves 4.

Chicken tidbits Chinese

2 whole chicken breasts, skinned and boned
3 tablespoons dry sherry
3 tablespoons dark soy sauce
2-3 teaspoons cornstarch
3-4 tablespoons butter or margarine
¼ teaspoon garlic powder
¼ teaspoon thyme
1 tablespoon finely chopped parsley

Cut chicken into bite-size tidbits or 1-inch wide strips. Combine sherry, soy sauce and cornstarch, add chicken tidbits and marinate 15-30 minutes.

Melt butter in a large skillet or Chinese wok over high heat. Add chicken. Sprinkle with seasonings.

Cook 5 minutes, stirring constantly. Sprinkle with parsley. To serve, turn into chafing dish and serve with toothpicks. Makes about 24 tidbits.

Dove hors d'oeuvre

2 dozen doves or quail
Milk
1 cup brandy
Louisiana hot sauce
Flour seasoned with salt, pepper and cayenne pepper
Cooking oil

Place doves in large bowl, cover with milk and add brandy. Let stand several hours at room temperature. Remove breast meat from birds with a sharp knife. Marinate dove breasts in a bowl of Louisiana hot sauce for several minutes, then dredge with seasoned flour.

Heat oil (about ½-inch) in heavy skillet and fry dove breasts on both sides until tender, drain on paper towels. Serve as a hot hors d'oeuvre. Serves 12-20.

Note: Also delicious served with biscuits and cream gravy.

Chicken salad Veronica

This an updated version of the old Waldorf salad, with chicken added. Best made when Thompson seedless grapes are in season, it's distinguished by delicious, curry flavored mayonnaise.

4 whole chicken breasts or 8 half breasts
2 teaspoons curry powder
3 tablespoons chicken broth
1 egg yolk
2 teaspoons Dijon mustard
3 tablespoons lemon juice
Salt and freshly ground white pepper
1½ cups salad oil
Dash cayenne pepper and Worcestershire sauce
¾ cup chopped pecans, walnuts or blanched almonds
4 ribs tender celery, sliced
2 cups Thompson seedless grapes, stems removed
2 tart apples, peeled and thinly sliced
Lettuce leaves to serve
Parsley sprigs or small bunches of grapes to garnish

Cover chicken breasts with lightly salted water, bring to a simmer, poach for 8 minutes, or until cooked through. Cool in the broth, then remove skin and bones and cut meat into neat, bite-size pieces. Reserve 3 tablespoons of the broth for this dish (the rest can be refrigerated for other uses).

Combine curry powder and the 3 tablespoons of broth in a small saucepan. Bring to a boil, stirring, then put aside to cool.

Place egg yolk in a bowl and beat in mustard, lemon juice and salt and pepper to taste. Gradually beat in oil — drop by drop, using a wire whisk. When mixture begins to thicken, add oil in a thin, steady stream, and continue beating until mayonnaise is thick. Beat in curry mixture, with cayenne and Worcestershire sauce to taste.

Place chicken pieces, nuts, celery, grapes and apples in a bowl and combine. Add curry mayonnaise and fold together. Arrange a bed of lettuce leaves on a pretty serving dish, spoon salad on top and garnish with parsley sprigs or small bunches of grapes. Serves 8-10.

Orange chicken

The orange marmalade combines with other flavorings to add a touch of magic to an easy chicken dish.

1 (3 lb) chicken
Flour seasoned with salt and pepper
4 tablespoons butter
2 tablespoons cooking oil
1 cup orange juice
½ cup medium sherry
4 tablespoons orange marmalade
1 small onion, finely chopped
1 tablespoon light soy sauce
Salt and freshly ground pepper

Cut chicken into serving pieces and pat dry with paper towels. Roll chicken in seasoned flour and shake off excess.

Heat butter and oil in a large, heavy frying pan and slowly brown chicken on all sides. Mix remaining ingredients together and pour over chicken. Cover and simmer for 35-40 minutes or until chicken is tender, turning pieces several times. If gravy seems to be thickening too much, thin with a little extra orange juice or water. Before serving, taste for seasoning and add more salt and pepper if necessary. Serves 4.

Double-celery chicken

(photograph right)

1 (4 lb) chicken
4 tablespoons butter
1 small onion, finely chopped
4 ribs celery, finely chopped
1½ cups soft breadcrumbs
2 teaspoons grated lemon rind
3 tablespoons finely chopped parsley
1 egg, beaten
Salt and freshly ground pepper
Extra 4 tablespoons butter, softened
2 cups chicken broth
½ bunch celery, cleaned and cut into short lengths

Wipe chicken inside and out with damp paper towels. Heat 4 tablespoons of butter in a frying pan and fry onion and celery until soft. Remove from heat and stir in breadcrumbs, lemon rind, parsley, egg and salt and pepper to taste. Stuff chicken with the mixture and truss into shape. Rub chicken all over with softened butter and place breast side up on a greased rack set in a greased baking dish. Pour broth into the dish.

Roast in a preheated 350° oven for 1 hour, basting occasionally with pan juices. Turn chicken over onto its breast and add celery to juices in pan. Continue cooking for another 40 minutes, or until chicken and celery are tender. (Add extra broth at any time if liquid in pan is drying up.)

Remove chicken to a warm platter and allow to rest for 10 minutes before carving. Remove celery with a slotted spoon and arrange around chicken. Adjust seasoning of pan juices, reheat, and serve as gravy. Serves 4-6.

Finger chicken

(photograph above)

Nothing beats chicken pieces for informal entertaining — economical and so easy to cook.

4 tablespoons butter or margarine
8-10 chicken pieces (thighs, drumsticks, etc.)
3 tablespoons finely chopped parsley
1 teaspoon salt
½ teaspoon each rosemary, thyme and oregano
1 teaspoon paprika
1 teaspoon crushed black peppercorns

Melt butter in a baking dish, and roll chicken pieces in butter. Combine remaining ingredients and sprinkle over all sides of chicken. Bake in a preheated 350° oven for 25 minutes. Turn pieces over and bake a further 25 minutes, or until crispy and golden brown. Serves 4-5.

Chicken pastries

You can make these fairly large for lunch and dinner, or small to serve as cocktail snacks.

| 2 pre-rolled sheets frozen puff pastry |
| 4 slices lean bacon |
| 2 cups finely chopped cooked chicken |
| 4 tablespoons mayonnaise |
| 4 green onions, finely chopped |
| 1 tablespoon finely chopped parsley |
| 1 tablespoon finely chopped sweet gherkins |
| 1 tablespoon finely chopped olives |
| Squeeze of lemon juice |
| Salt and freshly ground pepper |
| Beaten egg to glaze |

Roll each pastry sheet to measure 12-inches square. Pastry will be ⅛-inch thick. Cut pastry into 6-inch squares. Cook bacon until crisp, crumble into small pieces. Combine with remaining ingredients except egg (be sparing with the salt, as bacon is salty).

Place about a tablespoon of filling on each pastry square. Moisten the edges, fold pastry over and press firmly together, forming triangular or oblong pastries. Crimp edges with the tines of a fork. Make a slit in top of each pastry for steam to escape and glaze with beaten egg.

Bake on a cookie sheet in a preheated 400° oven for 15 minutes, or until crisp and golden brown. Makes about 8 luncheon-size pastries.

Note: Substitute your own favorite pastry recipe for frozen puff pastry.

Chicken and flour tortilla dumplings

| 1 (3 lb) chicken, cut in pieces |
| Water to cover |
| Salt and a few peppercorns |
| ½ cup chopped celery |
| ½ cup sliced carrot |
| ½ cup chopped onion |
| 2-3 teaspoons instant chicken bouillon (optional) |
| 4-5 flour tortillas, cut in strips |
| Flour |

Place chicken pieces in 3-quart pot with water to cover. Add salt, peppercorns, celery, carrot and onion. Add chicken bouillon if desired. Bring to a boil, reduce heat, cover and simmer 1 hour or until meat falls from bones, skimming as necessary. Meanwhile, dust tortilla strips with flour. With tongs, remove chicken bones from pot. Bring broth to a boil. Add floured tortilla strips and boil 5 minutes. Cover, lower heat and steam 5 more minutes. Serves 4.

Almond sherry chicken

A delicately flavored dish, ideal for a luncheon party.

| 4 whole chicken breasts, skinned and boned |
| Flour seasoned with salt and pepper |
| 4 tablespoons butter |
| ⅔ cup dry sherry |
| ½ teaspoon tarragon |
| ⅔ cup whipping cream |
| 3 tablespoons slivered toasted almonds |

Lightly pound chicken breasts with a mallet to flatten, coat with seasoned flour and shake off excess. Melt the butter, add chicken and cook over moderate heat about 5 minutes each side, or until tender. Remove from pan and set aside.

Add sherry and tarragon to pan and stir well to get up the brown bits from the bottom. When nearly boiling, stir in cream, replace chicken, and simmer until reheated. Taste for seasoning and add salt and pepper as required. Arrange on a heated serving platter and sprinkle with toasted almonds. Serves 4.

Honey chicken with tropical dip

A warm climate just naturally encourages outdoor cookery. Here's a sensational recipe for your next barbecue.

| 6 half chicken breasts |
| ½ cup honey |
| ¼ cup lime or lemon juice |
| ¼ cup cooking oil |
| 1 clove garlic, crushed |
| Salt and freshly ground pepper |

For tropical dip:

| 1 large ripe avocado, peeled and chopped |
| 2 teaspoons lime or lemon juice |
| 1 tablespoon honey |
| ¼ cup whipping cream |
| ¼ cup pineapple juice |
| ½ teaspoon mild curry powder |
| Salt and freshly ground pepper |

Place chicken breasts in a shallow dish. Combine honey, lime juice, oil, garlic and salt and pepper to taste and spoon over chicken. Cover and marinate for an hour, turning now and again.

Remove chicken from marinade and place in an oiled, hinged grilling rack. Grill over coals until brown on both sides and cooked through, brushing often with honey mixture. Serve with tropical dip. Serves 6.

Tropical dip: Mash avocado well and combine with remaining ingredients, seasoning to taste with salt and pepper. Cover and chill until serving time.

Chicken jambalaya

| 1 (3½ lb) chicken, cut in pieces |
| Salt and pepper |
| ¼ cup cooking oil |
| 2 medium onions, chopped |
| 1 green pepper, finely chopped |
| 2 ribs celery, finely chopped |
| ½ lb hot smoked sausage, sliced (optional) |
| 1 cup long grain rice |
| Pinch cayenne pepper |
| Chicken broth or bouillon to cover |
| 1 clove garlic, crushed |

Wash chicken, pat dry and season with salt and pepper. Fry in oil until golden brown over high heat in large saucepan. Lower heat and add onion, pepper and celery. Cook until onion is tender. Add sausage, rice and cayenne pepper, cook slowly about 15 minutes over low heat, stirring often. Add enough boiling broth to cover ingredients well and add garlic. Stir and cover.

Simmer over low heat for about 45 minutes or until chicken and rice are cooked. If necessary, remove lid from pan for a few minutes to dry out jambalaya. Serves 4-6.

Note: Other meats may be substituted for chicken.

Chicken and dumplings

| 1 (4 lb) chicken, cut in 8 pieces |
| 1 teaspoon salt |
| 10 peppercorns |
| 1 rib celery, chopped |
| 1 medium onion, chopped |
| 1 carrot, chopped |
| ½ bay leaf |
| 3 tablespoons flour mixed to a paste with water (optional) |

Dumplings:

| 1½ cups flour |
| 2 teaspoons baking powder |
| ¾ teaspoon salt |
| 2 tablespoons finely chopped parsley (optional) |
| ½ teaspoon rosemary (optional) |
| 3 tablespoons shortening |

| ¾ cup milk |

Place chicken pieces in heavy saucepan and just cover with water. Add salt, peppercorns, celery, onion, carrot and bay leaf. Cover and bring to a boil, lower heat and simmer gently for 30 minutes.

Combine flour, baking powder, salt, parsley and rosemary in a bowl. Cut in the shortening until mixture resembles coarse meal. Mixing with a fork, add enough milk to make dough hold together. Drop spoonfuls of dough from a wet tablespoon, letting dumplings rest on top of meat and broth. Cover tightly and simmer for an additional 15 minutes, not raising lid from pan.

To thicken broth, transfer dumplings to a warm plate and add flour paste to broth in pot. Stir constantly until thickened. Taste and adjust seasonings if necessary. Serve in soup bowls with dumplings floating on top. Serves 6.

Chicken in caper sauce

(photograph right)

| 1 (3½-4 lb) chicken |
| 2 cups water |
| 1 bay leaf and a few sprigs of thyme and parsley tied together |
| 1 small onion, stuck with 4 cloves |
| 1 small carrot, chopped |
| Salt and freshly ground pepper |

For sauce:

| 3 tablespoons butter |
| 3 tablespoons flour |
| 1¾ cups broth (from cooking chicken) |
| 3 tablespoons finely chopped parsley |
| 2 tablespoons chopped capers |
| ¼ cup whipping cream |

Place chicken in pan with water, herbs, onion, carrot and salt and pepper to taste. Bring to a boil, cover pan and lower heat, simmer chicken for 40 minutes or until tender, turning once or twice.

Remove chicken and strain broth. Skin chicken, cut into joints, and place on a serving dish in a warm oven until ready to serve.

Melt butter in a small saucepan, stir in flour, and cook 1 minute. Remove from heat, and stir in warm broth.

Return to heat and stir until smooth and thickened. Add parsley, capers and cream, taste for seasoning and spoon sauce over chicken. Serves 4.

Little chicken Wellingtons

(photograph right)

4 half chicken breasts
4 tablespoons butter
Salt and freshly ground pepper
½ lb mushrooms, finely chopped
1 tablespoon flour
4 tablespoons whipping cream
Squeeze of lemon juice
1 pre-rolled sheet frozen puff pastry
1 egg, beaten

Bone and skin chicken breasts. Heat butter in a heavy frying pan and cook chicken breasts over moderate heat for 3 minutes each side or until cooked through. Remove and season with salt and pepper. Add mushrooms to pan, stir until they are soft. Sprinkle flour over, and stir in. Add cream, lemon juice and salt and pepper to taste and continue stirring until mixture is smooth and thick. Allow to cool.

Roll out pastry sheet to measure 12-inch square (pastry will be ⅛-inch thick). Cut in four making 6-inch squares. Chop the chicken into bite-size pieces. Place a mound of chicken pieces on each square, and cover with mushroom mixture. Dampen edges of pastry and roll neatly around filling, tucking in the ends. Place seam-side down on a baking sheet and brush tops with beaten egg. Cut a small slit in the top for steam to escape. Bake in a preheated 400° oven for 25 minutes, or until golden brown and crisp. Serves 4.

Note: Substitute your own favorite pastry recipe for frozen puff pastry.

Backyard smoked turkey

Smoke a turkey on your own backyard grill and you'll find it is moist and juicy and delicately flavored. It's not difficult to do. As a bonus it is best served just warm, so it can be ready well before serving time, leaving the grill free for potatoes and other foods needing last minute preparation.

Serve the turkey with a spicy, smoke-flavored sauce made from the drippings. You'll enjoy it when first served, and any leftovers make delicious sandwiches.

You'll need a good-sized grill, about 24-inches in diameter. If rectangular shaped, about 24-inches x 14-inches. It should have a cover.

You will need about 2½ lb of charcoal, hickory chips and a foil pan a little larger

all around than the turkey. Make from double thickness of heavy-duty aluminum wrap by turning up foil on all sides and mitering corners.

Build the fire at one side or end of the grill in usual way. When the fire is burning evenly, place foil drip pan beside the fire under the place where the turkey will rest.

1 (12-15 lb) eviscerated turkey
1 rib celery with leaves, cut up
¼ cup chopped onions
¼ cup chopped parsley
2 sprigs fresh thyme or ½ teaspoon dried herbs
½ cup cooking oil and 1 cup cider or dry white wine, flavored with a sprinkling of herbs, salt and pepper

If turkey is frozen, defrost until pliable. Sprinkle cavity with salt and fill with celery, onion and herbs. Close openings with skewers, truss and brush all over with the flavored oil-cider basting liquid. Place turkey right on the grill with the foil pan underneath. Place a piece of foil against the side of the bird toward the fire for protection, if the fire seems quite hot.

Cover grill. Adjust damper so fire will burn slowly. Let turkey cook very slowly, allowing about 5 hours for a 12-15 lb bird. It should brown slowly. Lift the cover and brush with the herb-cider basting liquid once or twice. Add 3-4 damp hickory chips to the fire when first started, about half way through the cooking and toward the end. Add additional briquets once.

The turkey is done when the second joint moves easily and the breast meat is soft to the touch. A meat thermometer inserted in the thickest part of the thigh should read 190°.

Remove turkey to serving platter. Slip the foil pan with juices carefully onto a cookie sheet, pour the juices into a saucepan. Add any remaining basting sauce. Skim off the fat. Add broth (made from cooking giblets) to make 3 cups. Thicken with 1 tablespoon cornstarch mixed with ¼ cup of broth. Bring to a boil, stirring constantly and taste for seasoning. Simmer a few minutes. Serve a little sauce over each serving of turkey.

Wine-roasted duck

Cooked this way, duck is tender and beautifully glazed.

| 1 (6 lb) duck |
| Salt |
| Paprika |
| Ginger |
| 1 small onion, grated |
| 1 cup red wine |
| ⅓ cup brown sugar, firmly packed |
| 1 tablespoon cornstarch |
| ¼ teaspoon salt |
| 2 teaspoons grated lemon rind |
| ¼ cup toasted sesame seeds |

Cut duck into quarters and remove any excess fat. Arrange duck pieces in a single layer in a baking dish and bake uncovered in a preheated 400° oven for 30 minutes.

Remove duck from oven and pour off fat that has accumulated in dish. Season duck pieces generously with salt, paprika and ginger and return to the dish. Sprinkle with onion, pour in half a cup of the wine, and cover dish with a lid or aluminum foil.

Continue cooking until duck is tender (about an additional 45 minutes) turning pieces now and then.

In a small saucepan, combine sugar, cornstarch, salt, lemon rind, and remaining half cup of wine. Bring to a boil, stirring, lower heat and simmer until smooth and thickened. Spoon over duck and bake uncovered for another 10-15 minutes, basting often, until duck is glazed. Sprinkle with sesame seeds to serve. Serves 4.

Turkey enchiladas

| 2 (4 oz) cans green chilies |
| 2 tablespoons cooking oil |
| 1 large clove garlic, crushed |
| 1 (1 lb 12 oz) can tomatoes, drained |
| 1 cup tomato liquid or water |
| 2 cups chopped onion |
| 2 teaspoons salt |
| ½ teaspoon oregano |
| 3 cups shredded cooked turkey |
| 2 cups sour cream or non-dairy substitute |
| 2 cups grated Cheddar cheese |
| Extra ⅓ cup cooking oil |
| 15 large or 24 small corn tortillas |

Rinse seeds from chilies and chop (use rubber gloves and don't touch eyes). Heat oil in a saucepan and saute chilies and garlic for a few minutes. Drain and break up tomatoes, reserving 1 cup liquid (if necessary, add water to make up 1 cup). Add tomatoes, onion, 1 teaspoon of the salt, oregano and tomato liquid to pan. Lower heat and simmer, uncovered, for about 30 minutes or until mixture is thick.

Combine turkey, sour cream, cheese and remaining salt. Heat extra oil and dip in tortillas, one by one, until they become limp. Drain well on paper towels. Fill tortillas with turkey mixture, roll up and arrange side by side, seam side down, in a casserole or 13 x 9 x 2-inch baking dish. Pour sauce over top and place in a preheated 350° oven for 30 minutes or until hot. Serves 8-12.

Stuffed pork chops

| 6 butterfly pork chops, 1-inch thick |
| 4 tablespoons butter or margarine |
| ¼ cup chopped onion |
| ¼ cup chopped celery |
| 2 tablespoons chopped green pepper (optional) |
| 1 cup soft breadcrumbs |
| Salt and pepper to taste |
| ½ cup beef bouillon |
| **For gravy:** |
| 2 tablespoons drippings or butter |
| 2 tablespoons flour |
| 1 cup liquid, degreased casserole juices, bouillon or broth |
| Salt and pepper to taste |

Trim excess fat from chops. Melt 2 tablespoons of the butter in a small pan and saute onion, celery and pepper until tender. Combine with breadcrumbs and season to taste with salt and pepper. Stuff pork chops and close with small skewers or toothpicks.

Heat remaining butter in a skillet and brown chops. Place chops in a casserole, add bouillon, cover and cook in a preheated 350° oven for 1¼ hours or until tender. If desired, pan juices may be thickened. Remove chops from casserole, take out skewers and keep warm.

To make gravy, measure pan juices, use fat from top or butter, place in skillet, add flour, stir until smooth and cook 1-2 minutes. Add liquid and, stirring continuously, bring to a boil. Season to taste, simmer a few minutes and serve with chops.

Spareribs and sauerkraut

| 3 lb pork spareribs, cut into 3-4 rib pieces |
| Salt and pepper to taste |
| ½ cup water |
| 1 (1 lb 12 oz) can sauerkraut |

Season spareribs with salt and pepper, brown over medium heat in a heavy skillet. Add water, cover and cook slowly 1 hour. Remove ribs, reserve 2 cups meat drippings. Add sauerkraut and drippings to skillet, top with ribs and cook slowly 1 more hour or until ribs are tender. Serves 4.

Indo-American pork

*This is patterned after an
Indonesian dish called
Daging Ketjap*

1½ teaspoons cooking oil
1 lb boneless pork, cut into ½-inch cubes
½ cup chopped onion
1 clove garlic, crushed
⅓ teaspoon ground chile pepper
¼ cup soy sauce
1¼ teaspoons brown sugar
½ teaspoon lemon juice

Heat oil in skillet. Saute pork, onion, garlic and ground chile pepper 10 minutes, stirring often. Add soy sauce, sugar and lemon juice. Cook over low heat 10-15 minutes or until pork is tender. Serve over rice. Serves 2-3.

Note: Recipe doubles easily.

Pork and sauerkraut

1½-2 lb pork, cut in 1-inch cubes
Salt
Paprika
2 tablespoons cooking oil
1 onion, chopped
2 cups water
3-4 slices bacon
1 (1 lb 12 oz) can sauerkraut
4-6 juniper berries (optional)
¾ cup beer
1 cup sour cream or to taste

Season meat with salt and paprika. Heat oil in a heavy saucepan and brown pork on all sides. Add onion and water and simmer, covered, until pork is tender, approximately 1-1½ hours. Skim off excess fat.

Fry bacon in a skillet, drain off fat. Add sauerkraut, juniper berries and beer. Simmer, covered, 1 hour.

Transfer meat to a 2-quart casserole, mix sour cream into meat juices and sprinkle with paprika to taste. Spread sauerkraut over meat, pour sauce over, cover casserole. This can be prepared ahead up to this point.

Bake in a preheated 300° oven for 10-20 minutes or until hot. If made ahead of time and refrigerated, reheat at 350° for 1 hour or until hot. Serves 4-6.

Orange-ginger pork loin chops

Great for a barbecue!
8 thick pork loin chops
½ cup cooking oil
1 tablespoon grated lemon rind
Grated rind and juice of 1 large orange
½-inch fresh ginger, finely chopped
4 tablespoons light soy sauce
4 tablespoons brown sugar
Salt and freshly ground pepper
Orange wedges to garnish

Trim excess fat from chops and arrange in one layer in a shallow dish. Combine remaining ingredients except orange wedges, seasoning to taste. Spoon over chops and marinate for several hours or overnight in refrigerator, turning now and again.

Drain chops and grill over hot coals for 8-10 minutes each side, depending on thickness. Baste with marinade every couple of minutes as they cook. Garnish with orange wedges to serve. Serves 4.

Farmer's pork platter

*This is a lovely old-fashioned dish,
uncomplicated but full of flavor.
If you wish, you can use
thin pork chops instead of the more
expensive tenderloin.*

4 tablespoons butter
3 large potatoes, peeled and sliced
2 large onions, sliced
Salt and freshly ground pepper
4 tablespoons cooking oil
1½ lb pork tenderloin, cut into ½-inch slices
½ cup white wine or water
¼ lb mushrooms, finely chopped
1 clove garlic, crushed
½ cup finely chopped parsley
Extra 2 tablespoons butter, softened

Grease a square or oblong shallow casserole, and add potatoes and onions in layers. Season each layer with salt and pepper and dot with butter. Cover with aluminum foil and cook in a preheated 400° oven for 30 minutes, or until vegetables are tender.

Meanwhile, heat oil in a large frying pan and fry pork slices on both sides until golden brown and cooked through, about 10 minutes altogether. Season with salt and pepper and arrange over potatoes and onions.

Add wine or water to frying pan, and stir over medium heat until it boils. Pour over pork and vegetables.

Mix together mushrooms, garlic, parsley and softened butter and sprinkle over the top. Return to oven and bake 10 minutes longer. Serve from the casserole. Serves 6.

Pork'n beans with corn

(photograph right)

*A soup-stew that's hearty enough
for a main course — and with corn
for extra color and nutrition.
(When fresh corn is out of season,
use drained, canned shoepeg corn.)*

3 tablespoons oil
1½ lb lean pork, cut into cubes
2 medium onions, sliced
2 cloves garlic, crushed
1 teaspoon caraway seeds
1 tablespoon chopped fresh oregano, or 1 teaspoon dried
8 cups beef bouillon
Salt and freshly ground pepper
1 (15 oz) can kidney beans, chick peas or other beans, drained and rinsed
2 large carrots, sliced
3 ears corn, cut in thick slices
Plain yogurt, lemon wedges to serve

Heat the oil in a large, deep saucepan and fry pork over moderate heat until well browned. Add onions and garlic and cook until onion softens. Add caraway seeds, oregano, bouillon and salt and pepper to taste. Bring to a boil, cover the pan and cook until pork is tender, about 1 hour. (This can all be done the night before, and refrigerated until the next day.)

Add drained beans, carrots and corn to the pot, and simmer until vegetables are tender, about 15 minutes. Taste for seasoning and serve in deep bowls, with crusty bread. Provide bowls of yogurt to stir into the soup, and lemon wedges for added zest. Serves 8.

Note: If you don't like the flavor of caraway seeds, leave them out — but they do go well with pork.

serving pieces and secure with toothpicks. Roll in flour and shake off excess.

Melt the 3 tablespoons of butter in a heavy frying pan and fry tenderloins until golden brown on both sides. Add mushrooms and broth and stir to get up the brown bits from the bottom. Cover pan tightly and simmer until pork is tender, about 45 minutes.

Remove pork to a heated serving platter. Season sauce in pan with salt and pepper, stir in cream and heat gently. Spoon around pork and serve immediately. Serves 8.

Stuffed pork Wellington

(photograph right)

It's equally nice hot or cold
4 pork tenderloins of equal size, weighing about 3 lb altogether
Salt and freshly ground pepper
1 teaspooon dried rosemary
1 cup finely chopped parsley
3 tablespoons butter, softened
3 tablespoons grated Parmesan cheese
Extra 3 tablespoons butter
1 (1 lb 1 oz) package frozen puff pastry
1 egg yolk, beaten

Flatten pork tenderloins between two sheets of plastic wrap, and season with salt, pepper and rosemary.

Mix together parsley, 3 tablespoons of softened butter, Parmesan and salt and pepper to taste. Spread mixture on two of the tenderloins, top with the other two tenderloins and press firmly together. Tie into place with white string.

Heat the other 3 tablespoons of butter in a frying pan, and brown the stuffed tenderloins well on both sides. Remove, allow to cool, and remove string.

Roll the puff pastry out into two rectangles big enough to wrap around the tenderloins. Place a tenderloin on each, moisten the edges of the pastry, and press firmly together to enclose tenderloins completely. If desired, make decorations from surplus pastry, moisten, and press into place on top. Brush all over with beaten egg yolk.

Arrange on a baking sheet and bake in a preheated 400° oven for 20 minutes. Reduce heat to 350° and bake for a further 20 minutes. (If pastry is browning too much cover with foil.) Serve hot or cold, cut in thick slices. Serves 10.

Note: Substitute your own favorite pastry recipe for frozen puff pastry.

Rice-stuffed pork crown roast

· 1 (16-rib) pork crown roast, about 6½-7 lb
2 cups regular rice
1 cup combined wild and long grain rice
1 (4 oz) package dried apricots
½ teaspoon cinnamon
½ cup coarsely chopped pecans
½ (6 oz) can frozen orange juice concentrate, thawed
½ cup honey
2 tablespoons butter or margarine
Orange slices and fresh cranberries to garnish

Place roast, bone tips up, on a rack in a shallow roasting pan. Insert meat thermometer, not touching bone or fat. Cover ends of bones with a strip of foil. Roast in preheated 325° oven 3½ hours.

Meanwhile, cook rice according to package directions. Cook apricots according to package directions, adding cinnamon during the last 5 minutes of cooking time. Drain apricots and chop roughly. Combine rice, apricots and pecans, mix well. Combine orange juice concentrate and honey, mixing well.

Remove rack from roasting pan and fill roast cavity with rice mixture. Place the remaining rice mixture in a small baking dish. Dot the rice stuffing with butter. Brush roast with some of the orange juice mixture. Continue cooking roast 30 minutes-1 hour or until meat thermometer registers 160°. (Allow 35-40 minutes per lb.) Brush occasionally with the orange juice mixture. Let roast stand 10-15 minutes to allow juices to set.

Carefully transfer roast to a warm serving platter. Garnish with orange slices and cranberries. Serves 12-16.

Stuffed pork surprise

(photograph above)

4 pork tenderloins of equal length, about ¾ lb each
1 cup soft breadcrumbs
2 tablespoons melted butter
1 clove garlic, crushed
½ teaspoon sage
½ teaspoon rosemary
2 green onions, finely chopped
Salt and freshly ground pepper
Flour
Extra 3 tablespoons butter
¼ lb mushrooms, chopped
1 cup chicken broth
½ cup whipping cream

Trim the pork tenderloins and flatten out a little with a rolling pin. Mix together breadcrumbs, melted butter, garlic, herbs, green onion and salt and pepper to taste and spread over two of the tenderloins. Top with remaining tenderloins and press together. Cut into

Holiday spareribs

Just a few simple ingredients and you can plan on beautifully glazed, tender pork spareribs for dinner.

4 lb meaty pork spareribs, cut into serving pieces

½ cup medium sherry

4 tablespoons vinegar

3 tablespoons brown sugar

½ teaspoon ginger

6 tablespoons light soy sauce

Place spareribs in one layer in a shallow roasting pan. Bake uncovered in a pre-heated 350° oven for 1 hour, then pour off fat that has accumulated in pan.

Combine remaining ingredients and spoon over spareribs. Continue baking for another hour, turning frequently and basting with sauce. Serves 4-6.

Triple decker pork
(photograph page 60)

Use thin slices of pork and ask your butcher to beat them out very thinly, as for schnitzel.

6 thin slices pork of equal size, weighing about 2 lb altogether

3 teaspoons Dijon mustard

3 thick slices ham

6-8 slices Mozarella cheese

6 fresh sage leaves or 1 teaspoon dried sage

Salt and freshly ground pepper

2 eggs, beaten

About 1 cup fine breadcrumbs

4 tablespoons butter

4 tablespoons cooking oil

Spread 3 of the pork slices with mustard. Top with slices of ham, cut to fit, and then cheese. Place a couple of sage leaves on top or sprinkle with dried sage. Press remaining slices of pork in place to make 3 "sandwiches". Season both sides with salt and pepper. Dip in beaten egg, then in breadcrumbs, and chill for 20 minutes.

Heat butter and oil in a large frying pan and fry the pork on both sides until golden brown and tender, about 4 minutes each side. Cut in thick slices to serve. Serves 6.

Glazed pork roast
(photograph below)

4 lb pork rib roast

1 teaspoon grated fresh ginger

1 clove garlic, crushed

3 tablespoons soy sauce

3 tablespoons dry sherry

2 tablespoons brown sugar

1 tablespoon honey

1 cup chicken broth

Place pork in a baking dish, fat side up. Combine remaining ingredients in small saucepan and bring to a simmer. Pour over pork and bake in a preheated 350° oven for 1¾-2 hours or until internal temperature of pork is 160° on a meat thermometer. Baste with pan juices while pork is cooking and add extra broth to pan if it seems to be drying out. Serves 4.

Note: Sauce is delicious brushed over roast chicken, turkey halves, wild duck or goose.

Fruity stuffed pork loin

¾ cup chopped dried apricots

1 medium onion, finely chopped

2 tablespoons butter

¼ cup seedless raisins

1 cup soft breadcrumbs

4 tablespoons chopped walnuts

2 teaspoons grated lemon rind

Salt and freshly ground pepper

1 egg, lightly beaten

1 pork loin, about 3 lb, boned

For gravy:

1 tablespoon flour

1 cup beef bouillon

Salt and freshly ground pepper

Cover apricots with boiling water, leave for 30 minutes, drain. Fry onion in the butter until softened, stir in raisins, apricots, crumbs, walnuts, lemon rind, salt and pepper. Add the egg and mix in.

Spoon stuffing into the meat, hold firmly and tie in several places. Put into a greased baking dish and roast in a preheated 350° oven for about 2 hours, or until internal temperature is 160° on a meat thermometer. Put on a heated platter and leave in a warm place for about 15 minutes before carving. This sets the juices and makes the pork easier to carve.

Meanwhile, make gravy. Pour fat from pan, leaving about 1 tablespoon. Stir in flour over medium heat until well blended, remove from heat and stir in bouillon. Return to heat and stir until thickened and smooth. Season with salt and pepper to taste and serve with pork. Serves 6-8.

Honey glazed ham

The traditional gesture to lavish entertaining, a ham, is expensive. But after its initial display and consumption for a special event, it can be used in various ways to supply after-the-party meals, ending its use with pea soup made from the bone, so that not a scrap is wasted.

1 whole cooked ham, about 18 lb

¼ cup whole cloves

½ cup honey

2 tablespoons Dijon mustard

3 tablespoons dry sherry

2 tablespoons soy sauce

¼ cup brown sugar

Cut the ham fat in a diamond pattern and insert a clove in the centre of each diamond. Combine honey with remaining ingredients, brush over ham and place on a rack in a large baking pan. Bake in a preheated 350° oven for 3 hours, basting occasionally with pan juices. Serve warm or cold. A whole ham of this size should serve 30-40 people with other dishes.

Note: Please see The Changing Face of Texas chapter for pea soup recipe using ham bone.

Gingered ham slices

In this recipe, preserved ginger adds flavor to baked ham steaks.

4 ham steaks

4 pineapple slices, fresh or canned

2 tablespoons melted butter

2 tablespoons brown sugar

2 tablespoons finely chopped preserved ginger

1 teaspoon grated lemon rind

1 cup pineapple juice

Arrange ham steaks side by side in a shallow casserole dish. Put a slice of pineapple on top of each. Mix together remaining ingredients and spoon over ham and pineapple.

Bake in a preheated 400° oven for 10 minutes, or until ham is heated through and glazed. Baste with liquid in dish several times while cooking. Serves 4.

Creamy veal and mushrooms

Quickly made and beautifully flavored — a dinner party dish that's ready in 20 minutes.

2 lb veal steak

6 tablespoons butter

Salt and freshly ground pepper

2 cloves garlic, crushed

4 green onions, finely chopped

1 lb button mushrooms

½ cup dry white wine

2 cups sour cream

Trim fat from veal and cut meat into strips about 3-inches long and ½-inch wide. Heat butter and toss veal strips over moderately high heat for 6 minutes, or until golden brown. Season generously with salt and pepper and remove with a slotted spoon. Add garlic, green onions and mushrooms to pan, season, and saute for 5 minutes. Stir in wine and sour cream and heat, stirring.

Return veal to pan and stir gently through sauce to reheat. Taste for seasoning and spoon into a heated serving dish. Serves 6.

Venison pork casserole

(photograph left)

The combination of meats makes this casserole unusual and delicious.

| 1 lb venison steak |
| 1 lb pork tenderloin |
| 20 juniper berries |
| 1½ cups dry white wine |
| ¼ cup port wine |
| 25 soft prunes, pitted |
| Salt and freshly ground pepper |
| 3 tablespoons butter |
| ½ lb mushrooms, sliced |
| ⅓ cup whipping cream |

Trim meat and cut into 1-inch cubes. Crush juniper berries and mix with wine and port.

Place meat in a shallow dish with prunes and season with salt and pepper. Pour wine mixture over, cover with plastic wrap and refrigerate overnight.

Drain meat and prunes and dry on paper towels. Heat butter in a large, heavy frying pan and brown meat on all sides. Remove with a slotted spoon and place in a casserole.

Fry mushrooms lightly in pan juices and add to casserole. Strain marinade into a small saucepan and boil uncovered until reduced by half. Pour over meat and add cream and prunes. Cover and bake in a preheated 350° oven for 45-60 minutes, or until meat is tender. Serves 4-6.

Note: Check food import shops or specialty stores for juniper berries.

Veal patties in mushroom-brandy sauce

(photograph above)

| 1½ lb ground veal |
| ½ cup whipping cream or evaporated milk |
| 2 eggs |
| Salt and freshly ground pepper |
| 4 tablespoons butter |

For sauce:

| 3 tablespoons butter |
| ½ lb button mushrooms, sliced |
| Salt and freshly ground white pepper |
| 3 tablespoons brandy |
| ¾ cup whipping cream |
| Paprika to garnish |

Mix veal with cream, eggs and salt and pepper to taste until it forms a compact mixture. Shape into 6 patties and chill for 30 minutes. Heat the 4 tablespoons of butter in a heavy frying pan, and cook patties on both sides over moderate heat until golden brown all over and cooked through, about 8 minutes.

Meanwhile, make the sauce. Heat the 3 tablespoons of butter in a separate frying pan and toss mushrooms over moderately high heat until tender but still firm, about 3 minutes. Season with salt and pepper and stir in brandy and cream. Simmer until sauce is thickened, and taste for seasoning. Arrange patties on a heated platter, spoon sauce onto each, and sprinkle with a little paprika. Serves 6.

Venison stew

2 lb venison steak
3 tablespoons flour
1 teaspoon dried mixed herbs
2 medium onions, finely chopped
2 large tomatoes, peeled and chopped
Salt and freshly ground pepper
Small piece cinnamon stick
2 teaspoons Angostura bitters
¾ cup red wine
1 cup beef bouillon

Remove any sinews from venison, cut meat into cubes and roll lightly in flour. Arrange the cubes in a greased ovenproof casserole in layers, sprinkling each layer with herbs, onions and tomatoes and seasoning with salt and pepper. Add the cinnamon stick. Combine bitters, wine and bouillon and pour into the casserole.

Cover tightly and cook in a preheated 350° oven for 1½ to 2 hours or until venison is fork tender. Serves 6-8.

Butterflied leg of lamb with barbecue sauce

Ask your butcher to remove the bone from a leg of lamb.
The lamb is basted with a spicy sauce as it roasts. You can use the same sauce to baste chicken halves grilled on an outdoor barbecue. Allow 15-20 minutes each side.

1 butterflied leg of lamb
For sauce:
1 cup chicken broth
1 fat clove garlic, crushed
1 large onion, grated
3 tablespoons olive oil
3 tablespoons mild chili sauce
1 tablespoon vinegar
3 tablespoons brown sugar
1 teaspoon salt
½ teaspoon thyme

Place lamb on a greased rack set in a greased baking dish. Combine sauce ingredients in a saucepan and simmer 5 minutes.

Roast lamb in a preheated 350° oven until done, allowing about 25 minutes for each 1 lb and 25 minutes extra.

While lamb is cooking, baste frequently with sauce. If necessary, add a little water to baking dish to prevent sauce scorching. Transfer lamb to a platter and allow to rest 20 minutes.

Skim any fat from juices in roasting pan, and taste for seasoning. If too thick, stir in a little water or chicken broth. Heat, and serve as a sauce with the lamb. Serves 6-8.

Tarragon veal fricassee
(photograph right)

Pale, creamy stews were very popular in our grandmothers' day.
Chicken and veal were often "fricasseed" as a change from brown stews. Here's a streamlined version, using cream and sour cream to give richness and the necessary pale color to the sauce.

1½ lb stewing veal
Flour seasoned with salt and white pepper
4 tablespoons butter
1 large onion, finely chopped
1½ cups chicken broth
1 tablespoon chopped fresh tarragon, or 1 teaspoon dried
½ cup sour cream
½ cup whipping cream
1 tablespoon lemon juice
Finely chopped parsley to garnish

Remove any fat and gristle from veal and cut the meat into bite-size cubes. Roll in seasoned flour and shake off excess.

Heat butter in a heavy saucepan, and toss the pieces of veal until pale gold — don't let them brown. Add onion, broth and tarragon and bring to a boil. Lower heat, cover pan, and simmer until veal is tender, about 40 minutes. Stir in sour cream, cream and lemon juice and bring to a simmer. Taste for seasoning, and sprinkle generously with chopped parsley to serve. Serves 4.

Note: If you like a thicker sauce, stir in a paste of 1 tablespoon cornstarch mixed with a little water after adding the cream, and simmer, stirring, for 2 minutes.

Roast saddle of lamb with stuffed tomatoes

(photograph right)

1 saddle of lamb
3 cloves garlic, cut into slivers
Salt and freshly ground pepper
1 cup beef stock or bouillon
1 cup Madeira

For tomatoes:

8 medium tomatoes, peeled
Salt and freshly ground pepper
2 tablespoons butter
1 medium onion, finely chopped
¼ lb mushrooms, finely chopped
3 tablespoons finely chopped parsley

Cut tiny slits all over lamb, and insert slivers of garlic. Rub with salt and pepper. Place meat (back side upwards) on a greased rack in a greased baking dish, and roast in a preheated 350° oven until done, allowing 20 minutes for each 1 lb of lamb. Twenty minutes before conclusion of cooking time, pour off all fat that has accumulated, and place lamb directly in dish. Pour stock over and bake for the last 20 minutes, basting 2 or 3 times with the stock. Remove lamb to a heated platter and allow to rest for 15 minutes before carving. Skim as much fat as possible from liquid in the baking dish. Strain into a small saucepan, and taste for seasoning. Add Madeira. Reheat and serve as gravy with the lamb.

For tomatoes, cut a lid from each, scoop out flesh with a teaspoon and chop flesh roughly. Season tomato shells with salt and pepper. Heat butter and fry onion and mushrooms until onion is soft and liquid has evaporated. Add tomato and cook another minute. Stir in parsley and salt and pepper to taste and spoon into tomato shells.

Cook 20 minutes with the lamb, and keep warm while lamb is resting. Serves 8.

Note: You may like to use a meat thermometer when roasting lamb — make sure it doesn't touch bone. Lamb will be medium-rare when thermometer registers 145° and will be well done at 165°.

Rabbit casserole

Bacon, wine, herbs and mushrooms transform rabbit into a special-occasion casserole.

1 rabbit, cut in serving pieces
1 tablespoon vinegar
Flour seasoned with salt and pepper
2 tablespoons cooking oil
2 tablespoons butter
3 medium onions, coarsely chopped
3 slices lean bacon, diced
2 tablespoons flour
1 cup dry white wine
½ cup chicken broth
1 tablespoon tomato paste
2 sprigs parsley
1 sprig thyme
1 bay leaf
Salt and freshly ground pepper
¼ lb button mushrooms, halved or sliced
Extra 2 tablespoons butter
Chopped parsley to garnish

Soak rabbit for 6-8 hours in cold salted water with vinegar added. Drain pieces and dry thoroughly, then coat with seasoned flour.

Heat together oil and butter, add rabbit pieces and brown all over. Transfer rabbit to an ovenproof dish. Add onions and bacon to pan and gently fry until onions have softened.

Add flour, stir for a minute or two, then pour in wine and chicken broth. Add tomato paste and stir until boiling. Pour over rabbit in dish, add parsley, thyme and bay leaf, tied together, with salt and pepper to taste.

Cover and cook in a preheated 325° oven for about 1½ hours, or until tender. Just before cooking time is finished, quickly fry mushrooms in extra butter for a minute or two and mix into the casserole. Remove bundle of herbs and serve garnished with chopped parsley. Serves 4.

Oxtail stew

4 lb oxtail
3 tablespoons butter
2 large onions, finely chopped
1 large carrot, sliced
1 medium turnip, cut into dice
1 bay leaf
2 tablespoons chopped, fresh mixed herbs or 2 teaspoons dried mixed herbs (thyme and savory)
3 cups beef bouillon
Salt and freshly ground pepper
1 tablespoon flour mixed to a smooth paste with a little extra bouillon
Chopped parsley to garnish

Trim as much fat as possible from oxtail. Heat butter in a large, heavy saucepan and fry onion until starting to soften. Add oxtail, carrot and turnip and stir over high heat until oxtail starts to brown. Add remaining ingredients except flour paste and bring to a boil, stirring. Lower heat, cover, and simmer for 3 hours, or until oxtail is tender.

Stir a little hot liquid into the flour paste, then stir back into the stew. Simmer until sauce is smooth and thickened and taste for seasoning. Sprinkle with chopped parsley to serve. Serves 4.

Roast quail

12 quail
2 cups Thompson seedless grapes
1 cup red wine
2 sprigs fresh thyme, or pinch dried
¼ teaspoon salt
4 green onions, chopped
⅓ cup cooking oil
6 slices lean bacon, cut in half
Hard-boiled quail eggs and watercress to garnish

Stuff quail with the grapes. Bring wine to a boil with the sprigs of thyme, then remove from heat. When cool, mix with salt, green onion and oil and pour over quail. Marinate, covered, for several hours or overnight. Drain quail, pat dry, and wrap each one in half a slice of bacon. Arrange in a greased baking dish and bake in a preheated 350° oven for 15-20 minutes, until brown and tender. Serve at room temperature, garnished with quail eggs and watercress. Serves 6.

Liver marengo

1 lb beef or calf liver
¼ cup flour
1½ teaspoons garlic salt
¼ teaspoon pepper
2 tablespoons cooking oil
¼ cup dry white wine
1 cup beef bouillon
½ cup sour cream, sour cream dressing or imitation sour cream
1 (16 oz) can tomatoes, chopped
1 bay leaf
3 cups hot cooked rice (1 cup uncooked)

Cut liver in thin strips. Roll in combined flour, garlic salt and pepper. Brown in oil in skillet. Add wine, stir to loosen brown particles. Blend any remaining flour with bouillon and sour cream. Add tomatoes and bay leaf. Pour over meat, cover and simmer about 30 minutes or until meat is tender. Remove bay leaf. Serve over rice. Serves 6.

Texas pheasant

2 young pheasant, cut in pieces
¾ cup flour
1 teaspoon salt
¼ teaspoon pepper
2 eggs, beaten
6 tablespoons butter or margarine
Chicken broth or water
¼ teaspoon poultry seasoning
1½ cups whipping cream

Wipe pieces of pheasant with paper towels. Combine flour, salt and pepper. Dip pheasant in egg and dredge in flour. Heat butter in a frying pan and brown pheasant well. Place in a casserole. Pour chicken broth in casserole to a depth of ¼-inch. Add poultry seasoning, cover and cook in a preheated 325° oven for 1½ hours or until pheasant is tender. Additional chicken broth can be added if pheasant appears to be drying out. Add cream to casserole and return to oven for an additional 30 minutes. Gravy can be thickened by reducing it. Serves 4-6.

Green chile stew

3 lb boned venison or lamb, cut into 1½-inch cubes
Flour
2-4 tablespoons cooking oil
¼ teaspoon freshly ground black pepper
6 juniper berries, crushed
2 onions, chopped
5½ cups canned hominy with liquid
1 medium dried hot red pepper, crushed
1 tablespoon salt
2 cloves garlic, crushed
2 teaspoons oregano
½ cup finely chopped parsley
6 hot green peppers (such as fresh jalapenos, washed, seeded and quartered)
4 cups water

Dust meat lightly with flour. Brown slowly on all sides in oil in a large, heavy kettle. As meat browns, add pepper and juniper berries. Drain meat on paper

towels. In same kettle, saute onions slowly until golden.

Place all ingredients in kettle. Cover and simmer 1½ hours or until meat is tender, stirring occasionally. Serves 12-14.

Note: Juniper berries available at gourmet and food specialty shops. Expensive but excellent flavoring for wild game, especially venison.

Quail in a basket of cress

An easy quail dish, marvelous for a picnic or casual outdoor meal.

12 quail
3 lemons, quartered
1 cup butter
Freshly ground black pepper
3 bunches of watercress

Wipe quail with damp paper towels. Rub a piece of lemon over the skin of each quail, then place the lemon in the cavity. Melt butter and brush very generously over each bird, retaining any butter which isn't used.

Arrange quail in a baking pan and roast in a preheated 450° oven for 5 minutes. Reduce oven heat to 300° and roast for an additional 15 minutes. Frequently brush more butter on the quail, and baste with juices in the baking pan.

Remove quail when cooked, sprinkle with freshly ground pepper and allow to cool. Line a basket with watercress and arrange the cold quail among the cress. Serves 6.

Smothered doves

6-8 doves
3 tablespoons flour
½ teaspoon salt
¼ teaspoon pepper
½ cup olive oil
1-2 cloves garlic
1 cup red wine, Burgundy or claret
Water

Dust doves with flour seasoned with salt and pepper. In a heavy skillet, lightly brown doves in heated oil with garlic. When browned, remove garlic and discard. Add wine and enough water to barely cover birds. Simmer about 1½ hours or until tender. Thicken pan juices with a little of the remaining seasoned flour. Serve with a white rice-wild rice combination. Serves 3-4.

Goose stroganoff

2 geese breasts, cut in small pieces
¼ cup flour
Salt
Pepper
Butter or cooking oil
1 cup beef consomme or onion soup
1 (6 oz) can mushrooms, drained or 1 cup sliced fresh mushrooms
Pinch nutmeg
1 cup sour cream

Dredge goose in combined flour, salt and pepper. Heat butter in a skillet and brown meat. Add consomme, mushrooms and nutmeg. Cover and simmer about 1 hour, or until goose is tender. If necessary add a little more beef consomme.

When goose is tender, add sour cream, blending in well, but do not boil. Serve over wild rice or noodles. Serves 4-6.

Pan-fried liver in creamy sauce

For tenderness, liver should be cooked quickly, or long and slowly. Here's a quick approach, using calf liver.

1½ lb calf liver
Flour seasoned with salt, pepper and paprika
6 tablespoons butter
2 cloves garlic, crushed
¼ cup dry white wine
¼ cup whipping cream
2 tablespoons finely chopped chives or parsley to garnish

Remove any membrane and tubes from liver. Cut into thin slices, and then into finger-length strips. Toss in seasoned flour, leave for 10 minutes to dry.

Heat butter in a large frying pan, add garlic, and fry until garlic starts to soften. Add liver and toss over high heat until brown on all sides.

Reduce heat and add white wine to pan, stirring to get up the crusty bits from the bottom. Stir in cream and heat through (do not boil). Taste for seasoning, and add more salt and pepper if necessary. Sprinkle with chopped chives to serve. Serves 6-8.

East Texas stew

2-3 squirrels or rabbits or 10-12 doves or quail
Wine or salt water to cover
2½ quarts water
2 tablespoons salt
2 ribs celery, chopped
1 cup chopped onions
3 cups canned tomatoes
3 medium potatoes, chopped
3 tablespoons Worcestershire sauce
2 tablespoons garlic salt
1 teaspoon black pepper
3 tablespoons olive oil
1 jalapeno pepper, finely chopped
3 carrots, chopped

Cut cleaned, prepared animals or birds into serving pieces. Marinate in wine or salt water overnight. Next day, drain, place in large pot and add water, salt, celery, onion, tomatoes, potatoes, Worcestershire sauce, garlic salt, pepper, oil, jalapeno pepper and carrots. Bring to a boil, lower heat and simmer until meat is tender, 4-5 hours. Serves 6.

Fried quail

8 quail
Flour
1 teaspoon salt
⅛ teaspoon pepper
Cooking oil

Dredge quail with mixture of flour, salt and pepper. Heat oil (about 1-inch) in a heavy skillet. Add quail and brown birds on both sides. Cover skillet, lower heat and cook slowly until tender, about 20 minutes. Turn birds once or twice. Serves 4.

Overleaf: Celebration, San Antonio style.

TEX AND MEX

Hot is haute when it comes from Texas kitchens. That's not to mean all Tex and Mex food will set you on fire. The amount and kind of chile used and whether it is fresh, dried or ground determine the hotness of any particular dish. But there's a spice to Tex and Mex cooking that nothing can diminish.

Texas shared a common history with Mexico from the Spanish Conquest in the 1500s until Texas independence in 1836. And that common bond is nowhere more apparent than in the foods of Texas.

Although a nearly 900-mile border geographically separates Texas from Mexico, recipes have traveled back and forth across the Tex-Mex border with tasty results. That culinary swapping has led to some of the best eating to be found, including enchiladas, tacos, tamales, refried beans and nachos.

Although other nations have influenced Texas cuisine, the origin definitely is Mexican. With the possible exception of Chicken Fried Steak, every Texas favorite has its roots in Mexican food. Chili, that spicy beef concoction, may have originated in San Antonio in the mid-1800s, but what the dish showcased was the fiery hot Mexican chile.

The same is true of the recent favorite, fajitas. While the marinated skirt steak which is grilled and thinly sliced is a purely Texas invention, the serving of it tortilla-style with beans and salsa is rooted in Mexican cooking.

Even food we consider Texan bears that Mexican influence. Chili powder is added to barbecue and fried chicken for extra flavor. Cilantro is put in soups for more zing. Cumin is stirred into stews to impart that flavor Texans love.

All this leads to the question every non-Texan always wants answered. Exactly what is Tex and Mex food? Experts consider it a compromise among the cooking of the Indians, Spanish settlers and those who call Texas their home. It is the food Texans watched their mothers and grandmothers prepare, the foods they grew up on and the foods they learned to love.

Simply put, Tex and Mex food is good eating.

Mrs Gonzales cooking the meat filling for tamales

Chile peppers
(photograph right)

Chile peppers (chilies) are an intrinsic part of Texan and Mexican cooking. Here are a few facts which will make handling them trouble-free.

As a rule of thumb, green chilies, such as jalapenos and serranos, are hotter than red, although the tiny, round chile pequines (or chile petines) are firecracker hot. Generally, smaller chilies are hotter than larger ones.

Handling chile peppers: Chilies must be handled carefully because they have potent fumes and can burn eyes and skin if you touch them after handling the chilies, sometimes even after you have washed your hands. Knowledgeable cooks usually wear rubber gloves when handling hot peppers. If you do get a skin burn while handling chilies, apply a commercial burn ointment or a paste of baking soda and water. Don't use butter as it traps the heat.

. Although most people think the seeds provide the heat, it really comes from the veins, the fleshy, membranous walls. The more inner membrane and seeds present in the dish, the hotter it will be.

To prepare chilies, remove the stems, split the chilies in half and remove the seeds under cold running water. To prepare dried red chilies (such as ancho and pasillas), wash them in cold water and remove veins, stems and seeds. Tear them into rough pieces. Place in a bowl and soak in hot water (about 1 cup to 6 chilies) for about an hour. Puree in a blender, adding the water in which they have been soaked. Don't overload the blender.

Chilies soaked for several hours in cold, salted water will be milder. Chilies also can be broiled before using to give a smoky flavor.

Wash brine from canned chilies and remove seeds if they are present.

Pico de gallo

3 cups chopped sweet'n mild Texas onions
3 cups diced firm pink tomatoes
2 avocados, diced (optional)
1-2 teaspoons finely chopped serrano or jalapeno peppers
3 tablespoons finely chopped cilantro (fresh coriander or Chinese parsley)
Juice of 2 limes
Salt and pepper to taste
Pinch garlic salt

Combine all the ingredients and mix well. Refrigerate. Serve with tortilla chips, fajitas or Mexican egg dishes. Makes about 4 cups.

Nachos

Tortilla chips
Cheddar cheese, sliced
Jalapeno peppers, sliced

Spread tortilla chips on cookie sheet. Top each with a small slice of cheese. Top cheese with a slice of jalapeno pepper. Broil until cheese melts, serve hot.

Note: To make super nachos use round tortilla chips. Spread each with refried beans, taco meat, jalapeno strips or diced mild green chilies and top with the garnish of your choice — avocado slices, guacamole, chopped onion, sour cream, chopped tomato, chopped green onion and/or sliced ripe olives. Top with cheese. Broil until cheese melts or heat in microwave oven.

Guacamole
(photograph page 90)

2 large ripe avocados
1 tablespoon lime or lemon juice
½ teaspoon salt
1 tablespoon finely chopped cilantro (fresh coriander or Chinese parsley), optional
2 tablespoons finely chopped onion
1 medium firm tomato, finely chopped (optional)
⅛ teaspoon hot pepper sauce (optional)

Cut each avocado in half, remove seed and scoop out pulp. Mash avocado, mix with lime juice, salt, cilantro, onion, tomato and hot pepper sauce. Mix well, cover and chill. Serve with small crackers, as a dip with tortilla or corn chips, or as a topping for tacos, taco salad and other Mexican dishes. Makes 1½-2 cups.

Seviche Acapulco
(photograph page 91)

Tourists always come home raving about Seviche (or Ceviche), an appetizer of fish "cooked" by marinating in lime juice.

1 lb firm white fish, cut in small squares or julienne
Juice of 6 limes
1 large or 2 small tomatoes, peeled, seeded and chopped
1 small onion, finely chopped
2 or more canned jalapeno peppers, seeded and cut into strips
¼ cup olive oil
1 tablespoon white vinegar
Small handful of parsley, finely chopped
¼ teaspoon oregano
Salt
Freshly ground pepper
Green olives

Arrange fish in a deep dish and cover with lime juice. Refrigerate about 6 hours, turning once, about halfway through the process. At end of marinating period, drain and reserve juice.

Combine tomato, onion, peppers, oil, vinegar, parsley, oregano, salt and pepper to taste. Add the reserved lime juice. Pour the sauce over this fish, toss gently and refrigerate until ready to serve. Garnish with green olives. Serves 6.

Layered dip

1 (16 oz) can refried beans
1 large tomato, chopped
1 (4 oz) can chopped black olives
1 (4 oz) can green chilies, chopped
Guacamole, frozen or homemade
Grated sharp Cheddar cheese
1 (8 oz) jar picante sauce
2 cups sour cream

In a serving bowl, layer ingredients in the order given. Serve with tortilla chips. Serves 10.

Tortilla soup

6 (4-inch) tortillas

½ cup cooking oil

8 cups canned chicken broth

1 onion, finely chopped

½ cup tomato puree or tomatoes with green chilies, pureed

1 tablespoon chopped cilantro (fresh coriander or Chinese parsley)

Grated Monterey Jack cheese

Cut the tortillas into strips (about ¼-inch wide) or wedges and fry in hot oil on both sides until crisp and light brown. Drain on paper towels and keep warm.

Heat broth with onion and simmer until onion is tender. Add the tomato puree and simmer 5 minutes longer. Add cilantro. Pour soup in individual bowls or mugs and garnish with tortilla strips. Serve with grated cheese. Serves 6.

Huevos rancheros (Mexican style eggs)

Great for Sunday brunch or New Year's Day breakfast — said to have tremendous restorative powers if you've overindulged!

1 large onion, chopped

1 green pepper, chopped

2 tablespoons bacon drippings

2 fresh tomatoes, chopped, or canned tomatoes

1 small hot green chile, chopped

Salt and pepper to taste

Chili powder, hot pepper sauce and Worcestershire sauce to taste

6 eggs

6 tortillas

Grated cheese (optional)

Saute onion and pepper in bacon drippings. Add tomatoes with some juice (a small amount of water may need to be added with fresh tomatoes). Add chile and seasonings to taste and simmer slowly, at least 20 minutes until sauce is moderately thick. Prepare eggs as desired.

Heat tortillas on a hot dry griddle or hold over a gas burner. If you prefer tortillas crisp and crunchy, fry in shortening, taking care not to brown. Place 1 egg on each tortilla. Pour over 1 tablespoon sauce. Serve immediately. Top with grated cheese, if desired. Serves 6.

Flour tortillas

4 cups flour

2 teaspoons salt

6 tablespoons shortening

1¼ cups lukewarm water

Sift flour and salt together in a large mixing bowl. Cut in shortening with 2 knives or pastry blender. Add water and beat until dough forms a ball and cleans sides of bowl. Turn onto a floured board and knead 20 times. Shape into 6 balls and let rest 15 minutes. Roll out to dinner plate size and cook in ungreased skillet, allowing 2 minutes on each side. Makes 6.

Quesadillas

1 cup grated Monterey Jack cheese

1 cup grated Cheddar cheese

1 (4 oz) can chopped green chilies

6 (12-inch) or 12 (6-inch) flour tortillas

1 tablespoon melted butter

Sprinkle Monterey Jack and Cheddar cheeses and chopped green chilies onto open flour tortillas. Fold tortillas in half and place on large baking sheets. Brush tops with melted butter. Place in preheated 350° oven for 10-15 minutes, or until tops of quesadillas are golden brown. Cut each quesadilla in triangular quarters. Serves 6.

Guacamole (page 89)

Chilies rellenos

Poblano chilies are ideal for this dish.

12 large green chilies with stems, or 3 (4 oz) cans whole green chilies

1 lb Monterey Jack or Longhorn cheese, strips or grated

2 eggs

½ teaspoon salt

1½ cups flour ·

Oil for frying

Char and peel fresh chilies, make a small slit below the stem and remove seeds (optional). Chilies are hotter if seeds are left in. Fill chilies with cheese, being careful not to break them.

Beat eggs well, add salt to flour. Dip stuffed chilies in beaten egg, then in seasoned flour. Fry in hot oil (360°-365°) until golden brown. Drain on paper towels. Serve with taco sauce. Serves 6.

Fajitas

(photograph page 95)

This excellent fajitas marinade is from Carlos Rios, a Houston Chronicle photographer.

4 cups soy sauce (use light soy sauce, the dark imported Chinese type is too strong)

1 cup brown sugar, firmly packed

1 teaspoon garlic powder

1 teaspoon onion powder

8 tablespoons lemon juice

4 teaspoons ginger

1 skirt steak (about ¾-inch thick) for each 3 guests

Warm flour tortillas

Combine soy sauce, brown sugar, garlic powder, onion powder, lemon juice and ginger in jar, shake to mix well and dissolve sugar. Let marinade stand in sealed jar overnight.

Trim fat from beef and peel off any membrane. If meat is more than ¾-inch thick at the thickest part, cut in half lengthways so it will cook quickly.

Pour marinade over beef and marinate 2 hours or overnight in refrigerator in sealed container.

Remove fajitas from marinade and grill over very hot coals for a short time (should only take about 10 minutes per steak if meat is ¾-inch thick or less). Brush meat with marinade 2-3 times while cooking. Chop meat with a cleaver and fold into warm flour tortillas to serve.

Note: Refrigerate extra marinade in tightly sealed jar for future use.

Seviche Acapulco (page 88)

Taco salad

(photograph left)

1½ lb lean ground beef
1 cup chopped green pepper
1½ cups chopped onion
Salt and pepper to taste
1 tablespoon chili powder
6-8 pinches cumin powder (cominos)
1 lb pasteurized processed cheese spread loaf
1 (10 oz) can tomatoes with green chilies
1 head lettuce
2 medium tomatoes, chopped
1 (6 oz) bag corn chips

In a large skillet, brown meat well. Drain. Add chopped pepper and onion. Season to taste with salt and pepper. Brown a few minutes more. Add chili powder and cumin. Meanwhile, melt cheese over very low heat (or in microwave) and stir in tomatoes with green chilies.

In a large bowl, layer lettuce, torn in bite-size pieces, chopped tomatoes, crumbled corn chips, hot meat mixture and hot cheese sauce. Serve immediately. Serves 4-6.

Bonus burritos

8 (10 to 12-inch) flour tortillas
1½ cups shredded cooked beef
½ onion, chopped
3 tablespoons cooking oil
1 (20½ oz) can refried beans
1 (4 oz) can green chilies, chopped
⅓ cup ketchup
½ teaspoon chili powder
2 cups shredded Monterey Jack cheese
Garnishes (see below)

Wrap tortillas in foil, heat in a preheated 350° oven for 10 minutes until warm and soft. In a large skillet, saute beef and onion in oil until onion is transparent. Stir in beans, green chilies, ketchup and chili powder, heat thoroughly. Place half cup filling on each tortilla, sprinkle with cheese. Fold edges to inside and roll up. Garnish as desired. Makes 8.

Garnishes: Prepared salsa, shredded cheese, sliced olives.

Menudo

This is a classic tripe soup, thought to be beneficial "the morning after" overcelebrating. It's traditionally served on Christmas or New Year's Eve.

4-5 lb beef tripe
3 lb pigs' feet
1 tablespoon salt
4 cloves garlic
1 tablespoon finely chopped cilantro (fresh coriander or Chinese parsley) or oregano
6 tablespoons chili powder
1 (1 lb 13 oz) can white hominy
Lemon wedges
2 cups chopped onion
Extra finely chopped cilantro

Cut tripe in small pieces. Cut pigs' feet in 2-inch pieces if they have not been sliced through the middle by the butcher. Put meat in a large pan with about 1 gallon of water and simmer together with salt, garlic and cilantro for about 4 hours or until tripe and pigs' feet are tender.

While cooking, add more water if necessary and skim off white foam that forms on top. Add chili powder and hominy and simmer another 30 minutes. Serve with lemon wedges, chopped onion and cilantro. Serves 15-20.

Carne guisada

Tacos, like enchiladas, can be made with many different fillings. Tacos made with flour tortillas are frequently filled with carne guisada. It can also be served on a plate with rice and beans.

2-3 lb round steak, cubed
Cooking oil
1 tablespoon flour
2 tablespoons chopped green pepper
2 tablespoons chopped tomato
1-2 cloves garlic, crushed
¼-½ teaspoon cumin powder
⅛ teaspoon pepper
½ (8 oz) can tomato sauce
½ (10 oz) can tomatoes with green chilies
Salt to taste
¼ cup water

Brown steak in a small amount of cooking oil. After it is brown, add flour and stir into meat and juices in pan. Add remaining ingredients. Stir well, cover pan and simmer for about 30-45 minutes or until meat is tender and the sauce becomes thick.

If filling tacos, the sauce should be cooked longer so that it thickens even more. Serves 8-12.

Green enchiladas

1 whole chicken breast
1 large onion, chopped and divided in 3 parts
2 cloves garlic
Salt to taste
½ cup tomato sauce
Cooking oil
6 long green chilies, seeded and chopped
6 tomatillos (small Mexican green tomatoes), seeded and chopped
5-6 sprigs cilantro (fresh coriander or Chinese parsley)
Chicken broth or water
Cumin powder (cominos) to taste
12 corn tortillas
1 cup sour cream
½ cup milk
1½ cups grated Monterey Jack cheese

Place chicken breast in saucepan with one-third of the onion, 1 clove garlic and salt to taste. Barely cover with water and bring to a boil. Turn down heat, simmer, covered, until cooked, about 20 minutes. Saute another one-third of the onion and tomato sauce in a small amount of oil about 10 minutes. Remove chicken from pan and reserve broth. Skin, bone and cut chicken into small pieces. Add to tomato sauce.

Make green sauce by combining chilies, tomatillos, remaining onion, crushed garlic and cilantro in a saucepan, add a small amount of reserved chicken broth and simmer about 10 minutes. Cool a little, put in blender, add salt to taste and cumin powder. Blend, adding a little more chicken broth if too thick. Fry tortillas individually in oil. Fill with chicken mixture and roll up. Place in a row in an oblong 2-quart baking dish.

Blend sour cream and milk and pour over enchiladas. Pour green chile sauce over and sprinkle with grated cheese. Heat in a preheated 350° oven about 25 minutes until bubbly. Serves 4-6.

Note: Tomatillos and cilantro are available at Mexican food stores and in many supermarkets.

Texas style tacos

Meat filling:

1 onion, chopped
1 clove garlic, crushed
1 tablespoon cooking oil
1 lb ground round steak
½ teaspoon cumin powder (cominos)
¼ teaspoon chili powder
Salt and pepper to taste
1 large tomato, finely chopped

Taco sauce:

1 (4 oz) can green chilies
2 (8 oz) cans tomato sauce
2 (4 oz) cans taco sauce

Shells:

Peanut oil for frying
1-2 packages flat tortillas

To serve:

2 onions, chopped
1 small lettuce, shredded
2 tomatoes, chopped
1 lb Cheddar cheese, grated

Cook onion and garlic in oil in skillet until soft. Drain off oil. Add meat and fry until almost cooked, add spices and tomato. Cover and cook slowly 15-20 minutes.

Meanwhile, finely chop chilies by hand or in food processor. Add to tomato sauce and taco sauce and heat together.

Heat ½-inch peanut oil in skillet. Dip each tortilla in oil and fry about 3 seconds, flip tortilla over and fold. Fry until crisp. Drain on paper towels and keep warm in oven.

Each person takes a taco shell, puts in some meat filling, some onion, lettuce, tomato, grated cheese and tops it off with hot taco sauce.

Tell everyone to dress casually — tacos are messy but delicious eating! Serves 8-10.

Tamale pie

1½ cups yellow cornmeal
1½ cups cold water
1½ teaspoons salt
2 cups boiling water
1 lb ground beef
½ cup chopped onion
2 tablespoons flour
1½ teaspoons chili powder
1 (16 oz) can tomatoes, broken up
1 (8 oz) can tomato sauce
1 cup whole kernel corn, drained

Combine cornmeal and cold water. Add ½ teaspoon salt to boiling water. Slowly add cornmeal mixture, stirring constantly, bring to a boil. Lower heat, partially cover pan, cook slowly 7 minutes, stirring often. Line bottom and sides of greased 2-quart casserole with cooked cornmeal.

Saute beef and onion in a skillet until beef is brown and crumbly. Stir in flour, remaining 1 teaspoon salt and chili powder. Add broken up tomatoes. Stir in tomato sauce and corn. Spoon into casserole. Bake in a preheated 350° oven until hot and bubbly, 40-45 minutes. Serves 6.

Fajitas (page 91)

Enchiladas

Hot cooking oil
2 packages corn or flour tortillas (20-24)
2 tablespoons flour
2 tablespoons chili powder
½ teaspoon salt
Extra 2 tablespoons cooking oil
¾-1 cup warm water
2 onions, chopped
Canned or homemade chili
½-¾ lb grated Longhorn cheese

Place a little oil in skillet, heat and soften each tortilla one at a time. Make a chili sauce by stirring flour, chili powder and salt in extra cooking oil. Add water and blend until smooth.

On each tortilla place a small amount of chopped onion and chili. Roll and place in a greased baking dish. Pour chili sauce on top and sprinkle with remaining onion and cheese. Place in a preheated 350° oven until hot and cheese melts, about 20-30 minutes. Serves 10-12.

Barbecued young kid (Cabrito)

Cabrito, goat kid, shows up along the border, in San Antonio and in West Texas at barbecues; it's part of our Mexican heritage. Some people are put off by the thought of eating goat, but well prepared it is a great delicacy. It is occasionally featured by meat markets for holiday barbecues or your favorite butcher may be able to order it for you.

In Mexico it is commonly cooked whole on a stake stuck in the ground with the fire in front.

Allow 1 lb (dressed carcass weight) per person and about 30 minutes per lb cooking time.

Rub dressed cabrito, not over 15 lb, with garlic salt and freshly ground coarse black pepper. Place on barbecue spit over a medium hot fire. Turn every 30 minutes and thoroughly baste with a mopping sauce (see Texas Barbecue, Barbecue Mop Sauce) or beer. Baste towards end of cooking time with your favorite barbecue sauce or use following recipe. Barbecue sauce burns if used for whole cooking time. Serves 15.

Barbecue sauce

1 cup butter or margarine
3 medium onions, chopped
1½ cups wine vinegar
Juice and rind of 3 lemons
1 teaspoon coarsely ground black pepper
2 teaspoons garlic salt
½ cup ketchup
3 tablespoons Worcestershire sauce
Dash hot pepper sauce

Melt butter and saute onion until soft. Add remaining ingredients and simmer gently 15 minutes. Use to baste cabrito. Makes about 4 cups.

Frijoles refritos (Refried beans)

2 cups dried pinto or red kidney beans
2 medium onions, finely chopped
2 cloves garlic, chopped
1 bay leaf
2 or more serrano peppers, chopped (optional)
3 tablespoons lard or salad oil
Salt and freshly ground pepper
Extra lard (optional)

Cover beans with water and soak overnight. Drain beans.

Add fresh water to cover, 1 of the onions, 1 clove of garlic, bay leaf and peppers. Cover, bring to a boil, reduce heat and simmer gently, adding more boiling water as necessary. When beans begin to wrinkle, add 1 tablespoon of the lard. Continue cooking until beans are soft. Add salt and pepper to taste.

Cook another 30 minutes, but add no more water — there should not be much liquid when beans are cooked. Heat remaining lard in a skillet and saute remaining onion and garlic until limp. Add the beans and mash to make a smooth, fairly heavy paste. Return to low heat and stir until any remaining liquid has evaporated and the beans are hot throughout.

After basic frijoles are prepared, heat 2 tablespoons of the extra lard in a large skillet, add beans, tablespoon by tablespoon, and mash over low heat, adding lard from time to time, until beans are creamy and have formed a heavy, quite dry paste. Serves 6.

Jalapeno cornbread

2 cups cream-style corn
2 cups cornbread mix
⅔ cup cooking oil
4 eggs, beaten
2 cups sour cream
1½-2 cups grated Cheddar cheese
1 cup chopped onion
1 (4 oz) can jalapenos or green chilies, seeded and chopped

Combine all ingredients in a large bowl. Blend well. Pour into a greased 13 x 9 x 2-inch pan and bake in a preheated 350° oven for 1 hour or until cornbread tests done. Texture is between cornbread and spoon bread, moist but firm enough to cut.

Note: This recipe can be halved and baked in a smaller pan.

Ninfa's green sauce

One of the most famous recipes from Ninfa's Mexican restaurants.

3 medium-size green tomatoes, coarsely chopped
4 tomatillos (small Mexican green tomatoes), coarsely chopped
1-2 jalapeno peppers, stems removed and coarsely chopped
3 small cloves garlic
3 medium-size ripe avocados
4 sprigs cilantro (Chinese parsley)
1-2 teaspoons salt
1½ cups imitation sour cream

Place green tomatoes, tomatillos, jalapeno peppers and garlic in a saucepan, bring to a boil, lower heat, simmer 15 minutes or until tomatoes are soft. Remove from heat, cool slightly.

Peel, seed and slice avocados, set aside.

In food processor, place part of the green tomato mixture with part of the avocados, cilantro and salt, cover. Process until smooth, turn into large bowl. Repeat with remaining green tomato mixture and avocado. Add to mixture in bowl, stir in sour cream, cover with plastic wrap. Chill. Makes 5-6 cups.

Note: Real sour cream can be used instead of imitation.

Mexican chocolate cake (page 98)

Picante sauce

This is a good all-purpose hot sauce. Shredded carrot and/or chopped green pepper can be added if liked.

8 firm, ripe tomatoes

4 jalapeno peppers, seeded

1 large onion

Salt to taste

1 tablespoon red wine vinegar

1 tablespoon finely chopped cilantro (fresh coriander or Chinese parsley), optional

Chop tomatoes, jalapenos and onion in small pieces and combine with salt, vinegar and cilantro. Makes about 1 quart.
Note: Will keep about 2 weeks in refrigerator.

Jalapeno pepper jelly

Perfect for an appetizer when spread on a cracker with cream cheese.

¾ cup ground green pepper

¼ cup seeded and ground jalapeno peppers

5 cups sugar

1 cup apple cider vinegar

2 pouches liquid fruit pectin

Green food coloring (optional)

Mix peppers, sugar and vinegar in a large saucepan or kettle. Bring to a boil. Boil 5 minutes. Cool. Add pectin and boil hard 1 minute. Stir in food coloring. Pour into hot clean jars to within ½-inch of top. Screw on tops firmly. Process in a boiling water bath for 5 minutes. Makes about 5 (8 oz) jars.

Sopaipillas

4 cups flour

2 tablespoons baking powder

1 teaspoon salt

3 tablespoons shortening

1-1½ cups water

Cooking oil or shortening

Honey

Sift together flour, baking powder and salt. Cut in shortening. Add enough water to make a soft dough. Roll out dough on a floured board until it is ¼-inch thick or slightly thinner. Cut into 3-inch squares and deep fry in hot oil (400°) until golden brown and puffy. Fry only a few at a time so that oil remains hot. Drain on paper towels. Serve warm with honey. Makes about 4 dozen.

Flan

Caramel:

¾ cup sugar

3 tablespoons cold water

Custard:

4 large eggs

2 tablespoons sugar

2 cups milk

½ teaspoon vanilla

Prepare caramel by heating sugar and water together in a small pan over low heat until sugar is completely dissolved. Bring to a boil and without stirring, boil until golden brown, (once it starts to turn color, it burns easily, so watch carefully). Pour caramel into 6 individual custard cups, twist around until base and sides are well coated.

Combine eggs and sugar, warm milk and add to eggs with vanilla. Strain custard into custard cups. Place cups in large baking pan containing 1-inch of warm water. Cook in a preheated 350° oven for 35-40 minutes or until knife comes out clean. Cool, chill and unmold to serve. Serves 6.

Mexican chocolate cake

(photograph page 97)

The cinnamon and cocoa, historically associated with Mexico, inspire the title of this rich, luscious cake.

½ cup margarine

½ cup cooking oil

2 squares (2 oz) unsweetened chocolate or 4 tablespoons cocoa

1 cup water

2 cups flour

1 teaspoon baking soda

2 cups sugar

½ cup sour milk (place 1½ teaspoons vinegar in ½ cup measure, fill with milk)

2 eggs, beaten

1 teaspoon cinnamon

1 teaspoon vanilla

Mexican chocolate frosting:

½ cup margarine

2 squares (2 oz) unsweetened chocolate

6 tablespoons milk

1 lb powdered sugar

1 teaspoon vanilla

½ cup chopped pecans

Combine margarine, oil, chocolate and water in a saucepan and heat until chocolate is melted. Combine flour, baking soda, sugar, milk, eggs, cinnamon and vanilla in a large bowl and blend with first mixture. Pour batter into a greased 11½ x 4 x 3-inch sheet cake pan and bake in a preheated 350° oven for 40-50 minutes or until cake is done. Frost while cake is warm with Mexican chocolate frosting.

Mexican chocolate frosting: Combine margarine, chocolate and milk in a saucepan and heat until bubbles form around the edge. Remove from heat. Add powdered sugar, a little at a time, vanilla and pecans. Beat well.

Bunuelos (Mexican cookies)

2¼ cups flour

½ teaspoon baking powder

½ teaspoon salt

2 tablespoons sugar

Frozen Margaritas
(photograph bottom left)

1 cup freshly squeezed lime or lemon juice (preferably lime)
1½ cups Triple Sec liqueur
¾ cup tequila
Crushed ice
Lime wedges
Salt (optional)

Combine all ingredients except lime wedges and salt in a blender, using enough crushed ice to form a slush-like consistency. Moisten the rim of each cocktail glass with a lime wedge and dip the rim of the glass into a plate of salt. Pour the margarita mixture into the glass and squeeze a lime wedge over the top of the drink. Drop the rind into the glass and serve. Serves 6-8.

Rio sangria

3 grapefruit
3 oranges
1 cup sugar
2 (25 fl oz) bottles Texas white wine
1 (1 quart) bottle club soda, chilled (optional)

Squeeze 2 grapefruit and 2 oranges. Combine juices with sugar. Stir well and chill. Cut remaining grapefruit and orange into ½-inch slices, quarter the slices.

Just before serving, combine chilled fruit juice, wine, sliced fruit and if desired, chilled club soda. Serves 10-12.

1½ tablespoons shortening
About ⅔ cup hot water
Cooking oil or shortening
Extra ½ cup sugar
½ teaspoon cinnamon

Mix flour, baking powder, salt and sugar in a medium size bowl. Add shortening and rub in with fingertips. Add water, a little at a time, enough to form a dough, knead for half a minute. Set aside for 15 minutes, covered with a cloth. Cut off small pieces of dough and form into small balls about 1-inch in diameter. On a floured board, work each ball of dough into a round flat cookie, 5-inches in diameter. Half fill a 10-inch skillet with oil and when hot, fry one side of cookie, then the other (turn only once). When crisp and golden in color, drain on paper towels and dust with combined sugar and cinnamon. Makes 2 dozen.

Sangria

1 lemon, thinly sliced
1 lime, thinly sliced
1 orange, thinly sliced
½ cup brandy
¼ cup superfine sugar
1 (25 fl oz) bottle Texas red wine
2 tablespoons lemon juice
1 (1 quart) bottle club soda, chilled

Place fruit slices in a large pitcher. Add brandy which has been mixed with sugar. Let stand at room temperature 1 hour.

Add wine and lemon juice. Stir sangria thoroughly and chill for 1 hour. Just before serving, add ice cubes and fill pitcher with club soda. Stir briskly and serve in chilled glasses. Serves 6-8.

Overleaf: *Shrimp boat near the shore of Sea Rim State Park*

COASTAL BOUNTY

There is a wealth of seafood in the waters along the Texas coast. A wondrous selection of redfish, flounder, pompano, shrimp, crab and oysters from the Gulf of Mexico finds its way to tables throughout the state, as far west as the Panhandle and as far north as Dallas-Fort Worth.

Fifty miles south of Houston lies Galveston, a city known for its seafood bounty. This is where Cabeza de Vaca, the first European to set foot on Texas soil, landed in 1528. It is also the point of entry for many of the immigrants who settled the rest of Texas. The inlets of Galveston Bay are prime breeding grounds for seafood, including oysters and shrimp.

Almost everyone loves fresh shrimp, and Texans are no exception. Jumbo shrimp are frequently butterflied and fried, barbecued, or boiled in beer and served with a spicy sauce.

Of course there are some Texans who will tell you there is only one way fish is worth eating and that's fried, and only one fish worth frying and that's catfish. Connoisseurs recommend the fish be rolled in cornmeal, fried in hot oil and served with crispy hush puppies.

Fish frys have always been popular events in Texas. They usually get started when a group returns home from the coast after deep-sea fishing. The end result — crispy, succulent snapper or grouper chased with beer — is some of the best eating around.

The popularity of fish and seafood is on the rise in Texas, probably because of the trend toward lighter meals. Fish is fast and easy to prepare and low in calories and fat when grilled or steamed. Generally it is an inexpensive source of protein. If you opt for the more expensive varieties, serve smaller portions and accompany them with tasty side dishes.

Eggs with chutney shrimp (main dish; page 108), *shrimp risi bisi* (top; page 108) *and tomato garlic shrimp* (left; page 109)

103

Oyster stew

| 1 (10 oz) jar oysters |
| 2½ cups milk |
| ½ cup whipping cream |
| 1 onion slice |
| 1 rib celery, sliced |
| 1 bay leaf |
| 2 strips lemon rind |
| 2 tablespoons butter |
| 2 tablespoons flour |
| Freshly grated nutmeg |
| Salt and freshly ground white pepper |
| 4 tablespoons dry sherry |

Drain oyster liquor into a saucepan. Chop oysters into pieces, add to saucepan and bring to simmering point. Pour into a bowl and set aside. In same saucepan, scald milk and cream with onion, celery, bay leaf and lemon rind. Leave to infuse for 5-10 minutes, strain.

Melt butter in a clean saucepan over low heat and stir in flour. Gradually stir in flavored milk and continue stirring until mixture boils and thickens.

Season with a pinch of nutmeg, salt and pepper. Add oysters and their liquid and sherry and heat but do not boil. Taste for seasoning, and serve in heated bowls. Serves 4.

Creamy shrimp soup

| *A very special soup.* |
| 2 lb raw shrimp in shells |
| 6 tablespoons butter |
| 1 small onion, finely chopped |
| 1 small carrot, finely chopped |
| 1 rib celery, finely chopped |
| 2 cups stock made with shrimp shells |
| Salt and freshly ground pepper |
| 1 cup dry white wine |
| 1 cup whipping cream |

Peel and devein shrimp, chop finely. Place shrimp heads and shells in a saucepan with 3 cups water. Bring to a boil, simmer until reduced to about 2 cups. Strain and put aside. Discard shells.

Heat butter in a clean saucepan and gently fry onion, carrot and celery until soft, about 6 minutes. Add shrimp and stock, and simmer 15 minutes. Season with salt and pepper.

Puree the mixture in a blender or food processor, or push through a sieve. Return to saucepan with wine, and heat through. Add cream and stir just to simmering point. Taste for seasoning, serve at once in heated bowls. Serves 4-6.

Last-minute salmon soup

| *Keep this recipe in mind when six hungry people demand something hot and filling in 10 minutes. It can happen!* |
| 4 tablespoons butter |
| 3 tablespoons flour |
| 2 cups evaporated milk |
| 2 cups water |
| 1½ cups flaked, drained salmon |
| Salt and freshly ground pepper |
| 1 teaspoon Worcestershire sauce |
| 1 tablespoon lemon juice |
| Finely chopped parsley to garnish |

Melt butter in a heavy saucepan. Stir in flour and blend well. Gradually stir in milk and water mixed together, and continue stirring over low heat until smooth and creamy. Add salmon, season with salt and pepper to taste, and stir in Worcestershire sauce and lemon juice. Simmer 3 minutes and serve sprinkled with chopped parsley. Serves 6.

Crab bisque

| 3 tablespoons butter |
| 1 tablespoon grated onion |
| 1½ cups crabmeat, fresh, canned or frozen |
| 2 tablespoons flour |
| 2 cups chicken broth |
| 2 cups half and half |
| Salt and freshly ground white pepper |

Melt butter in a saucepan and cook onion until soft. Add crabmeat and cook slowly. Add flour and stir until well blended. Add chicken broth and stirring continuously, bring to simmering point. Simmer for 10 minutes. Add half and half and season to taste with salt and pepper. Cook over low heat for 5 minutes and serve in heated soup bowls. Serves 4.

Andrea Bowen's crab puffs
(photograph right)

| **Tea party puffs:** |
| ½ cup butter or margarine |
| 1 cup boiling water |
| ½ teaspoon salt |
| 1 cup sifted flour |
| 4 eggs |
| **Filling:** |
| 1 (6½ oz) can crabmeat, drained |
| 1 (8 oz) package cream cheese |
| 1½ teaspoons prepared horseradish |
| 1 teaspoon minced onion |

Combine butter and boiling water in medium size saucepan and heat over high heat until butter melts. Turn heat to low, add salt and flour together and stir vigorously until mixture leaves sides of pan in a smooth, compact ball, about 2 minutes. Turn off heat. Add eggs, one at a time, beating with spoon until mixture has a satin-like sheen.

Drop by teaspoonfuls, 1½-inches apart on greased cookie sheets, shaping each into a mound that points up in the center. Bake in a preheated 400° oven 20-25 minutes without opening the oven door. Puffs should be puffed and golden. Remove with spatula to wire rack to cool.

Meanwhile, combine crabmeat, softened cream cheese, horseradish and onion in mixing bowl. Mix until blended. Slice tops off tea party puffs, fill and replace tops. Serve warm or at room temperature. Makes 3-3½ dozen.

Shortcut crab bisque

1 (6½ oz) can or 1 cup
flaked crabmeat

¼ cup dry sherry

1 (11¼ oz) can condensed
green pea soup

1 (10¾ oz) can condensed
tomato soup

1¼ cups milk or half and half

Soak crabmeat 5 minutes in sherry. Combine and heat soups to boiling point. Stir milk in slowly. Add the crabmeat. Heat, but do not boil. Serves 4.

Grilled lemon oysters

12-16 oysters

4 tablespoons butter, softened

2 cloves garlic, crushed

1 teaspoon grated lemon rind

¼ cup finely chopped parsley

½ cup fine breadcrumbs

Salt and freshly ground pepper

A little extra grated lemon rind
or parsley

Arrange oysters in small ramekins or scallop shells. Place on a baking sheet. Combine remaining ingredients and spoon over oysters. Place under a preheated hot broiler for 3-4 minutes, or until oysters are heated through and topping is crisp and bubbly. Sprinkle with a little extra grated lemon rind or parsley to serve. Serves 4.

Oysters casino
(photograph center right)

48 oysters on the half shell

1 lb sliced lean bacon

½ cup finely chopped green pepper

½ cup finely chopped onion

¾ cup butter

¼ cup finely chopped parsley

1 (4 oz) jar pimientos, drained
and chopped

Freshly ground pepper

Arrange oysters in a single layer on a large shallow baking pan. Fry bacon, drain and crumble. Saute pepper and onion in ¼ cup of the butter and add to remaining softened butter, parsley and pimiento. Top each oyster with a spoonful of the butter mixture, a grind of pepper and pieces of bacon.

Bake in a preheated 450° oven until oysters are heated through. Serve with garlic toast. Serves 8.

Oysters the natural way
(photograph bottom right)

Allow 6 oysters per person when serving them as a first course. If the oysters have not been opened, open them and make sure there are no pieces of shell inside. Wash as quickly as possible. Do not wash oysters for a long time under a running tap, you will lose a lot of the natural flavor. If they have been bought opened, they will probably not need washing. Always cover opened oysters with a sheet of wax paper before chilling. The refrigerator tends to dry them out. For the best flavor, remove oysters from refrigerator 15 minutes before serving.

Serve oysters on dinner plates with a small container in the center of each for sauce. Red cocktail sauce, tartar sauce or remoulade sauce are all suitable accompaniments. Also garnish with wedges of lemon and have a salt and pepper grinder handy.

Angels on horseback
(photograph top right)

A charming name for a simple yet distinguished course of broiled oysters wrapped in bacon.

24 oysters

6 slices lean bacon

Freshly ground pepper

4 slices hot, buttered toast

Lemon wedges to garnish

Remove oysters from shell, or drain well if from a jar. Cut bacon into 24 squares, wrap each one around an oyster.

Thread 4 bacon-wrapped oysters on each of 6 metal skewers. Season with a little freshly ground pepper.

Place under a preheated hot broiler, and broil for 3 minutes each side, or until bacon is crisp. Serve on toast, garnished with lemon wedges. Serves 6.

Shrimp Victoria

1 lb raw, peeled and deveined shrimp,
fresh or frozen

¼ cup finely chopped onion

¼ cup butter or margarine

1 (6 oz) can sliced mushrooms,
drained or 1 cup sliced fresh mushrooms

1 tablespoon flour

¼ teaspoon salt

Pinch cayenne pepper

1 cup sour cream

Thaw shrimp if frozen. In a 10-inch frying pan, saute shrimp and onion in butter over medium heat for 3-5 minutes or until shrimp are opaque. Add mushrooms and heat. Sprinkle in flour, salt and pepper, stir to mix, reduce heat. Stir in sour cream and cook gently 5 minutes, not allowing mixture to boil. Serve over rice. Serves 4-6.

Oysters Ernie

These oysters were a classic at Ernie Coker's Ye Olde College Inn in Houston in the '50s and '60s.

24 oysters
Salt and pepper
Flour
4 tablespooons melted butter
¼ cup lemon juice
1 cup bottled steak sauce
2 tablespoons Worcestershire sauce
Sherry or Madeira wine
Extra 2 tablespoons flour
3 tablespoons water

Season oysters with salt and pepper and dredge in flour. Cook on lightly buttered griddle or in heavy skillet until crisp and brown on both sides. Sprinkle oysters with 2 tablespoons of the melted butter while cooking. Sprinkle on both sides — it browns and crisps them.

In a small saucepan, melt remaining butter over low heat. Add lemon juice, steak sauce, Worcestershire sauce and sherry. Heat thoroughly but do not allow to boil. Blend flour and water together, add to pan and stir until sauce thickens. Season to taste by adding steak sauce if too thin or sherry if too thick and highly seasoned.

Place freshly cooked oysters on a hot serving plate and spoon over some of the heated sauce. Serves 4 or 8 as an appetizer.

Note: This sauce can be strained, reheated and used again.

Shrimp cocktail

Its success depends on using crisp lettuce, the freshest shrimp, and a sauce that's well-flavored but does not overwhelm the delicate taste of the shrimp themselves.

1 lb cooked, peeled shrimp
2-3 teaspoons lemon juice
Salt and freshly ground white pepper
8 slices brown bread
Butter for spreading
Red cocktail sauce:
½ cup ketchup or chili sauce
2 tablespoons lemon juice

1 tablespoon prepared horseradish
1 teaspoon grated onion
1 teaspoon Worcestershire sauce
3-4 drops hot pepper sauce
Pinch salt

If the shrimp have been refrigerated, let them come to room temperature before serving. It they have prominent dark veins in the back, carefully remove them — small to medium size shouldn't need deveining. Toss in a bowl with juice and a little salt and white pepper.

Make 4 sandwiches of the brown bread and butter, trim the crusts, cut each sandwich into 4 triangles. Line 4 glass dishes with lettuce leaves or shredded lettuce. Pile shrimp on top. Add a spoonful of sauce, or pass sauce separately, serve with triangles of bread and butter. Serves 4.

Sauce: Combine ingredients and chill thoroughly. Makes ¾ cup.

Crabmeat chantilly

1 (6 or 7 oz) package frozen king, snow or other crabmeat
2 tablespoons chopped green onion
2 tablespoons margarine or cooking oil
1 tablespoon flour
½ teaspoon salt
Pinch cayenne pepper
1 cup half and half or milk
¼ cup salad dressing (not mayonnaise)
1 (10 oz) package frozen asparagus spears, cooked and drained, or 1 lb fresh asparagus, cooked and drained
1 tablespoon grated Parmesan cheese

Thaw crabmeat, drain and cut in chunks. Cook green onion in margarine until onion is tender but not brown. Stir in flour, salt and cayenne pepper. Add half and half, cook, stirring constantly, until thickened. Remove from heat.

Stir in salad dressing. Fold in crabmeat. Arrange asparagus spears on heatproof platter or in shallow 1½-quart baking dish. Spoon sauce over asparagus. Sprinkle with Parmesan cheese. Broil about 4-inches from heat, 3-5 minutes or until lightly browned and hot. Serves 4.

Note: 1 (6 or 7 oz) can king, snow or other crabmeat may be used instead of frozen.

Eggs with chutney shrimp

(photograph page 102)

Hard-boiled eggs are served with a spicy-sweet shrimp sauce.

8 hard-boiled eggs, shelled
4 tablespoons butter
1 small onion, finely chopped
1 large tart apple, peeled and finely chopped
2 teaspoons curry powder
2 tablespoons flour
1½ cups chicken broth
4 tablespoons chopped mango chutney
1 tablespoon lemon juice
Salt and freshly ground pepper
1 lb cooked, peeled shrimp

Cut eggs in half lengthways and arrange cut-side down on an ovenproof serving platter. Keep warm in oven while preparing sauce. Heat butter and fry onion and apple until soft. Stir in curry powder and cook for a minute, then sprinkle flour over and stir again. Gradually add broth, stirring all the time. Bring to a boil, lower heat and simmer 2 minutes. Add chutney, lemon juice, salt and pepper to taste and shrimp. Simmer until shrimp are heated through, spoon over eggs. Serves 6-8.

Shrimp risi bisi

(photograph page 102)

One of the easiest shrimp dishes to assemble — and very pretty on a buffet table.

4 tablespoons butter
1 clove garlic, crushed
3 cups cooked rice (1 cup uncooked)
1 lb cooked green peas
1 lb cooked, peeled shrimp
Salt and freshly ground pepper
Dill sprigs and Parmesan cheese (optional)

Heat butter in a large, heavy frying pan and fry garlic for a minute or two. Add rice, peas and shrimp, season to taste with salt and pepper. Toss gently over low heat until heated through.

Spoon into a heated serving bowl and garnish with dill if desired. Parmesan cheese may also be sprinkled over the top. Serves 4-6.

Tomato-garlic shrimp

(photograph page 102)

4 tablespoons butter

1 large onion, finely chopped

2 large ripe tomatoes, peeled and chopped

¼ cup dry white wine

1 teaspoon sugar

Salt and freshly ground pepper

1½ lb cooked, peeled shrimp

Extra 4 tablespoons melted butter

2 fat cloves garlic, crushed

½ cup finely chopped parsley

1 cup breadcrumbs

Heat butter and fry onion until it starts to soften. Add tomatoes and fry another minute or two, then add wine, sugar and salt and pepper to taste. Simmer with lid on for 5 minutes, then spoon mixture into a shallow, greased ovenproof dish. Scatter shrimp over tomatoes. Mix melted butter with garlic, parsley, breadcrumbs and salt and pepper to taste and sprinkle over shrimp.

Bake in a preheated 400° oven for 8-10 minutes, or until topping is crisp and golden. Serve with rice and a salad. Serves 4.

Dipping sauces for shrimp

Remoulade sauce

2 cups mayonnaise

½ cup Creole mustard

2 tablespoons prepared mustard

Salt to taste

1 tablespoon prepared horseradish

1 teaspooon Worcestershire sauce

Juice of ½ lemon

1 clove garlic, crushed

Dash hot pepper sauce

½ cup finely chopped celery (optional)

½ cup finely chopped green pepper (optional)

½ cup finely chopped onion (optional)

Mix all ingredients together and blend well. Keep in covered container in refrigerator. Makes about 4 cups.

Tartar sauce

½ cup mayonnaise or salad dressing

1 tablespoon chopped onion

1 tablespoon chopped pickle

1 tablespoon chopped parsley

1 tablespoon chopped stuffed olives

Mix thoroughly and chill. Makes ¾ cup.

Buttermilk tartar sauce

2 tablespoons flour

½ teaspoon paprika

½ teaspoon salt

1 cup buttermilk

1 cup sour cream

¼ cup chopped parsley

1 tablespoon chopped stuffed olives

1 tablespoon capers, drained

Combine flour, paprika and salt in a saucepan. Stir in buttermilk and sour cream, parsley, olives and capers. Cook over low heat, stirring constantly, until thickened. Do not boil. Makes about 2 cups.

Crab imperial

1 tablespoon English mustard

1 teaspoon salt

1 teaspoon seasoned salt

½ teaspoon white pepper

2 eggs, lightly beaten

1 cup mayonnaise

1 green pepper, finely chopped

2 pimientos, finely chopped

3 lb lump crabmeat

Extra mayonnaise

Paprika

Mix mustard, salt, pepper, eggs, and mayonnaise. Add pepper and pimiento. Mix in crab lightly. Prepare 8 crab shells by scrubbing and soaking them in baking soda water 15 minutes to sterilize and deodorize them. Alternatively, use 8 individual ovenproof dishes. Fill each with the mixture. Top with a light coating of extra mayonnaise and sprinkle with paprika. Bake in preheated 350° oven 15 minutes or until hot. Serve hot or cold. Serves 8.

Gulf Coast oyster souffle

2 (10 oz) jars oysters

½ cup chopped onion

⅓ cup margarine

½ cup flour

1½ teaspoons salt

½ teaspoon paprika

Pinch pepper

Pinch nutmeg or allspice

1 cup milk

4 eggs, separated

Creamy lemon sauce:

2 tablespoons margarine

2 tablespoons flour

½ teaspoon salt

¼ teaspoon paprika

1¼ cups milk

½ cup salad dressing or mayonnaise

1 tablespoon lemon juice

Drain oysters, reserve ½ cup liquor. Coarsely chop oysters or process briefly in blender. Saute onion slowly in margarine until tender, but not brown. Stir in flour, salt, paprika, pepper and nutmeg. Add milk and reserved oyster liquor. Cook until thickened, stirring constantly. Remove from heat.

Beat egg yolks until thick and lemony colored. Add yolks slowly to hot mixture, stirring constantly. Fold in oysters. Beat egg whites until they hold soft peaks. Fold into oyster mixture. Pour into ungreased 2-quart souffle dish or deep casserole. Bake in a preheated 325° oven about 60-70 minutes or until souffle is puffed, browned and set. Serve immediately with sauce.

Creamy lemon sauce: Melt butter in saucepan. Stir in flour, salt and paprika. Add milk, cook until thickened and smooth, stirring constantly. Blend in salad dressing and lemon juice, heat. Serve with souffle.

Crab in pastry parcels

(photograph right)

2 pre-rolled sheets frozen puff pastry

1 egg, beaten

For filling:

1 (8 oz) can cream-style corn

1 lb lump crabmeat

1 small green pepper, finely diced

½ cup sour cream

3 tablespoons chopped parsley

Pinch cayenne pepper

Salt and freshly ground pepper to taste

Prepare filling by mixing all ingredients together. Roll each pastry sheet to measure 12-inches square (pastry will be ⅛-inch thick). Cut each in four, making 6-inch squares. Divide filling among the 8 pieces of pastry. Moisten edges with water and fold pastry over the filling, pressing edges together firmly. Place the parcels on baking sheets. Brush with beaten egg and bake in a preheated 400° oven for 20-30 minutes, until golden brown. Serves 8.

Spiced cold fish

6 fish steaks about 1-inch thick

¼ cup olive oil

4 green onions, finely chopped

2 cloves garlic, crushed

2 cups water

3 tablespoons lemon juice

1 teaspoon grated lemon rind

1 teaspoon ground cumin

1 teaspoon curry powder

Salt and freshly ground pepper

2 teaspoons sugar

Remove any skin and bones from fish. Heat oil, and fry green onions and garlic until softened, about 3 minutes. Add remaining ingredients, bring to a boil, lower heat and simmer for 3 minutes.

Add fish steaks and simmer 25 minutes, or until fish is cooked. Arrange fish in a shallow serving dish. Taste liquid for seasoning, strain over fish, and chill. Delicious with cucumber salad. Serves 4.

Shrimp in beer

4 cups beer

4 tablespoons lemon juice

2 teaspoons salt

1 teaspoon whole peppercorns

1 teaspoon tarragon

2 lb raw shrimp in shells

Combine beer with seasonings in a saucepan. Bring to a boil and simmer 10 minutes. Add shrimp and bring back to a boil. Lower heat and simmer 2-5 minutes, until shrimp turn pink. Drain, cool and shell shrimp. Serves 4-6.

Shrimp mold

1 (10¾ oz) can condensed tomato soup

3 (3 oz) packages cream cheese, softened

1 envelope unflavored gelatin

¼ cup cold water

2 cups cooked, peeled shrimp, cut up

1 cup mayonnaise

1 small onion, grated

½ cup finely chopped celery

Pinch garlic powder

Salt and pepper

1 tablespoon lemon juice

2 tablespoons finely chopped parsley

Heat soup and dissolve cheese in it. Soak gelatin in cold water, dissolve in hot cheese mixture. Cool about 30 minutes. Add remaining ingredients. Pour in 2-quart oiled fish mold, chill. To unmold, run a knife blade around edge and dip mold quickly in hot water. Invert on a serving plate. Serve with unsalted crackers. Serves 10-12.

Note: Substituting one package of chive cream cheese for one package of plain cheese gives a nippier flavor. If desired, add 2 teaspoons prepared horseradish to mayonnaise.

Greek style baked snapper

2 lb snapper or flounder filets

1 tablespoon lemon juice

Salt and pepper to taste

Pinch oregano

1 medium onion, chopped

¼ cup olive or cooking oil

1 clove garlic, crushed

2 tomatoes, chopped

¾ cup finely chopped parsley

½ cup water

4 tablespoons breadcrumbs

2 tablespoons butter

Sprinkle fish with lemon juice, salt and pepper. Place in well greased baking dish. Sprinkle with oregano. Saute onion in oil until golden. Add garlic, tomatoes, parsley and water. Pour over fish. Sprinkle with breadcrumbs. Dot with butter. Bake in a preheated 350° oven 40-45 minutes or until fish is tender.

Beer batter fried shrimp

*2 lb raw shrimp
in shells or 1½ lb raw, peeled and
deveined shrimp*

1 cup flour

2 teaspoons paprika

Pinch cayenne pepper

1 teaspoon salt

1½ cups beer

Extra flour

Peanut oil

Clean shrimp if necessary. If frozen let thaw on paper towels. Combine flour, paprika, cayenne and salt in mixing bowl.

Gradually beat in beer until batter is quite thin. Dip shrimp first in extra flour, then into beer batter. Deep fry in oil at 400° for 2 minutes. Drain on paper towels and keep warm. Serve as soon as possible. Serves 4-6.

Grilled crabs

There's no better way to eat them.

12 dressed crabs

¾ cup chopped parsley

½ cup melted butter or cooking oil

1 teaspoon lemon juice

¼ teaspoon nutmeg

¼ teaspoon soy sauce

Dash hot pepper sauce

Lemon wedges to garnish

Clean, wash and dry crabs. Place in well greased, hinged wire grills. Combine remaining ingredients except the lemon wedges. Heat. Baste crabs with sauce. Cook about 4-inches from moderately hot coals for 8 minutes. Baste with sauce.

Turn and cook 7-10 minutes longer or until lightly browned and cooked when tested. Serve with lemon wedges. Serves 6.

Pickled Texas shrimp

2 lb raw, peeled and deveined shrimp

2 medium onions, sliced

1½ cups salad oil

1½ cups white vinegar

½ cup sugar

1½ teaspoons salt

1½ teaspoons celery seed

4 tablespoons capers with juice

Place shrimp in boiling salted water, turn off heat and let stand, covered, 3-5 minutes, or until pink and tender. Drain and rinse with cold water. Chill. Alternate layers of shrimp and sliced onion rings in a sealable container. Mix remaining ingredients and pour over shrimp and onions.

Chill 6 or more hours, shaking and inverting occasionally. Remove shrimp from marinade and serve. Serves about 6-8 as an appetizer.

Rice shrimp party pie

2 tablespoons finely chopped parsley

2 tablespoons finely chopped pimiento

1 tablespoon grated onion

¼ teaspoon salt

⅛ teaspoon pepper

2 tablespoons butter

3 cups hot cooked rice

Shrimp filling:

1½ lb raw, peeled and deveined shrimp

2 tablespoons butter or margarine

1 (10¾ oz) can condensed cream
of mushroom soup

1 teaspoon lemon juice

¼ teaspoon pepper

Mix parsley, pimiento, onion, salt, pepper, butter and hot rice until butter is melted. Press firmly and evenly around sides and bottom of a 10-inch pie plate.

Brown shrimp in butter and put into rice shell. Add soup, lemon juice and pepper to shrimp skillet. Stir until smooth and heated, pour over shrimp. Bake in a preheated 350° oven for 30 minutes or until lightly browned. Serves 6-8.

Lazy Lil's fish stew

It's ready in 30 minutes.

¼ cup olive oil

1 small carrot, finely chopped

1 medium onion, finely chopped

4 ribs celery (with leaves)
finely chopped

1 fat clove garlic, chopped

1 bay leaf

1 tablespoon tomato paste

1 cup dry white wine

Salt and freshly ground pepper

2 lb firm fish filets — cut in
2-inch pieces

3 tablespoons finely chopped parsley

Heat oil in a large, heavy saucepan and fry vegetables until tender, about 6 minutes. Add bay leaf, tomato paste and wine and simmer 5 minutes. Season with salt and pepper to taste, add fish pieces, and cover pan. Simmer until fish is cooked through, 6-8 minutes. Taste for seasoning, and sprinkle with chopped parsley. Serves 6.

Crab sunshine salad

1 large lettuce

1 lb cooked crabmeat

1 large papaya or cantaloupe

4 hard-boiled eggs, peeled

2 tablespoons finely chopped
chives or green onions

For dressing:

½ cup mayonnaise

¼ cup French or vinaigrette dressing

2 teaspoons finely chopped
sweet gherkin

1 tablespoon ketchup

Salt, freshly ground pepper and
sugar to taste

Wash and dry lettuce leaves and shred finely. Make mounds of lettuce on 4 plates, and pile crabmeat in the center.

Peel and seed papaya or cantaloupe, cut into thin crescents, and arrange around crab.

Separate whites from yolks of the eggs. Push yolks through a sieve, sprinkle over crab. Chop whites finely and sprinkle around the lettuce. Scatter chopped chives over all, and serve with dressing. Serves 4.

Dressing: Combine all ingredients, seasoning to suit your own taste with salt, pepper and sugar.

Seafood gumbo

3 ribs celery

1 small green pepper

1 lb okra

2 bunches green onions

1 large onion

4 slices lean bacon

4 tablespoons flour

1 (1 lb 12 oz) can tomatoes with liquid

Salt and freshly ground pepper

2 lb raw, peeled and deveined shrimp,
halved

2 lb crabmeat

2 tablespoons gumbo file

Chop celery, pepper, okra and onions (not green onion tops). Chop ½ cup green onion tops and set aside. Fry bacon in skillet, drain on paper towels.

Stir flour into bacon drippings in skillet and brown. Add chopped vegetables and cook 15 minutes, stirring constantly. Stir in tomatoes and simmer 5-10 minutes.

Place mixture in a large black iron pot or steamer kettle and add 2-3 tomato cans of water. Bring to a boil. Season to taste with salt and pepper. Add shrimp and cook until they turn pink. Add crabmeat and green onion tops and simmer 2 hours or more. Thirty minutes before serving, stir in file (or reserve and sprinkle over gumbo in individual bowls). Serve with rice. Serves about 12.

Note: Fresh crabs which have been scrubbed, cleaned and broken in two may be added with the seafood if desired.

Fish in shrimp sauce

(photograph right)

1½ lb firm white fish filets

¼ cup dry white wine

Few sprigs parsley

1 bay leaf

Salt and freshly ground pepper

Water to cover

4 tablespoons butter

3 tablespoons flour

1 cup stock from cooking fish

½ cup milk

¼ cup whipping cream

½ lb cooked, peeled shrimp

1 small bunch spinach, cooked
and finely chopped

1 lb potatoes, boiled and mashed

Remove any skin and bones from fish and cut into serving pieces. Place in a large frying pan with wine, parsley, bay leaf, salt and pepper to taste and just enough water to cover.

Bring to a simmer, cook for 15 minutes, or until fish is white and opaque and flakes easily when tested with a fork. Drain fish, reserving 1 cup of stock. Melt butter in a heavy saucepan, stir in flour and cook for 1 minute. Slowly stir in fish stock, then milk. Stir until mixture boils, then remove from heat, stir in cream and season with salt and pepper. Add shrimp and fold through.

Place a layer of spinach in a 9-inch pie plate. Arrange fish on top, and spoon shrimp sauce over. Pipe or spoon potatoes around the edge of the dish. Place in a preheated 400° oven for 15 minutes, or until heated through. Serves 4-6.

Salmon croquettes
(photograph left)

Some good cooks make a white sauce with 2 tablespoons butter, 2 tablespoons flour and 1 cup milk and add to the salmon, egg and crumb mixture with a small chopped onion, salt and pepper.

1 (16 oz) can salmon with liquid

1 large egg, slightly beaten

1½ cups (approximately) crushed cracker crumbs

Cooking oil

Drain salmon and reserve the liquid. Discard skin and bones from salmon. Combine salmon, a little salmon liquid, egg and enough crushed cracker crumbs to make mixture hold together. It should be moist — use reserved salmon liquid as needed. Roll portions of the mixture into cylinders about 3-inches long. Roll in remaining finely crushed cracker crumbs and fry in hot oil in large skillet, turning as they cook. Drain on paper towels.

Note: Chilling croquettes before frying is a good idea. Croquettes can be re-coated with cracker crumbs before frying.

Shrimp casserole

1 (10¾ oz) can condensed cream of shrimp soup

2 tablespoons chopped green pepper (optional)

2 tablespoons chopped onion

2 tablespoon melted margarine

1 tablespoon lemon juice

2 cups cooked white rice or 1 (6 oz) package long grain and wild rice, cooked

1½ teaspoons Worcestershire sauce

½ teaspoon dry mustard

½ teaspoon black pepper

¾ cup American cheese, cubed

1 lb or more raw, peeled and deveined shrimp, cut in pieces

½ teaspoon salt

Combine all ingredients and mix thoroughly. Pour into a 1½ to 2 quart greased casserole. Bake in a preheated 350° oven for 30-35 minutes or until hot. Serves 5-7.

Gulf Coast fish stew

If you can get them, use 4 or 5 kinds of Gulf Coast fish in this easily-made, delectable stew. Pompano, redfish, red snapper, flounder and trout are all suitable.

6 tablespoons butter

1 large onion, finely chopped

2 cloves garlic, crushed

½ lb mushrooms, sliced

Salt and freshly ground pepper

3 lb assorted fish, cut into 2-inch slices

1 bay leaf

2 sprigs thyme

4 sprigs parsley

1 cup fresh breadcrumbs

1 (25 fl oz) bottle dry white wine

3 tablespoons brandy

4 tablespoons finely chopped parsley

Heat butter in a deep, heavy saucepan and fry onion, garlic and mushrooms 3-4 minutes, or until they soften. Season with salt and pepper. Add half the fish slices, season them, and top with bay leaf, thyme and parsley tied together. Sprinkle breadcrumbs over, add remaining fish, and season. Pour in wine, and bring to a boil.

Heat brandy, pour into the saucepan and ignite it. Lower heat, cover pan and simmer fish for 10-15 minutes, or until white and opaque. Remove fish with a slotted spoon to a heated platter. Take bundle of herbs from the broth.

Taste broth for seasoning, stir in parsley, then spoon over the fish. Serve with crusty bread. Serves 4-5.

Fish stroganoff

1½ lb filets of garfish

3 tablespoons butter

½ cup flour

⅛ teaspoon garlic powder

1 teaspoon salt

½ teaspoon freshly ground pepper

½ lb mushrooms, sliced

½ cup chopped onion

½ cup chopped green pepper

½ cup chopped celery

1 tablespoon Worcestershire sauce

½ teaspoon cayenne pepper or to taste

¼ cup finely chopped parsley

2 cups warm sour cream

1 cup warm water

Slice filets into ¼-inch slices. Cut into bite-size chunks. Melt 1 tablespoon of the butter in a skillet. Combine flour, garlic powder, ½ teaspoon of the salt and pepper. Sprinkle over fish and toss until all pieces are well coated (have fish slightly moist so seasoned flour will stick). Saute fish in butter quickly, about 5 minutes or until lightly brown, turning so it browns evenly. Remove from pan, cover and keep warm. Add remaining butter to pan, melt, and saute mushrooms, onion, pepper and celery. Stir in Worcestershire sauce. Add fish.

Season with remaining salt, cayenne pepper and parsley. Add sour cream and water and heat, do not boil. Cover and let simmer over low heat 15-20 minutes, stirring occasionally. Serve over rice. Serves 6.

Note: If reheating leftovers, heat in double boiler and add milk to desired thickness.

Garnished steamed fish

A slimmer's special — steamed fish garnished with julienne vegetables.

4 thick filets white fish (red snapper or redfish)

A little butter

Salt and freshly ground pepper

Squeeze lemon juice

2 medium carrots

3 ribs celery

Arrange fish on a buttered, heatproof plate. Dot with a little butter and season with salt, pepper and lemon juice. Cover with another plate or aluminum foil, place on top of a saucepan of boiling water. Steam for 10 minutes, or until fish is white and opaque and flakes easily.

Meanwhile, cut carrots and celery into matchstick-size strips (julienne). Cover with boiling, salted water and boil just until tender-crisp, about 3 minutes. Drain and season. Serve fish on a hot plate, with juices that have collected in the plate poured over, and a garnish of the vegetables. A boiled or baked potato is a good accompaniment, and acceptable in a slimming routine if you eat it as is or with a little plain yogurt. Serves 4.

Kingfish in foil

6 kingfish steaks

2 green peppers, sliced

2 medium onions, sliced

¼ cup melted margarine

2 tablespoons lemon juice

1 teaspoon paprika

Salt and pepper to taste

Thaw fish if frozen. Place each steak on a lightly greased square of heavy-duty aluminum foil. Top with peppers and onions. Combine remaining ingredients and pour over fish. Wrap foil packages tightly and grill about 5-inches from heat for 45 minutes-1 hour, or until fish flakes easily. For a more natural flavor, omit green peppper and onion. Fish packages can also be baked in a preheated 350° oven for 30 minutes or until fish is cooked when tested.

Whole baked fish with herbed stuffing

1 large snapper or other whole fish

½ cup butter

2 cups bread cubes

4 slices lean bacon, chopped

1 small clove garlic, crushed

1 rib celery, sliced

3 green onions, finely chopped

3 tablespoons chopped fresh herbs, or 2 teaspoons dried (chives, tarragon, dill or fennel)

Salt and freshly ground pepper

A little melted butter

Sliced limes or lemons to garnish

Wipe cavity of fish and place fish in an oiled baking dish. Heat butter in a large pan, add bread cubes and fry until crisp and golden. Remove from pan and set aside to cool. Place bacon in same pan, and fry until the fat runs. Add garlic, celery and green onions and cook until soft, about 5 minutes. Combine with bread cubes, herbs, salt and pepper.

Spoon filling into fish and brush fish with melted butter. Bake in a preheated 350° oven for about one hour, or until flesh is white and opaque and flakes easily when tested with a fork. To serve, cut fish into slices and serve each with a spoonful of herbed bread stuffing. Garnish with lime or lemon slices. Serves 4-6, depending on size of fish.

Padre Island filets

(photograph left)

8 filets firm white fish
¾ cup dry white wine
½ cup water
Salt and freshly ground pepper
Few sprigs parsley and thyme
3 tablespoons butter
3 tablespoons flour
½ cup fish stock
1 (10½ oz) can oyster stew
3 tablespoons whipping cream
1½ tablespoons brandy
12-15 steamed mussels, or 1 jar mussels, drained (optional)
½ lb cooked, peeled shrimp

Remove any skin and bone from filets and cut into serving pieces. Bring wine and water to a simmer, add fish, salt and pepper and herbs, poach fish gently for 5 minutes, or until flesh is white and opaque. Drain fish and keep warm on a serving plate. Reserve ½ cup of fish stock. Melt butter in a heavy saucepan, stir in flour over low heat and cook 1 minute. Stir in warm stock, then undiluted soup, cream and brandy. Cook for a few minutes, stirring continuously. Add mussels and shrimp and heat through. Taste for seasoning and pour sauce over fish. Serves 4-6.

Poached trout with green mayonnaise

A beautiful cold main course for a summer party.

4-5 whole, medium-size trout
Lemon juice
Salt and freshly ground pepper
1 teaspoon dill
1½ cups dry white wine
1½ cups chicken broth
4 green onions, finely chopped
Green mayonnaise (see below)

Remove heads from trout if desired and trim fins with kitchen scissors. Make two or three diagonal slashes on each side of fish, through the skin. Season inside and out with lemon juice, salt and pepper and dill and allow to stand 10 minutes.

Place wine, broth and green onions in a shallow pan and bring to simmering point. Add trout in a single layer and poach just until flesh is tender and opaque, about 15 minutes.

Cool fish in the liquid, then carefully lift out and remove skin. Arrange on a platter and spoon a little green mayonnaise over. Serve remaining mayonnaise separately. Serves 4-5.

Green Mayonnaise: In a blender or food processor fitted with the steel blade, combine 1 cup mayonnaise with half a cup of watercress leaves, 1 tablespoon lemon juice and salt and pepper to taste. (If watercress isn't available, use equal parts chopped parsley and chopped young spinach leaves instead.)

Crunchy filets

Coat filets in cornmeal for extra crunchiness.
6 medium fish filets
Flour seasoned with salt and pepper
1 cup evaporated milk
About 1 cup cornmeal
4 tablespoons butter
3 tablespoons cooking oil
Lemon wedges to serve

Pat filets dry, roll in flour and shake off excess. Dip in evaporated milk, then in cornmeal. Chill 15 minutes to firm the crust.

Heat butter and oil in a heavy frying pan, and fry filets on both sides over medium heat until brown and crisp, about 3 minutes each side. Drain on paper towels and serve piping hot with lemon wedges. Serves 4-6.

Note: For a change, use equal amounts of cornmeal and wheat germ.

Barbecued whole fish

A lovely way to cook trout or any firm-fleshed fish. A hinged, double-sided griller makes it easy to turn the fish without breaking them.

4 whole fish, each weighing about 1 lb
Cooking oil
Salt and freshly ground pepper
4 thick slices onion
4 sprigs parsley
4 thin slices lemon
Lemon wedges to garnish

Make sure fish are thoroughly cleaned and scaled. Make 3 diagonal slashes on each side and brush inside and out with oil. Season generously with salt and pepper, and place an onion slice, a sprig of parsley and a slice of lemon in the cavity of each.

Brush 2 hinged grillers generously with oil, and place fish inside. Grill over glowing coals for about 5 minutes each side, or until flesh is white and opaque and flakes easily. Serve with lemon wedges. Serves 4.

Overleaf: 'Making bread is one of the things Texans do best'

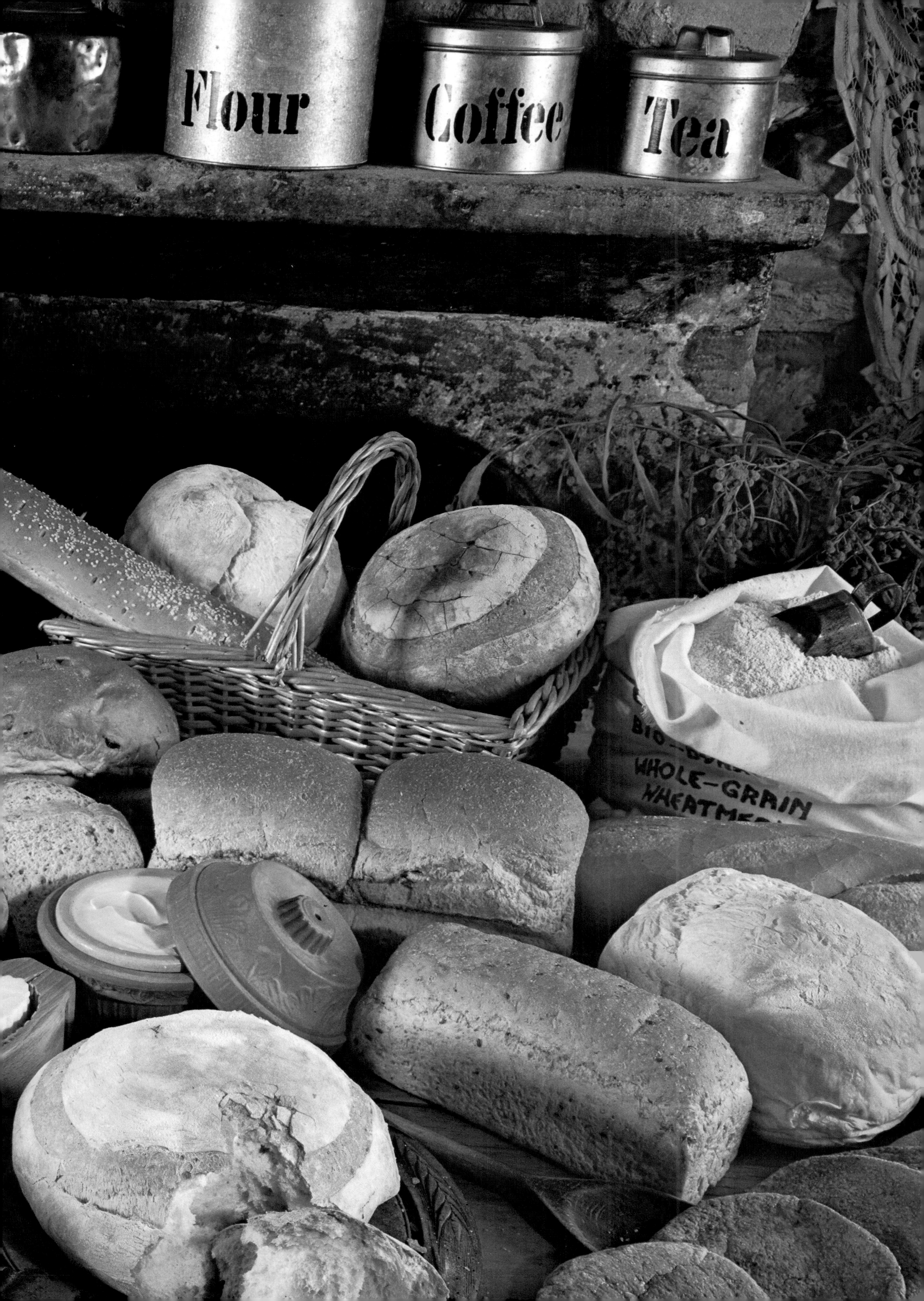
Flour
Coffee
Tea
WHOLE-GRAIN

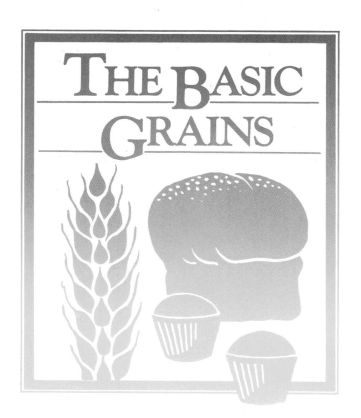

THE BASIC GRAINS

Even in today's sophisticated world, there are few foods as appealing as a loaf of freshly baked bread. Better yet, few are as satisfying to make.

Perhaps the most fundamental of all foods, bread really has not changed all that much from its earliest form when it was baked on rough stones to modern versions, which include buttery croissants and chewy sourdough.

Making bread is one of the things Texans do best. The need to be a good baker arose early among Texas settlers and the tradition has carried through to today.

Along the way, Texas cooks simplified the baking process to coincide with busy schedules. That simplification, however, did nothing to detract from flavor. Quick breads, flavored with pumpkin, garden zucchini or fresh strawberries, are appetizing additions to any Texas table. So are cakes flavored with fresh apples, grapefruit or freshly grated carrots. Also popular are cookies, particularly those with a Mexican or "Deep South" influence.

Grains play an important role in another area of Texas cooking. The state's mixed ancestry means there is an array of authentic Mexican, German, Czech, Italian, Oriental and Middle Eastern foods. Each culture has its own unique way with grains — pasta, corn cakes and jalapeno pepper rice are just a few tasty examples.

Rice is one of the state's major crops. It flourishes in the coastal lands along the Gulf of Mexico, particularly in the Houston area. Texans frequently use rice as a side dish to both gourmet and everyday meals.

Panhandle wheatfields

Fruit muesli

Some historians believe that muesli is almost as old as man himself — that our caveman ancestors lived mostly on a mixture of crushed grains, raw fruits and nuts. The combinations are almost limitless, so experiment.

½ cup chopped dried apricots
½ cup seedless raisins
1 cup quick-cooking rolled oats
¼ cup wheat germ
¼ cup bran, processed or unprocessed
¼ cup chopped walnuts, hazelnuts or almonds
¼ cup bulgur
2 tablespoons brown sugar

Mix all together and store in an airtight container. To serve, top with grated fresh apple or other fruits, and add milk, cream, buttermilk or yogurt. Makes 8-10 servings.

Rice pancakes

(photograph right)

Delicious for breakfast with bacon, and honey or maple syrup. For dessert, top with strawberry jam and whipped cream.

1 cup flour
½ teaspoon salt
2 teaspoons baking powder
1 cup milk
1 egg, beaten
2 tablespoons cooking oil
2 cups cooked, short grain rice
Extra oil for cooking

Sift flour, salt and baking powder into a bowl and make a well in the center. Pour milk into the well and gradually incorporate flour, using a wooden spoon. Add the beaten egg and oil, mix to a smooth batter. Stir in rice and allow to stand for 20 minutes.

Grease a crepe pan or small frying pan with oil, heat. Using about 1½ tablespoons of batter for each pancake, cook one side until golden underneath and bubbly on top, then turn and cook the other side. Keep cooked pancakes warm in a folded towel while cooking remainder. Serves 4-6.

Vegetable rice soup

5 cups beef stock or bouillon
1 (16 oz) can tomatoes, with their juice
2 cloves garlic, crushed
½ cup brown rice
2 teaspoons sugar
Salt and freshly ground pepper
1 (16 oz) can baby lima beans, drained and rinsed
½ small white cabbage (about 1½ cups), shredded
2 teaspoons chopped fresh thyme or ½ teaspoon dried
2 tablespoons butter

Bring stock to a boil and add chopped tomatoes with their juice, garlic, brown rice, sugar, and salt and pepper to taste. Cover and simmer until rice is tender, about 40-50 minutes. Add drained beans, cabbage and thyme and simmer another 10 minutes until cabbage is cooked. Taste for seasoning, stir in butter, serve in deep bowls with plenty of whole grain bread. Serves 4-6.

Sandwiches for lunch at home

At home, you can indulge in luscious fillings for freshly-made sandwiches. Here are some of our own favorites.

Crunchy salmon sandwiches

1 (7½ oz) can red or pink salmon
1 tablespoon finely chopped parsley
2 tablespoons chopped celery
6 large green olives, pitted and chopped
1 small onion, grated
2 teaspoons lemon juice
3 tablespoons mayonnaise
Salt and freshly ground pepper
6 slices buttered whole grain bread

Drain salmon, remove skin and bones and flake. Combine with remaining ingredients. Spread on 3 slices of bread and top with remaining slices. Makes 3 hearty sandwiches.

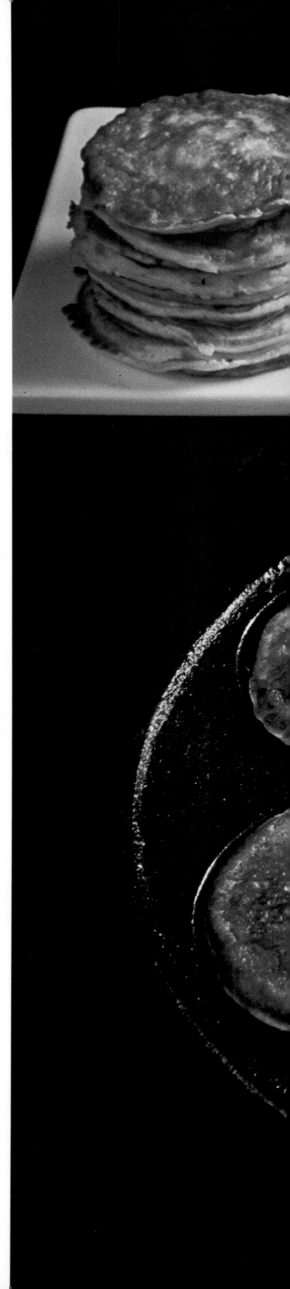

4 slices cheese

4 tablespoons butter for frying

For batter:

2 eggs, lightly beaten

½ cup flour

Pinch salt and pepper

1 cup milk

Spread 4 slices of bread thinly with chutney, top with a slice of ham and cheese, press top slices into place. Beat batter ingredients together with a rotary beater, pour into a shallow dish. Heat the butter in a large frying pan. Dip sandwiches on both sides into the batter, and fry on both sides until batter is crisp and golden. Drain on paper towels, and cut into diagonal halves to serve. Serves 4.

Super curried egg sandwiches

3 hard-boiled eggs, finely chopped

4 tablespoons sour cream

½ teaspoon salt

1 teaspoon mild curry powder

2 green onions, finely chopped

1 tablespoon chopped chutney

6 slices buttered white bread

Combine all filling ingredients and chill until ready to use. Pile on 3 slices of bread and top with remaining slices. Makes 3 sandwiches.

Peanut butter and bacon sandwiches

2 slices crisp lean bacon, crumbled

½ cup peanut butter, at room temperature

1 tablespoon mayonnaise

1 tablespoon finely chopped sweet gherkin

Freshly ground pepper

4 lettuce leaves

8 slices buttered rye bread

Combine bacon, peanut butter, mayonnaise, gherkin and pepper to taste. Spread filling on 4 slices of bread, top with a lettuce leaf, and then remaining slices. Makes 4 sandwiches.

Chicken and almond sandwiches

2 cups finely chopped cooked chicken

½ cup chopped, toasted almonds

3 tablespoons finely chopped celery

2 teaspoons soy sauce

¼ cup mayonnaise or sour cream

Pinch each sugar and cayenne pepper

10 slices buttered white sandwich bread

Small bunches of grapes to garnish

Combine filling ingredients, seasoning to taste with sugar and cayenne pepper. Spread filling on 5 slices of bread and top with remaining slices. Trim crusts. Wrap in plastic wrap and chill for 1 hour, or until serving time. Cut in fingers or triangles to serve and garnish the platter with small bunches of seedless grapes. Makes 20 small sandwiches.

Cheese-ham pancake sandwiches

Once you get the basic idea of these sandwiches, you can change the fillings to suit yourself. Serve as a substantial (not to say fattening!) snack, or for lunch.

8 slices lightly buttered white sandwich bread

Fruit chutney

4 slices ham

Tabbouleh

Tabbouleh is traditionally served on individual dishes, with vine leaves, lettuce or cabbage leaves on the side to be used as scoops. A little finely chopped cucumber and tomato (previously salted and drained of any excess juice) — may be added to the salad. If served in a large bowl, it can be decorated with black olives, tomato sections, slices of cucumber and sprigs of parsley.

1½ cups bulgur

4 tablespoons finely chopped green onion, or 1 small onion, finely chopped — or both

1½ cups finely chopped parsley

½ cup finely chopped mint

¾ cup olive oil

4 tablespoons lemon juice

Salt and freshly ground black pepper

Soak the bulgur in plenty of cold water for about an hour to allow it to soften and expand. Drain, and squeeze out excess water with your hands. Spread the bulgur on a clean towel or paper towels and dry off for 20 minutes.

Place bulgur, onions, parsley and mint in a large bowl and mix well, squeezing with your hands so that the onion juice mixes with the bulgur. Gradually add oil, then lemon juice and mix well. Season with salt and pepper and add additional lemon juice if necessary — tabbouleh should be quite tart. Serves 8.

Fettucine with blue cheese sauce

(photograph page 128)

The simple sauce has a gourmet touch.

½ lb green fettucine (ribbon noodles)

2 tablespoons butter

1 medium onion, thinly sliced

4 oz blue vein cheese, diced

½ cup whipping cream

3 tablespoons chopped walnuts

¼ cup dry white wine

2 egg yolks, lightly beaten

2 tablespoons finely chopped parsley

Cook fettucine in plenty of boiling salted water until tender. While pasta is cooking, prepare the sauce.

Melt butter in a saucepan and add onion and cheese, stirring until cheese melts. Gradually stir in cream, walnuts and wine. Bring to a boil, then whisk a little of the sauce into the egg yolks. Return mixture to the saucepan and stir over gentle heat until thickened, but do not allow to boil. Stir parsley into sauce. Pour sauce over cooked and drained fettucine and serve immediately. Serves 2-4.

Rice and vegetable bake

(photograph page 131)

Brown rice is nutritious and has a pleasantly nutty texture and flavor. Combined with vegetables, milk and cheese, it makes a meal in itself.

3 cups cooked brown rice (1 cup uncooked)

4 ribs celery, sliced

2 medium parsnips, thinly sliced

1 small leek or onion, sliced

4 tablespoons butter

½ lb mushrooms, sliced

4 tablespoons flour

¾ cup liquid from cooking vegetables

¾ cup milk

Salt and freshly ground pepper

1 cup grated Jarlsberg cheese

Spread rice in a greased casserole dish. Cook celery, parsnips and leek in salted water to cover until just tender, about 5 minutes. Drain, reserving ¾ cup of liquid. Arrange vegetables over rice. Heat butter in a saucepan and toss mushrooms until beginning to soften. Lower heat, stir in flour, and cook 1 minute. Combine vegetable water and milk and stir in. Continue stirring until mixture is smooth and thickened, then season with salt and pepper to taste.

Spoon sauce over vegetables, and sprinkle with cheese. Bake in a pre-heated 400° oven for 15 minutes, or until heated through and cheese is melted. Serves 4.

Green rice

1 cup rice

6 tablespoons butter

1 green pepper, chopped

1 onion, chopped

1 rib celery, chopped

1 (10¾ oz) can condensed cream of mushroom soup

Salt and freshly ground pepper

½ cup grated mild Cheddar cheese

½ cup grated sharp Cheddar cheese

Cook rice in 3 cups of water until tender. Saute pepper, onion and celery in butter. Dilute mushroom soup with ¾ can water, heat to a boil. Add sauteed pepper, onion and celery. Add salt and pepper to taste. Mix with rice and transfer to a buttered baking dish. Top with the cheeses and bake in a 350° oven for 20 minutes or until hot. Serves 6-8.

Dirty rice

*More often than not, this is what
the Cajun selects to serve with
turkey or chicken.*

| 1 lb ground beef |
| 1 lb chicken giblets, ground |
| ½ cup butter |
| 1 cup chopped onion |
| ½ cup chopped green pepper |
| ½ cup chopped celery |
| 1 clove garlic, chopped |
| 1 bunch green onions including tops, chopped |
| 1 tablespoon parsley, finely chopped |
| Salt, pepper and hot pepper sauce to taste |
| Pinch thyme and basil |
| 4 cups cooked rice |
| Chicken broth or bouillon |

Saute ground beef and giblets in 2 tablespoons butter in a skillet until brown.
Set aside. Saute onion, pepper, celery,
garlic, green onion, parsley and seasonings in remaining butter in skillet. Combine with rice and meat, moisten with
chicken broth and place in a 3-quart
casserole and bake in a preheated 350°
oven 20-30 minutes. Serves 6.

Jalapeno pepper rice

| 4 cups cooked long grain rice |
| 2 cups sour cream |
| 1 (4 oz) can jalapeno peppers, seeded and chopped |
| ½ cup grated Cheddar cheese |

Blend cooked rice with sour cream. Stir
in jalapenos. Place in buttered 1¾ or 2-
quart shallow casserole. Top with grated
cheese. Bake in a preheated 350° oven
for 20 minutes or until heated through.
Serves 4-6.

Fettucine with blue cheese sauce (page 127)

Wild rice with mushrooms and almonds

| 1 cup wild rice |
| ¼ cup butter or margarine |
| ½ cup slivered almonds |
| 2 tablespoons chopped chives or green onions |
| 1 can (8 oz) mushrooms, drained |
| 3 cups chicken broth or bouillon |

Wash and drain rice. Melt butter in a
large skillet. Add rice, almonds, chives
and mushrooms. Cook and stir until
almonds are golden brown, about 20
minutes.

Pour rice mixture into ungreased
1½-quart casserole. Heat chicken broth
to boiling, add to casserole. Cover
tightly. Cook in a preheated 325° oven
for 1½ hours or until all liquid is
absorbed and rice is tender and fluffy.
Serves 6-8.

Note: This can have many variations.
Add ½ chopped green pepper to skillet
when frying wild rice. Add some cubed
cooked chicken and/or ½ cup sauterne,
15 minutes before serving.

Pumpkin bread

| 3½ cups sifted flour |
| 3 cups sugar |
| 1 teaspoon each ginger and cinnamon |
| 1 teaspoon each nutmeg and allspice |
| 1½ teaspoons salt |
| 2 teaspoons baking soda |
| 2 cups (16 oz can) cooked pumpkin |
| 1 cup cooking oil |
| 4 eggs |
| ⅝ cup (½ cup plus 1 tablespoon) water |

Combine flour, sugar, spices, salt and
baking soda. Make a well in the center of
the mixture and add pumpkin, oil, eggs
and water, mix. Pour into 2 (9 x 5 x 3-
inch) greased and floured loaf pans and
bake in a preheated 350° oven for 1 hour
or until bread tests done. Makes 2 loaves.

Note: To freeze, when bread is cool,
wrap in vapor and moisture-proof freezer
wrap and freeze. Thaw, but for ease in
slicing, slice before bread is completely
thawed.

Strawberry bread with cream cheese spread

3 cups flour
2 cups sugar
1 teaspoon baking soda
1 teaspoon cinnamon
1 teaspoon salt
2 (10 oz) packages frozen strawberries, thawed and drained (reserve ½ cup juice)
1 cup cooking oil
4 eggs, well beaten
Cream cheese spread:
1 (8 oz) package cream cheese, at room temperature
Reserved ½ cup strawberry juice

Combine all dry ingredients and mix well. Make a well in the center of mixture and add all liquid ingredients. Mix by hand. Pour mixture into 2 (8 x 4 x 2-inch) greased and floured loaf pans. Bake in a preheated 350° oven for 1 hour or until toothpick inserted in center comes out clean.

Combine cream cheese and enough strawberry juice to make a spreadable consistency. Cut bread very thin and spread with cream cheese spread. Sandwich each 2 slices together as sandwiches. Chill until ready to serve. Makes 2 loaves.

Note: Loaves freeze well; slice thinly before completely thawed.

Whole wheat muffins

2 cups whole wheat flour
⅔ cup wheat germ
1 teaspoon salt
4 teaspoons baking powder
⅔ cup brown sugar
1 cup milk
1 egg
4 tablespoons cooking oil

Combine flour, wheat germ, salt and baking powder. Add sugar, milk, egg and oil all at once. Mix well. Put paper baking cups in cupcake pans, fill two-thirds full and bake in a preheated 400° oven for 15-20 minutes. Makes 12-14 muffins.

Whole wheat orange bread

6 medium oranges
3 cups water
2 cups honey
5½ cups whole wheat flour
2 tablespoons plus 2 teaspoons baking powder
2 teaspoons salt
2 cups cold milk
1 cup chopped walnuts
2 tablespoons flour

Cut rind from oranges and discard inner white pith from rind. Cut rind into long thin strips. Add to water and bring to a boil. Lower heat and cook slowly until rind is tender, about 30 minutes. Pour off all but ½ cup liquid, keeping orange rind. Add honey to liquid, bring to a boil and simmer until syrup is thick. Let cool. Sift whole wheat flour, baking powder and salt.

Add milk to the orange-honey syrup, mix well. Add gradually to dry ingredients and beat well. (Some of the orange rind may be added, if desired.) Dredge walnuts with flour. Mix into batter. Let batter rest 10 minutes.

Divide batter equally between 2 (9 x 5 x 3-inch) well greased loaf pans and level with spatula. Bake in a preheated 325° oven for 1 hour. Test to see if done with toothpick in several places. Remove loaves from pans onto a wire rack to cool. Serve cool or cold. Loaves get better with age. Serve thinly sliced. Makes 2 loaves.

Zucchini nut bread

3 eggs, well beaten
2-2¼ cups sugar
3 teaspoons vanilla
1 cup cooking oil
2 cups shredded zucchini
3 cups flour
¼ teaspoon baking powder
1 teaspoon salt
1 teaspoon baking soda
1 tablespoon cinnamon
1 cup chopped nuts

Beat eggs in a bowl until light and fluffy. Add sugar, vanilla and oil and blend well. Stir in zucchini. Sift flour, baking powder, salt, baking soda and cinnamon together. Stir into sugar mixture. Fold in nuts. Turn into 2 (9 x 5 x 3-inch) greased and floured loaf pans. Bake in a preheated 325° oven for 1 hour or until bread tests done. Makes 2 loaves.

Quick monkey bread

½ cup chopped nuts
3 (10 biscuit) cans biscuits
1 teaspoon cinnamon
½ cup sugar
½ cup butter or margarine
1 cup brown sugar, firmly packed

Grease a large bundt pan. Pour nuts evenly into pan. Cut biscuits into quarters. Combine cinnamon and sugar. Roll each piece of biscuit in cinnamon-sugar mixture. Arrange biscuits in bundt pan. Melt butter and add brown sugar (the microwave is terrific for this). Pour over sugared biscuits. Bake in a preheated 350° oven for 30-40 minutes (depends on size of biscuits). Remove from pan and everyone will think you've been in the kitchen all morning. Serves 12.

Rice and vegetable bake (page 127)

Monkey bread

1 cake compressed yeast or
1 package dry yeast

1 cup milk, scalded and cooled
to lukewarm

4 tablespoons sugar

1 teaspoon salt

½ cup melted butter or margarine

3½ cups sifted flour

Extra melted butter or margarine

Dissolve yeast in lukewarm milk in a large bowl. Stir in sugar, salt, melted butter and flour. Beat well. Cover and let rise in a warm place until almost double in bulk, about 1 hour. Punch down and roll out on lightly floured board to ¼-inch thickness. Cut into diamond shaped pieces, about 2½-inches long. Dip each piece in extra melted butter and arrange in layers in a 9-inch ring mold. The mold should be about half full. Let rise until almost doubled in bulk. Bake in a preheated 400° oven for 30 minutes, or until golden brown. Serves 12.

Can-do-quick bread

The whole process takes about
3 hours.

2 packages dry yeast

1½ cups warm water (105°-115°)

2½ cups buttermilk

9-10 cups flour

½ cup shortening

4 tablespoons sugar

4 teaspoons baking powder

4 teaspoons salt

Soft butter

Dissolve yeast in water in large mixer bowl. Add buttermilk, 4½ cups of the flour, shortening, sugar, baking powder and salt. Blend 30 seconds on low speed, scraping sides and bottom of bowl. Beat 2 minutes on medium speed. Stir in remaining flour. Dough should remain soft and slightly sticky. Turn out on generously floured board and knead 5 minutes or about 20 turns. Divide dough in three.

Roll each portion into an 18 x 9-inch rectangle. Roll up from short side, jelly roll fashion. With side of hand, press down each end to seal. Fold ends under loaf. Place, seam side down, in 3 loaf pans, 9 x 5 x 3-inches. Brush loaves

lightly with soft butter. Let rise in warm place (85°) until double in size, about 1 hour. Dough in center should come up above pan about 2-inches.

Bake loaves in a preheated 425° oven for 30-35 minutes, oven rack should be in lowest position. When bread tests done, remove from pans and brush with butter. Cover with towel if soft crust is desired. Cool on wire rack. Makes 3 loaves.

Note: To make raisin bread, add 1½ cups seedless raisins to mixture.

Whole wheat quick bread

2 cups whole wheat flour

½ teaspoon salt

1 teaspoon baking soda

1 egg, well beaten

1 cup buttermilk

2 tablespoons honey

Mix flour, salt and baking soda. Combine egg, buttermilk and honey. Add wet ingredients to dry, mixing as little as possible to form a sticky dough. Do not overbeat. Shape into 2 small flat round loaves on a greased baking sheet and cut 2 parallel slashes on top, about ½-inch deep. Bake in a preheated 375° oven for 25 minutes. Makes 2 loaves.

Best and easiest rolls

½ cup butter

5 tablespoons sugar

½ cup boiling water

1 egg, well beaten

1 cake compressed yeast

½ cup cold water

Pinch salt

3 cups flour

Cream butter and sugar. Add boiling water and let cool. Add egg. Dissolve yeast in cold water, add salt with flour. Mix, cover and refrigerate overnight or longer. Divide dough into 2 balls. Roll into circles, ¼-inch thick and 12-inches in diameter. Cut into 8 pie-shaped pieces. Roll up, beginning at rounded edge, bend in a crescent shape. Place on greased cookie sheet with point underneath. Let rise in warm place about 3 hours. Bake in a preheated 400° oven 20 minutes, or until golden brown. Makes 16.

Redeemer bread

¾ cup cooking oil or shortening

¾ cup sugar

1 tablespoon salt

1 cup bran cereal, such as All-Bran

2 cups boiling water

2 packages dry yeast

½ cup lukewarm water (110°-115°)

2 eggs

7½-8½ cups flour

Mix oil, sugar, salt and cereal in a large mixing bowl. Pour boiling water over, let cool. Soften yeast in lukewarm water. When bran mixture has cooled to lukewarm, add eggs, softened yeast and flour. Turn out on floured board. Knead 8-10 minutes, drawing in more flour as needed to keep it from being sticky. Place in greased bowl. Let rise until double in size (about 1¼ hours), punch down. Knead 2 minutes, shape into loaves or rolls. Let rise in greased pans, (9 x 5 x 3-inch pans for loaves) until double in size (about 45 minutes). Bake in a preheated 350° oven, about 30 minutes for loaves, 12-15 minutes for rolls. Makes 3 loaves or 2 loaves and 1 dozen rolls.

Town crier orange cookies

1 cup shortening

1½ cups brown sugar, firmly packed

Grated rind 1 orange

2 eggs

3½ cups flour

2 teaspoons baking powder

½ teaspoon salt

1 teaspoon soda

1 cup sour milk

Glaze:

2 cups powdered sugar

2 tablespoons butter

¼ cup orange juice

Cream shortening and sugar and orange rind. Add eggs. Sift dry ingredients. Add them alternately with sour milk. Drop by spoonfuls on greased cookie sheet. Bake in a preheated 375° oven about 10 minutes.

Meanwhile, combine powdered sugar, butter and orange juice. While cookies are still hot, spread with glaze. Makes 6½ dozen.

Peanut butter cookies

1 cup shortening

1 cup brown sugar, firmly packed

1 cup sugar

1 cup peanut butter

2 eggs

1 teaspoon vanilla

3¼ cups flour

1 teaspoon baking powder

½ teaspoon salt

Cream shortening and sugars with peanut butter. Beat in eggs and mix well. Add vanilla. Sift flour with baking powder and salt. Work into peanut butter mixture. Dough will be firm enough to roll into balls the size of large marbles. Place on ungreased cookie sheet. Press flat with fork tines to make a crosshatch design. Don't let cookies touch. Bake in a preheated 350° oven, 12-15 minutes or until lightly browned. They burn easily, so watch them carefully. Cool on a wire rack. Makes 7-8 dozen.

Lemon butter cookies

1 cup butter or margarine

¾ cup sugar

Rind of 1 lemon, grated

2 cups flour

Cream butter and sugar. Add grated lemon rind. Add flour and blend. Drop by teaspoons on ungreased cookie sheets. Bake in a preheated 350° oven for 15 minutes. Cool on a wire rack. Makes 5 dozen.

Bisquick bars

This mixture makes a bar relatively like a brownie with the same consistency but a different taste.

*2 cups Bisquick
(buttermilk baking mix)*

2¼ cups brown sugar, firmly packed

4 eggs, well beaten

2 cups chopped pecans

Combine Bisquick mix and brown sugar. Add eggs and then chopped pecans. Grease and flour a 13 x 9 x 2-inch pan. Pour mixture into pan and bake in a preheated 325° oven for 30-35 minutes. Remove from oven and let cool before cutting into bars. Makes 2 dozen.

Fudge peanut oaties

2 cups sugar

3 tablespoons cocoa

½ cup butter or margarine

½ cup milk

½ cup peanut butter

3 cups quick cooking oats

1 tablespoon vanilla

Mix sugar, cocoa, butter and milk together in a pan. Bring to a boil and boil 1 minute. Add immediately to combined peanut butter, oats and vanilla. Stir well and drop by teaspoonfuls on wax paper or foil to set. Makes 5 dozen.

Strawberry shortcake biscuits

2 cups flour

½ teaspoon salt

4 teaspoons baking powder

1 tablespoon sugar

⅓ cup shortening

1 egg, well beaten

⅔ cup milk

Sift and mix flour, salt, baking powder and sugar. Cut shortening in until it is the size of crumbs. Combine egg with milk and stir into flour mixture until just blended. Knead lightly. Roll out on a floured board, ½ to ¾-inch thick. Cut with a 3-inch round cutter, place on greased cookie sheets and bake in a preheated 425°-450° oven until lightly browned, 10-12 minutes. Fill and/or top with strawberries and sweetened whipped cream. Makes about 6 (3-inch) biscuits.

Old-fashioned teacakes

1 cup butter or shortening

1½ cups sugar

1 teaspoon baking soda

*½ cup buttermilk or
1½ teaspoons vinegar or lemon juice
in ½ cup measure filled with milk*

3 eggs

5 cups flour

2 teaspoons baking powder

1 teaspoon vanilla

Cream butter and sugar well. Dissolve soda in buttermilk. Add eggs, then flour, baking powder and vanilla to creamed butter and sugar. Mix in buttermilk. Chill several hours until firm. Roll out dough to ¼-inch thick on lightly floured board, cut with a 3-inch cookie cutter and place on cookie sheets. Bake for 10 minutes until lightly browned in a preheated 400° oven. Makes 5-6 dozen.

Truly different cupcakes

1 cup butter or margarine

4 squares (4 oz) semi-sweet chocolate

¼ teaspoon butter flavoring

1-1½ cups chopped nuts

1 cup flour

1¾ cups sugar

4 eggs

1 teaspoon vanilla

In a saucepan, melt butter and chocolate. Add butter flavoring and chopped nuts. In a bowl mix flour, sugar, eggs and vanilla. Combine the two mixtures with a spoon. Put paper baking cups in cupcake pans, fill two-thirds full. Bake in a preheated 325° oven for 25-30 minutes. Do not overbake. Makes about 16 (2-inch) cupcakes.

Deluxe pound cake

1 cup butter
½ cup shortening
3 cups sugar
5 eggs
3 cups cake flour or 3 cups less 3 tablespoons all-purpose flour, sifted
½ teaspoon baking powder
1 cup milk
2 teaspoons vanilla
1 teaspoon coconut flavoring

Have ingredients at room temperature. Cream butter, shortening and sugar together. Add eggs one at a time, beating well after each addition, cake requires about 30 minutes beating in all. Sift flour with baking powder. Add flour alternately with milk, ending with flour. Blend in flavorings. Pour into a greased and lightly floured 10-inch tube pan and bake in a preheated 325° oven for 1 hour or until cake tests done. Cool a few minutes in the pan before turning out.

Fresh apple cake

(photograph right)

2 cups sugar
1½ cups cooking oil
2 tablespoons vanilla
2 eggs, well beaten
1 teaspoon salt
Juice of ½ lemon
3 cups flour
1¼ teaspoons baking soda
3 cups tart apples, peeled and chopped
1½ cups pecans, broken

Mix sugar, oil, vanilla, eggs, salt and lemon juice. Beat well. Sift flour and baking soda together and add gradually to first mixture. Batter is quite stiff before apples and pecans are added. Add apples and pecans. Blend well. Bake in a greased and floured tube pan in a pre-heated 325° oven for 1½ hours or until cake tests done. Cool on a wire rack.

Italian cream cake

1 teaspoon baking soda
1 cup buttermilk
½ cup margarine
½ cup shortening
2 cups sugar
5 eggs, separated
2 cups sifted flour
1 teaspoon vanilla
1 cup chopped pecans
1 (3½ oz) can flaked coconut
Cream cheese frosting:
1 (8 oz) package cream cheese
½ cup margarine
1 teaspoon vanilla
1 lb powdered sugar

Combine baking soda and buttermilk and let stand a few minutes. Cream margarine and shortening with sugar. Add egg yolks, one at a time, beating well after each addition. Add buttermilk alternately with flour to creamed mixture. Stir in vanilla. Beat egg whites until stiff. Fold in egg whites, then gently fold in pecans and coconut.

Divide cake mixture between 3 (9-inch) greased, floured layer pans. Bake in a preheated 325° oven for 25 minutes or until cake tests done. Frost cooled cake with cream cheese frosting.

Cream cheese frosting: Have ingredients at room temperature. Cream cheese and margarine well and add vanilla. Beat in sugar a little at a time until of spreading consistency.

Bundt cake

2 cups sugar
2 cups flour
1 cup margarine
5 eggs
1 tablespoon flavoring (1 teaspoon each vanilla, almond, lemon, if desired)

Have ingredients at room temperature. This is most important to the success of the cake. Combine all ingredients in mixer bowl, beat until smooth, about 10 minutes in all. Pour into a well greased bundt pan (even grease Teflon-lined pan). Bake in a preheated 325° oven for 1 hour or slightly longer if needed, until cake tests done. Cool on a wire rack.

Pumpkin nut cake

2 eggs
2 cups (16 oz can) cooked pumpkin
¾ cup cooking oil
¼ cup water
2½ cups flour
2¼ cups sugar
1½ teaspoons baking soda
½ teaspoon salt
¾ teaspoon nutmeg
¾ teaspoon cinnamon
1 cup golden raisins
½ cup chopped walnuts
Extra chopped walnuts to decorate
Cream cheese frosting:
4 oz cream cheese
3 tablespoons butter
1 teaspoon lemon juice
2 cups powdered sugar

Beat eggs, pumpkin, oil and water together. Add flour, sugar, soda, salt, nutmeg, cinnamon, raisins and nuts, folding in well. Pour into a greased and lightly floured 13 x 9 x 2-inch baking pan and bake in a preheated 350° oven for 20-25 minutes or until cake tests done. Cool cake and frost with cream cheese frosting. Decorate with extra chopped walnuts.

Cream cheese frosting: Have ingredients at room temperature. Cream cheese and butter. Add lemon juice and beat in powdered sugar.

Orange carrot cake

1 cup butter or margarine, at room temperature
2 cups sugar
1 teaspoon cinnamon
½ teaspoon nutmeg
1 tablespoon grated orange rind
4 eggs
1½ cups grated or finely shredded carrots
⅔ cup finely chopped walnuts or pecans
3 cups flour
3 teaspoons baking powder
½ teaspoon salt
⅓ cup orange juice
Orange slices to decorate
Orange glaze:
1⅓ cups sifted powdered sugar
1 tablespoon butter or margarine
½ teaspoon grated orange rind
2-3 tablespoons orange juice

In large bowl of electric mixer, cream butter and sugar. Add cinnamon, nutmeg and orange rind. Beat in eggs one at a time. Add carrots and nuts. Sift flour, baking powder and salt, add alternately with the orange juice. Pour into a greased and floured 10-inch tube pan. Bake in a preheated 350° oven for 1 hour or a little longer, until toothpick inserted in cake comes out clean. Cool in pan 15 minutes, then turn out of pan and cool completely on wire rack. Cover top of cake with orange glaze and decorate with orange slices.

Orange glaze: In small bowl, beat powdered sugar with butter, orange rind and enough orange juice to make a slightly runny glaze.

Texas grapefruit cake

2 cups cake flour
2 teaspoons baking powder
½ teaspoon salt
½ cup fresh grapefruit juice
⅓ cup cooking oil
4 eggs
⅛ teaspoon cream of tartar
1 cup sugar
Grapefruit sections to decorate
Cream cheese frosting:
2 (8 oz) packages cream cheese
1 cup powdered sugar
2 tablespoons finely grated grapefruit rind
½ teaspoon vanilla
⅓ cup fresh grapefruit juice

Combine flour, baking powder and salt. Sift into bowl. Strain grapefruit juice and combine with oil. Set aside. Separate eggs. Beat egg whites and cream of tartar until stiff peaks form, set aside.

In large mixing bowl, beat egg yolks and sugar until mixture is thick. Beat in about half cup of flour mixture then one-fourth cup of the juice-oil mixture. Repeat, alternating flour mixture with liquid, beating well after each addition. Gently fold beaten egg whites into batter thoroughly.

Pour batter into 2 (9-inch) or 3 (8-inch) greased and floured cake pans. Bake in a preheated 350° oven for 25 minutes or until toothpick inserted in center comes out clean. Let cakes cool in pans 5 minutes. Turn out onto wire racks and cool thoroughly.

When cool, frost cake layers with cream cheese frosting and sandwich together. Decorate with grapefruit sections and refrigerate until ready to serve.

Cream cheese frosting: Have cream cheese at room temperature. Combine cream cheese and powdered sugar. Add grapefruit rind and vanilla. Add juice gradually, beating until mixture is fluffy.

German chocolate potato cake

½ cup butter or margarine
½ cup shortening
2 cups sugar
2 cups mashed potatoes, unseasoned
1 teaspoon salt
1 teaspoon cloves
2 teaspoons cinnamon
1 teaspoon nutmeg or allspice
4 eggs
2 teaspoons baking soda
1 cup buttermilk
½ cup cocoa
2 cups flour
½ cup seedless raisins (plumped in water, well drained)
1 cup chopped nuts

Cream butter and shortening together with sugar. Beat in potatoes, salt and spices. Add eggs and beat thoroughly. Combine soda and buttermilk, let stand a few minutes. Add to creamed mixture alternately with cocoa and flour which have been sifted together. Stir in raisins and nuts. Bake in a lightly greased and floured large tube or bundt pan, in a preheated 350° oven for 50 minutes-1 hour, or until toothpick inserted in center comes out dry and cake is just beginning to pull away from pan. Do not overbake.

Note: Raisins are optional.

Cream of coconut cake

1 (2-layer size) package white cake mix
1 (3½ oz) can flaked coconut
1 (15½ oz) can cream of coconut
Coconut frosting:
1 (8 oz) carton frozen whipped topping, thawed
1 (3½ oz) can flaked coconut
2 tablespoons coconut liqueur (optional)

Prepare cake mix according to package directions, adding coconut to the batter. Bake in a greased, floured 13 x 9 x 2-inch cake pan. When baked, remove from oven and punch deep holes in cake with a fork. Pour the cream of coconut into holes. Cool about 5 minutes or until just

warm before frosting. Spread frosting over cake, cover and store in refrigerator.

Coconut frosting: Mix ingredients together well.

7-Up pound cake

1 cup butter or margarine,
½ cup shortening
2 cups sugar
5 eggs
3 cups flour
¾ cup 7-Up
1 teaspoon vanilla or lemon flavoring
1 teaspoon butter flavoring
Powdered sugar to decorate

Have ingredients at room temperature. Cream butter and shortening with sugar. Add eggs, one at a time, beating well after each addition. Fold in flour alternately with 7-Up and flavorings. Bake in a greased tube pan in a preheated 325° oven for at least 1 hour or until a toothpick inserted in center comes out clean. Leave in pan for a few minutes then turn out on a wire rack to cool. Before serving, dust with powdered sugar.

Overleaf: Iron wheels, mules and sandy road in deep East Texas north of Nacogdoches

COUNTRY FARE

The jalapeno isn't the state vegetable of Texas. But you might think so judging by the number of ways it is used. Eaten out of hand, fried, stuffed or as a primary ingredient in salsa, the fiery hot jalapeno is a state speciality. Jalapeno Pie, a cocktail party staple, is a favorite Texas way to show off this versatile veggie.

The Lone Star State produces a number of other lush vegetables which show up on Texas tables in salads, pickles, relishes, casseroles and side accompaniments.

A dazzling array of fruits also is harvested in the state. Two of the best known are watermelon and cantaloupe. The small town of Pecos, located on the Pecos River in West Texas, grows some of the best cantaloupe in the world. This dry area, used mainly for cattle ranching, produces a juicy, sweet and tender melon which must be tasted to be believed.

Also well known for its fruit-growing ability is the Rio Grande Valley. Grapefruit and oranges are prime crops. Any visitor to the area invariably goes home with suitcases loaded with Texas' fine citrus. Boxes of the juicy fruit also make their way north through the mails, especially at Christmas time.

Cheese and eggs are other important elements for meals or for side dishes. A basic ingredient, eggs sustained many an early Texas family when there was little else to go around. Today, when your larder is bare, eggs and a bit of cheese still go a long way toward making a meal, be it an omelet, crepe, souffle or taco.

Both eggs and cheese should be cooked on low to moderate heat. Excessive heat toughens the protein in eggs and cheese and causes them to curdle.

The general store in Jonesville

Quick vegetable soup

(photograph page 145)

You can really add any vegetables you have on hand, and it's ready in 20 minutes.

| 5 cups beef bouillon (made with cubes) |
| 1 large onion, chopped |
| 2 large carrots, chopped |
| 1 medium turnip, chopped |
| 4 ribs celery, chopped |
| (You may add also chopped potatoes, parsnips, leeks) |
| 6 cloves |
| Salt and freshly ground pepper |
| 1/4 cup finely chopped parsley |

Bring bouillon to a boil and add all the ingredients except parsley. Cover pan and simmer for 20 minutes, or until vegetables are tender. Taste for seasoning and serve in heated bowls, sprinkled with parsley. Serves 4-6.

Hot broccoli dip

| 1 (6 oz) roll jalapeno cheese |
| 1 (6 oz) roll garlic cheese |
| 1 (10¾ oz) can condensed cream of chicken soup |
| 1 (10 oz) package frozen chopped broccoli |

Melt cheeses over very low heat or in top of double boiler. Combine chicken soup and frozen broccoli with cheese mixture. Continue to cook over very low heat until broccoli thaws. Keep warm in a chafing dish. Serve with pieces of crisp vegetables or tortilla chips. Serves 8-12 as an appetizer.

Jalapeno cocktail pie

| 2-3 fresh jalapeno peppers |
| 1 lb sharp Cheddar cheese |
| 6 eggs |

Cut jalapenos into slivers and spread over the bottom of a lightly greased 8 or 9-inch square pan. Grate cheese over jalapenos. Beat eggs and pour over the cheese. Bake in a preheated 350° oven for 30 minutes or until just set when pan is shaken. Cut into 1-inch squares. Serve on toothpicks on a large plate. Serves 12 as an appetizer.

Yogurt and spinach iced soup

Deliciously light, cool and refreshing.

| 2 cups chicken broth |
| 1 large onion, finely chopped |
| 6 large spinach leaves, stalks removed |
| 1½ cups plain yogurt |
| 2 tablespoons finely chopped mint |
| Salt and freshly ground pepper |
| Grated lemon rind to garnish |

Bring chicken broth to a boil, add onion and spinach. Cover pan, and simmer until vegetables are soft, about 5 minutes. Process until smooth in a blender or food processor fitted with steel blade. Cover and chill.

At serving time, stir in yogurt and mint and season to taste with salt and pepper. Spoon into bowls and sprinkle each bowl with a little grated lemon rind. Serves 4.

Garnished cheese soup

(photograph page 144)

| 4 tablespoons butter |
| 3 tablespoons flour |
| 3 cups chicken broth |
| 1 cup milk |
| Salt and freshly grated pepper |
| Pinch freshly grated nutmeg |
| 2 egg yolks |
| 1 cup whipping cream |
| 1 cup grated Cheddar or Parmesan cheese |
| Garnishes (see below) |

Melt butter in a heavy saucepan, stir in flour, and cook over low heat for 1 minute. Gradually stir in broth and milk, and continue stirring over medium heat until mixture boils and thickens. Season with salt and pepper and nutmeg.

Beat egg yolks with cream and gradually stir into the hot soup. Reheat, but do not allow to boil. Stir in cheese until it melts, and taste for seasoning. Serve from a tureen surrounded by garnishes, which each person adds to his soup to suit his own taste. Serves 4-6.

Garnishes: Peeled shrimp, thinly sliced radishes or green peppers, thinly sliced cucumber or celery, chopped ham mixed with chopped leeks, etc.

Creamy tomato soup

| 1½ lb ripe tomatoes, roughly chopped |
| 4 green onions, chopped |
| 2 teaspoons sugar |
| 1 cup water |
| Salt and freshly ground pepper |
| 3 tablespoons butter |
| 3 tablespoons flour |
| 2 cups milk |
| ½ cup coffee cream |
| 2 tablespoons each finely chopped parsley, mint and fresh basil |

Place tomatoes, green onions, sugar, water and salt and pepper to taste in a saucepan. Cover, and cook over low heat for 30 minutes, or until tomatoes are very soft. Puree in a blender or food processor. Wash and dry saucepan.

Melt butter in the saucepan, add flour, and stir over very low heat until well blended. Gradually stir in milk, then the tomato puree. Continue stirring until soup comes to a boil, stir in cream and herbs. Taste for seasoning, and serve in heated bowls. Serves 4-6.

Brie surprise

(photograph right)

A circle of creamy Brie cheese baked in a puff pastry crust.

| 10-12 celery leaves |
| 1 pre-rolled sheet frozen puff pastry |
| 1 whole Brie or Camembert cheese (5 to 7-inches diameter) |
| Beaten egg to glaze |

Pour boiling water over celery leaves, leave for 2 minutes, drain and pat dry. Roll pastry out ⅛-inch thick, big enough to wrap around cheese. Place half the leaves in the center of the pastry. Put cheese on top, then the rest of the leaves. Wrap cheese completely in pastry, sealing edges with beaten egg and trimming excess pastry off. Brush with beaten egg and place on a baking sheet. Bake in a preheated 400° oven until pastry is puffed and golden, about 20 minutes. Stand 15 minutes before cutting. Serve cut in small wedges. Serves 6-10, depending on size of cheese.

Note: Substitute your own favorite pastry recipe for frozen puff pastry.

Artichoke balls

2 cloves garlic, crushed

2 tablespoons olive oil

1 (14 oz) can artichoke hearts, drained and mashed

2 eggs, slightly beaten

½ cup grated Parmesan cheese

1 cup Italian seasoned breadcrumbs

Saute garlic in oil. Add artichokes and eggs. Cook over low heat about 5 minutes, stirring constantly. Remove from heat and add cheese and ½ cup of the crumbs.

Roll into balls using 1 teaspoonful of mixture for each ball. Roll each ball in remaining breadcrumbs. Chill until firm. Makes 4 dozen.

Chilled carrot-orange soup

An unusual soup with a subtle, spicy-sweet taste.

6 medium carrots, chopped

3 cups chicken broth

1½ teaspoons ground cumin

1 teaspoon ground cardamom

2 teaspoons sugar

2 tablespoons grated orange rind

1 cup orange juice

1 cup coffee cream

Salt and freshly ground white pepper

Thin orange slices to garnish

Place carrots in a saucepan with all ingredients except orange juice, cream and salt and pepper. Bring to a boil, then simmer covered for 45 minutes, or until carrots are very soft.

Process in batches in a blender then stir in orange juice and cream. Cover and chill for several hours.

When ready to serve, taste for seasoning and add salt and pepper and perhaps a little extra sugar. Soup must be well-flavored. Float a slice of orange on top of each bowl. Serves 6-8.

Left: Garnished cheese soup (page 142)

Easy marinated mushrooms

1 lb medium-size fresh mushrooms

¾ cup salad oil

¼ cup lemon juice

1½ teaspoons grated lemon rind

1 teaspoon oregano

1 teaspoon garlic salt

⅛ teaspoon pepper

Wash mushrooms under cold running water, drain well. Cut lengthways though mushrooms into 3-4 slices, about ¼-inch thick. Place in plastic bag or glass dish. Combine remaining ingredients, pour over mushrooms. Seal bag or cover dish and marinate for several hours in the refrigerator, turning bag or stirring occasionally. Drain before serving. Serves 6-8.

Note: Save marinade for use in a salad dressing or for marinating other food.

Dill carrots

¼ cup Green Goddess salad dressing

¼ cup Italian salad dressing

¼ cup grated onion

1 tablespoon finely chopped parsley

1 tablespoon dill weed

¼ teaspoon salt

¼ teaspoon pepper

2 cups cooked sliced carrots (can use 16 oz can), drained

Combine dressings, onion, parsley, dill weed, salt and pepper as marinade. Pour over drained carrots and marinate for one day in refrigerator. Serves 4.

Below: Quick vegetable soup (page 142)

Yogurt potato salad

Great with ham!

8 medium potatoes

1 bay leaf

1 teaspoon caraway seeds

1 medium onion, sliced

6 hard-boiled eggs, chopped

1 medium onion, chopped

2 cups chopped celery

1 teaspoon salt

Pinch of pepper

1 teaspoon celery salt

1 (8 oz) carton plain yogurt

½ cup mayonnaise

1 tablespoon prepared mustard

Hard-boiled egg slices, green pepper rings, and paprika to garnish

Cover potatoes with water. Add bay leaf, caraway seeds and onion slices. Cover and cook until potatoes are tender. Drain and cool. Peel and cut into cubes. Add eggs, chopped onion, celery, salt, pepper and celery salt.

Blend yogurt, mayonnaise and mustard together. Add to potato mixture and toss lightly until well mixed. Chill several hours. Garnish with hard-boiled egg slices, green pepper rings and paprika. Serves 8.

Gold coast salad bowl

1 clove garlic, halved

1 medium iceberg lettuce

1 small Romaine or bibb lettuce

1 cup sliced fresh mushrooms or 1 (4½ oz) jar sliced mushrooms, drained

Avocado dressing

Freshly ground pepper

3 slices crisp bacon, crumbled

Rub inside of large salad bowl with cut garlic. Coarsely tear lettuce into bowl. Add mushrooms, avocado dressing, then toss lightly. Sprinkle with ground pepper and crumbled bacon. Serves 6-8.

Avocado dressing

1 large ripe avocado, peeled

¼ cup lemon juice

½ cup salad oil

1 teaspoon sugar

¾ teaspoon salt

½ teaspoon dry mustard

Cut up avocado into blender container, add lemon juice, oil, sugar, salt and dry mustard. Blend until smooth. If you don't have a blender, sieve or mash the avocado

to a smooth pulp. Immediately stir in lemon juice. Place in a pint jar with tight-fitting cover. Add oil, sugar, salt and mustard, cover and shake well. Will dress enough salad greens for 6-8.

Island salads

A trio of easily prepared salads for sunny days.

Melon and shrimp salad

1 small cantaloupe, halved and seeded

¼ small watermelon, seeded

2 grapefruit, peeled and separated into segments

2 kiwi fruit, peeled and sliced

1 (11 oz) can mandarin segments, drained

½ lb cooked, peeled shrimp

Lettuce leaves

¾ cup mayonnaise, thinned with a little mandarin syrup

Lemon wedges to garnish

Scoop cantaloupe and watermelon into balls with a melon baller, or cut into cubes (about 1 cup of each). Combine with remaining fruits and shrimp, cover and chill.

At serving time, spoon into a bowl lined with lettuce leaves. Serve mayonnaise to accompany salad in a small bowl. Garnish salad with lemon wedges. Serves 4-6.

Sunshine salad

1 small lettuce, washed and dried

1 small cucumber, thinly sliced

1 (11 oz) can mandarin segments, drained

1 small onion, thinly sliced

1 banana, thinly sliced

2 teaspoons lemon juice

½ cup French or vinaigrette dressing

Tear lettuce into pieces and place in a bowl with cucumber, mandarins and onion. Sprinkle banana slices with lemon juice and add to bowl. Chill until serving time, then toss with the French dressing. Serves 4.

Harlequin tomatoes

| 4 medium-size, ripe tomatoes |
| Salt and freshly ground pepper |
| 1 cup cooked long grain rice |
| ¼ cup cooked green peas |
| ¼ cup drained, shoepeg corn |
| 1 medium-size red or green pepper, finely chopped |
| ½ cup French or vinaigrette dressing |
| ¼ teaspoon oregano |
| Lettuce leaves to serve |

Cut a slice from the top of each tomato and scoop out seeds and some of the flesh. Season inside with salt and pepper. Chop flesh and mix with remaining ingredients. Fill tomato shells with the mixture and arrange on lettuce leaves. Chill until serving time. Serves 4.

Cucumber and yogurt salad

An excellent salad to serve with fish.

| 1 large cucumber |
| 2 teaspoons salt |
| 2 tender ribs celery, chopped |
| 1 (8 oz) carton plain yogurt |
| 3 tablespoons finely chopped mint |
| Freshly ground pepper |

Peel cucumber, cut in half lengthways and scrape out the seeds with a teaspoon, cut into very thin slices. Place in a colander, sprinkle with salt and leave for 30 minutes. Drain well, pushing down on cucumber slices to extract as much moisture as possible.

Dry cucumber on paper towels, then mix with remaining ingredients. Chill before serving. Serves 4.

Salad bouquets

A trio of salads that look as pretty as flowers, and are especially easy to prepare.

For Rice Platter: Make a bed of lettuce leaves. Toss together 3 cups cooked rice (1 cup uncooked), 1 cup drained, whole kernel corn, and ½ cup French or vinaigrette dressing. Pile on top of lettuce and garnish with tomato wedges, cucumber slices, and strips of red pepper. Serves 4.

For Celery and Olive Salad: Slice ½ bunch of tender celery, and combine with ½ cup of mayonnaise, a squeeze of lemon juice, 2 teaspoons sugar and ¼ cup whipping cream. Spoon into a serving dish and garnish with wedges of ripe pineapple and black olives. Serves 4.

For Tomato-Onion Salad: Cut 4 medium-size, firm tomatoes into slices. Arrange on a serving plate and drizzle with French or vinaigrette dressing. Thinly slice a large onion (the large purple type if available), separate into rings, and scatter over the top. Serves 4.

Spinach-mushroom-bacon salad

The intriguing thing about this salad is the hot bacon dressing. It must be served the moment it's made, so it's a good idea to toss it at the table.

| 10-12 small spinach leaves |
| 1 small onion, thinly sliced |
| ¼ lb button mushrooms, sliced |
| Salt and freshly ground pepper |
| 3 tablespoons cooking oil |
| 3 slices lean bacon |
| 1 clove garlic, crushed |
| 1 tablespoon wine vinegar |

Remove stalks from spinach. Wash leaves, pat dry, and tear into small pieces. Place in a bowl with onion and mushrooms and season with salt and pepper.

Heat oil in a frying pan. Chop bacon into small pieces and add to pan with garlic. Cook for a few minutes, stirring, until bacon is crisp. Add vinegar to the pan and bring to a boil. Pour hot dressing over the salad, toss lightly and serve at once. Serves 3-4.

French dressing (Sauce vinaigrette)

| 6 tablespoons salad or olive oil |
| 2 tablespoons vinegar or lemon juice |
| ¼ teaspoon salt |
| ¼ teaspoon pepper |
| ¼ teaspoon dry mustard |
| 1 clove garlic (optional) |

Combine all ingredients in a jar. Shake well to combine. Store in refrigerator and remove garlic after 1 day. Shake well before using. Makes about ½ cup.

Helen Corbitt's poppyseed dressing

| 2 teaspoons dry mustard |
| 1½ cups sugar |
| 2 teaspoons salt |
| ⅔ cup vinegar |
| 1 tablespoon onion juice |
| 2 cups salad oil |
| 3 tablespoons poppyseed |

Mix mustard, sugar, salt and vinegar together. Stir onion juice in thoroughly. Add oil slowly, beating constantly and continue beating until thick. Add poppyseed and beat a few minutes. Store in a covered container in refrigerator. Makes 3½ cups.

Pink lagoon dressing

If you like a touch of the exotic, here's a dressing for you — clear, pink and sweet. Toss through crisp salad greens, or spoon over fruit salad.

| ⅓ cup sugar |
| 1 tablespoon paprika |
| 1 teaspoon dry mustard |
| 2 teaspoon tomato paste |
| ½ teaspoon salt |
| ½ cup white vinegar |
| 1⅓ cups salad oil |
| 1 tablespoon celery seeds |

Place all ingredients except oil and celery seeds in a saucepan. Bring to a boil stirring, reduce heat and simmer 2 minutes. Allow to cool. Gradually beat in oil, adding very slowly and beating constantly. Stir in celery seeds.

Chill dressing before serving. Makes about 2 cups.

Fluffy mayonnaise

A lovely dressing for coleslaw, sliced fresh fruits, and cold fish dishes.

| 1 cup mayonnaise (homemade or bought) |
| ½ cup whipping cream, whipped with 2 teaspoons sugar |
| 1½ tablespoons lemon juice |
| 2 teaspoons grated lemon rind |

Gently fold all ingredients together, and chill. Makes about 2 cups.

Blender lime mayonnaise

A quickly-made mayonnaise with refreshing flavor. If you haven't fresh limes, use lemon juice.

2 egg yolks, at room temperature
½ teaspoon salt
½ teaspoon dry mustard
Pinch cayenne pepper
4 tablespoons lime juice
About 1½ cups oil (a mixture of olive oil and sunflower is good)

Put egg yolks, salt, mustard, cayenne, lime juice and ¼ cup of oil in the blender. Cover and blend at low speed. Remove cover and with the motor running, add a steady stream of oil from a jug. Blend just until very thick and smooth — don't use all the oil unless it's necessary. Cover and store in refrigerator. Makes about 2 cups.

Spinach Madeleine

2 (10 oz) packages frozen chopped spinach
4 tablespoons butter
2 tablespoons flour
2 tablespoons chopped onion
½ cup evaporated milk
½ cup liquid from spinach
¾ teaspoon garlic salt
¾ teaspoon celery salt
½ teaspoon salt
½ teaspoon pepper
1 teaspoon Worcestershire sauce
1 (6 oz) roll jalapeno cheese, softened and cut in small chunks
Buttered breadcrumbs (optional)

Cook spinach as directed on package, drain well and reserve liquid. Melt butter in saucepan over low heat. Add flour and stir until smooth. Add onion and cook until soft, but do not brown. Slowly add liquids and cook, stirring constantly, until smooth and thickened. Stir in seasonings and cheese and cook, stirring, until cheese is melted and sauce is smooth. Combine with spinach.

If serving as a casserole, pour into 1½-quart casserole and top with buttered breadcrumbs. Bake in a preheated 350° oven for 10-15 minutes or until heated through and bubbly. Serves 6-8.

Red wine salad dressing

A simple green salad becomes a talking-point when you toss it with this spicy wine dressing.

½ cup olive oil
½ cup safflower or sunflower oil
3 tablespoons red wine vinegar
4 tablespoons red wine
1 teaspoon salt
½ teaspoon freshly ground pepper
¼ teaspoon each of paprika and dry mustard
1 clove garlic, crushed

Place all ingredients in a screwtop jar and shake vigorously until well blended. Taste and adjust seasoning to suit your own preference. Store in refrigerator and shake well before using. Makes about 1½ cups.

Eggplant casserole

1 medium to large eggplant, peeled and diced
½ teaspoon salt
½ cup margarine, divided
1 small onion, chopped
1 small green pepper, chopped
1 tablespoon brown sugar
Extra 1 teaspoon salt
2 tablespoons flour
1 (16 oz) can tomatoes, cut up, with liquid
1 cup cornbread crumbs
Grated Cheddar cheese

Cook eggplant in a small amount of water with salt 8-10 minutes until tender, drain well. In saucepan, melt half the margarine and saute onion and green pepper. Add remaining margarine and melt. Add sugar, salt and flour, stirring to blend. Add tomatoes. Cook, stirring for 5 minutes. Add cornbread crumbs and eggplant. Pour into greased 1½-quart casserole and bake in a preheated 350° oven for 15 minutes. Top with cheese and bake 10-15 minutes longer. Serves 4-6.

Note: This recipe can easily be increased by adding more eggplant and/or cornbread crumbs or it can be successfully doubled.

Chinese stir-fried asparagus

1 lb fresh asparagus
¼-½ cup chicken stock or bouillon
1 tablespoon soy sauce
½ teaspoon sugar
½ teaspoon salt
2 tablespoons peanut oil
1 green onion, cut in ½-inch pieces

Discard tough fibrous ends of asparagus. Cut stalks diagonally in 1 to 1½-inch sections. Blanch the stalks if young and tender, if not, parboil them (do not blanch or parboil the tips). Combine stock, soy sauce, sugar and salt. Heat oil in a wok. Add asparagus (it may be necessary to adjust heat to prevent scorching). Stir-fry to coat with oil and heat through. Add stock mixture and heat quickly. Add green onion. Simmer, covered, over medium heat until asparagus is crisp-tender, about 3 minutes. Serves 3-4.

Herbed creole cabbage

1 medium head cabbage
1 (16 oz) can tomatoes, broken up
¼ cup sweet pepper flakes
2 tablespoons minced onion
1 teaspoon salt
1½ teaspoons sugar
¾ teaspoon oregano
2 teaspoons lemon juice

Shred cabbage. Place ½-inch boiling water in a medium saucepan. Add cabbage, cover and cook 10 minutes, drain well. Meanwhile, in another saucepan combine tomatoes, pepper flakes, minced onion, salt, sugar and oregano. Bring to boiling point. Reduce heat and simmer, uncovered, 15 minutes. Stir in lemon juice. Add tomato mixture to cabbage, toss gently. Serve hot. Serves 8.

Stir-fried radishes

3 tablespoons cooking oil
2 onions, quartered and sliced
2 cups sliced radishes
2 cups sliced mushrooms (optional)
2 tablespoons soy sauce

Heat oil in large, heavy skillet or wok. Combine onions, radishes and mushrooms in skillet and cook in oil until onion is yellow and tender (radishes will remain crisp). Stir in soy sauce and serve as a vegetable or main dish. Serves 6.

Fried okra

1½ lb okra
1 egg, beaten
½ cup cornmeal
½ teaspoon salt
Cooking oil

Wash okra. Dry on paper towels, remove stems and cut in ¼-inch slices. Dip in egg, then roll in cornmeal which has been combined with salt. Fry in hot oil until golden brown. Drain. Serves 4.

Lemon butter potatoes

3 lb small red potatoes
1 medium onion, sliced
3 slices lemon
1 teaspoon salt
¼ cup melted butter or margarine
1 tablespoon lemon juice

Wash unpeeled potatoes. Put in a saucepan with onion, lemon and salt. Cover with boiling water, cook until tender. Drain. When ready to serve, remove lemon slices and pour hot lemon butter sauce over potatoes. Make sauce by combining melted butter and lemon juice. Serves 6.

Broccoli in garlic and wine

This way of cooking broccoli results in a rich, peppery sauce, lovely with veal dishes, meat loaf or barbecued meats.

2 lb bright green broccoli
⅓ cup olive oil
2 cloves garlic, crushed

1 small dried red chile, seeded and finely chopped
1 cup dry white wine
Salt

Cut off tough bottom stalk ends from broccoli, slice remaining stalks into thin pieces. Separate heads into florets. Heat oil in a heavy saucepan and fry garlic and chopped chile for a minute or two, until softened. Add broccoli stalks and wine, season with salt, and cook five minutes or until stalks are softened. Place broccoli florets on top and cook covered for 8-10 minutes, or until florets and stalks are tender. Turn once or twice during this time. With a slotted spoon, put broccoli in a warm serving bowl.

Remove lid from pan, raise heat and reduce liquid to about half a cup. Taste for seasoning, pour over broccoli and serve very hot. Serves 6-8.

Candied sweet potatoes

6 sweet potatoes
½ teaspoon salt
1 cup dark brown sugar, firmly packed
½ cup water
4 tablespoons butter
1 tablespoon lemon juice

Cook potatoes in their jackets in boiling salted water until nearly tender. Drain, peel and cut in ½-inch slices. Place in a greased, shallow baking dish and sprinkle with salt.

Combine sugar, water and butter in a separate pan and cook several minutes until sugar is dissolved. Stir in lemon juice and pour over potatoes. Bake in a preheated 375° oven for 20-30 minutes, basting occasionally with the syrup. Serves 6-8.

My mama's purple hull peas

From the mother of legendary Texas football pro Earl Campbell.

2 ham hocks or bacon end pieces (about 1 lb)
3 quarts water
10 cups fresh-shelled purple hull peas
1 onion, sliced
¼ cup sugar
2 tablespoons salt

Add ham hocks to water, bring to a boil. Add peas, onion, sugar and salt. Cover, lower heat and simmer 2½ hours. Serves 1 running back and 3 rookies.

Green beans oregano

3 cups green beans (frozen are fine)
4 slices crisp bacon, crumbled
1 (10¾ oz) can condensed cream of mushroom soup
1 (3-4 oz) can sliced mushrooms
1 envelope onion soup mix
¼ teaspoon oregano

Cook beans until barely done. Drain. Mix with remaining ingredients, save half the bacon for garnish. Refrigerate overnight to blend flavors. Bake in a 1½-quart casserole in a preheated 350° oven for 30-40 minutes. Garnish with bacon. Serves 6.

Stir-fried snow peas

Try them raw, with a creamy dip — or in this easy, Chinese-style recipe.

½ lb snow peas
3 tablespoons cooking oil
1 small clove garlic, crushed
1 slice fresh ginger, chopped
2 teaspoons light soy sauce
Freshly ground white pepper
Pinch sugar

Trim ends of snow peas and string if necessary. Rinse pods in cold water and dry.

Heat oil in a large, heavy frying pan and fry garlic and ginger for a minute. Add peas and toss for 3 minutes, or until tender-crisp. Sprinkle with soy sauce, pepper and sugar and toss for another few seconds. Serve at once. Serves 2-3.

Asparagus with basil crumb butter

3 lb fresh asparagus or 2 (10 oz) packages frozen asparagus spears
2 tablespoons instant minced onion
2 tablespoons water
½ cup butter or margarine
1 cup soft breadcrumbs
2 teaspoons basil or tarragon
⅓ cup lemon juice
1 teaspoon salt
½ teaspoon ground black pepper
Sliced lemon to garnish

If using fresh asparagus, trim stems and wash well. Place in a skillet containing ½-inch boiling salted water. Cook, uncovered, 5 minutes, cover and cook 8 minutes more or until lower part of stalk is just crisp-tender.

If using frozen asparagus cook as label directs.

Combine onion with water, let stand 10 minutes to rehydrate. Meanwhile in skillet melt butter and add breadcrumbs and basil, brown lightly. Stir in onion along with remaining ingredients, reheat. Arrange asparagus on a heated platter, pour sauce over asparagus. Garnish with sliced lemon. Serves 8.

Green beans with ham and almonds

1 lb young green beans
4 tablespoons butter
2 teaspoons chopped fresh oregano or ½ teaspoon dried
Salt and freshly ground pepper
Pinch sugar
2 slices cooked ham, cut in strips
3 tablespoons toasted, slivered almonds

Snip the ends off beans, but leave whole. Cook uncovered in rapidly boiling, salted water until just tender, about 5 minutes. Drain. Refresh beans in cold water for a minute or two after cooking to set the bright green color and stop the cooking. Heat butter in a frying pan and add the beans, oregano, salt and pepper to taste, a pinch of sugar and ham strips.

Toss just until heated through, about 2 minutes. Serve in a heated dish, sprinkled with almonds. Serves 3-4.

Almond potatoes

These tempting smooth and crunchy potato balls give an elegant touch to dinner party menus, accompanying fish, meat and poultry.

1½ lb potatoes, peeled
2 egg yolks, beaten
2 tablespoons butter
Salt and white pepper
1 large egg, beaten
1 cup chopped or crushed almonds
Cooking oil

Cook potatoes in salted water until tender. Drain and shake over low heat to dry thoroughly. Mash until very smooth with egg yolks, butter, pepper and salt. (You can add extra flavor with chopped parsley, grated Parmesan or chives if you wish.) Allow to cool, then form into balls with floured hands — approximately 8-16, depending on required size. Dip them in beaten egg and roll firmly in crushed almonds. Heat enough oil in a heavy frying pan to give a depth of about 1-inch. Fry balls, turning constantly with 2 spoons, until crisp and golden brown all over. Drain on paper towels and keep hot in a warm oven until ready to serve. Serves 8-10.

Zesty carrots

6-8 carrots, cooked and cut in strips
1/4 cup liquid from carrots or water
2 tablespoons grated onion
2 tablespoons prepared horseradish
1/2 cup mayonnaise
1/2 teaspoon salt
1/4 teaspoon pepper
1/4 cup cracker crumbs
1 tablespoon butter
Pinch paprika
Finely chopped parsley to garnish

Arrange carrot strips in a shallow dish. Mix liquid from carrots, onion, horseradish, mayonnaise, salt and pepper and pour over carrots. Top with a mixture of cracker crumbs, butter and paprika. Bake in a preheated 375° oven for 15-20 minutes. Serves 6.

Potato pancakes

1 lb potatoes
2 eggs, beaten
3 tablespoons self-rising flour
3 tablespoons chopped chives or green onions
1 tablespoon finely chopped parsley
Salt and freshly ground pepper
Cooking oil

Peel and grate potatoes. Squeeze tightly in a towel to extract as much moisture as possible, mix with eggs, flour, chives, parsley, salt and pepper to taste. Heat enough oil in a frying pan to give a depth of about 1/4-inch and drop in large spoonfuls of mixture.

Cook over medium heat until brown and crisp on the bottom, turn and cook the other side — about 8 minutes altogether. Drain on paper towels, and serve at once. Serves 4.

Breakfast scramble

4 tablespoons butter
1 cup whole kernel corn, drained
1/2 cup finely chopped green pepper
1/4 cup finely chopped pimiento
1/2 teaspoon salt
Freshly ground pepper
6 eggs

Melt butter in a skillet, add corn and stir over moderate heat for 1-2 minutes until corn glistens. Add pepper, pimiento, salt and pepper and cook uncovered, stirring frequently for 5 minutes, or until vegetables are soft but not brown.

Break eggs in a bowl, beat lightly with a fork, pour into skillet. Cook over low heat, stirring until eggs are soft and creamy.

Serve immediately with slices of crisp bacon. Serves 4.

Garden omelet

4 eggs

3 tablespoons water

Salt and freshly ground pepper

½ cup cooked ham, cut in fine strips

2 tablespoons butter

4 asparagus spears, heated in a little butter

¼ cup grated Cheddar cheese

1 tablespoon finely chopped parsley or chives

Beat eggs and water with a fork, and stir in salt and pepper to taste and ham. Heat butter in a medium-size frying pan until it sizzles. Pour in egg mixture over high heat. As soon as the edges set (almost immediately) draw them towards the center, and tilt pan so uncooked egg runs underneath. Repeat until the omelet is set underneath, but the top is still moist. Arrange asparagus spears on one half of the omelet, and sprinkle with cheese and parsley. Fold the other half of the omelet over, and roll onto a heated plate. Serve at once. Serves 2.

Bacon and egg puff

(photograph right)

5 eggs

6 tablespoons flour

1½ cups evaporated milk

1 tablespoon finely chopped chives or green onion

Salt and freshly ground pepper

1 tablespoon butter

4-6 slices lean bacon

¼ lb button mushrooms

Chopped chives to garnish

Beat eggs and flour together until smooth, stir in evaporated milk, chives and salt and pepper to taste. (Don't over-mix.) Allow batter to stand 20 minutes or so.

Put butter in a 9-inch iron skillet, and place in a preheated 400° oven for 3-4 minutes or until butter is sizzling. Pour batter into skillet and bake for 15-20 minutes, until well puffed and golden brown. Meanwhile, fry bacon until crisp, remove from pan and toss mushrooms in bacon fat until tender. Season with salt and pepper. Place bacon and mushrooms in center of puff and serve immediately. Serves 3-4.

Curried eggs and bacon

(photograph left)

*Here's a new way of presenting a popular dish —
the eggs are cut in half, coated with curry sauce, and sprinkled with crisp bacon.
Good for any casual meal.*

6 hard-boiled eggs, shelled

3 tablespoons butter

1½ teaspoons mild curry powder

Pinch sugar

3 tablespoons flour

1½ cups chicken broth

2 teaspoons lemon juice

4 slices lean bacon

Finely chopped parsley to garnish

Cut eggs in half lengthways, and arrange cut-side down in a greased, shallow casserole dish.

Melt butter in a saucepan, stir in curry powder, sugar and flour, and cook 1 minute. Remove from heat and stir in broth and lemon juice. Return to heat and gradually bring to a boil, stirring constantly. Taste for seasoning (add salt and pepper if required) and spoon over eggs.

Bake in a preheated 400° oven for 5 minutes, or until eggs are heated through and sauce is bubbly. Meanwhile, chop bacon and fry until crisp. Sprinkle bacon over eggs and garnish with parsley. Serves 3-4.

Egg cheese brunch

8 slices day-old bread

8 eggs, beaten

2 teaspoons salt

1 teaspoon dry mustard

4 cups milk

8 oz American cheese, grated

Topping:

2 cups crushed cornflakes

¼-½ cup melted butter

Remove crusts from bread and cut into cubes. Spread in a greased 13 x 9 x 2-inch baking pan. Mix remaining ingredients and pour over bread cubes. Cover pan with foil and refrigerate overnight. Take out of refrigerator 1-1½ hours before baking. Bake in a preheated 350° oven for 45 minutes. Combine topping ingredients and sprinkle over eggs and return to oven for an additional 15 minutes. Serves 10-12.

Cheese souffle

Make it with your favorite Cheddar cheese for lunch, or as a first course for dinner.

| Butter and dry breadcrumbs to prepare dish |
| 4 tablespoons butter |
| 3 tablespoons flour |
| Salt and freshly ground pepper |
| Pinch each of cayenne pepper and nutmeg |
| 1 cup milk |
| 3 eggs, separated |
| 1½ cups grated Cheddar cheese |

Grease a 4-cup souffle dish or straight-sided dish with butter and sprinkle with breadcrumbs. Tie a collar of doubled, aluminum foil or wax paper around out-side of the dish to extend about 2-inches above the rim. Melt butter over medium heat, stir in flour, salt and pepper, cayenne and nutmeg, and cook for a minute. Gradually stir in milk and con-tinue stirring until mixture is smooth and thickened. Remove from heat and cool a little. Beat egg yolks and add little by lit-tle, then stir in cheese.

Whisk egg whites until stiff peaks form and fold a couple of spoonfuls through cheese mixture, then fold in the rest. Pour into prepared dish and place dish on a bak-ing sheet that has been heated in a 375° oven.

Bake for 35 minutes, or until souffle is puffed and golden and feels firm to the touch. Serve immediately. Serves 4.

Baked eggs with cream and cheese

| Butter |
| 4 eggs |
| Salt and freshly ground pepper |
| 4 tablespoons sour cream |
| 4 tablespoons grated Gruyere or Swiss cheese |
| Hot buttered toast to serve |

Butter 4 small ramekins or souffle dishes and break an egg into each. Season with salt and pepper. Spoon a tablespoon of sour cream over each egg, and sprinkle with cheese. Bake in a preheated 350° oven for 10 minutes, or until whites are firm and yolks still a little runny. Serve in the ramekins, with hot buttered toast. Serves 4.

Cheese souffle omelet

This is the very fluffy omelet, in which yolks and whites are beaten separately.

| 4 eggs, separated |
| 3 tablespoons whipping cream |
| Salt and freshly ground pepper |
| ½ cup Mozarella cheese, cut in tiny cubes |
| 2 teaspoons chopped chives |
| 2 tablespoons butter |

Beat egg yolks with cream and salt and pepper. Beat whites until they hold soft peaks, and fold into yolks with cheese and chives.

Heat butter in a heavy frying pan, and pour in the mixture. Cook over medium heat, without stirring, until set on the bottom.

Place pan under a preheated medium broiler, and cook until the top is golden brown and puffy. Slide onto a heated serving platter, and cut in half with a fork to serve. Serves 2.

Light 'n easy drinks

(photograph left)

Six freshly different drinks made with healthy ingredients — perfect pick-me-ups for humid days.

Orange flip

| 1 orange, peeled and sectioned |
| 1 egg |
| 1 cup plain yogurt |
| Pinch sugar |

Place all in a blender and blend until combined. Serves 2-3.

Avocado smoothie

| 1 large, ripe avocado, peeled and chopped |
| ½ small cucumber, peeled, seeded and chopped |
| 3 tablespoons lemon juice |
| ⅓ cup plain yogurt |
| Salt and freshly ground pepper |

Combine all ingredients in a blender, and blend until combined. Serves 2-3.

Bloody Jane

There's no alcohol in this version of a Bloody Mary.

| 2 large ripe tomatoes, peeled and chopped |
| ¾ cup tomato juice |
| 3 tablespoons lemon juice |
| 2 teaspoons sugar |
| Salt and freshly ground pepper |
| 1 teaspoon Worcestershire sauce |
| Pinch cayenne pepper |
| Celery sticks to serve |

Place all ingredients except celery in a blender, and blend until combined. Taste for seasoning and serve with a celery stick stirrer. Serves 2-3.

Strawberry sundae drink

| 1 pint strawberries, hulled |
| ½ cup strawberry or vanilla ice cream |
| 2 cups milk |

Place all in a blender and blend until combined. Serves 4.

Grapefruit mint cooler

| 1 grapefruit, peeled and sectioned |
| ½ cup milk |
| ½ cup vanilla ice cream |
| 6-8 mint leaves |

Place all in a blender and blend until smooth. Serves 2.

Golden fizz

| 1 medium carrot, chopped |
| 1 large sweet apple, peeled and chopped |
| ½ cup orange juice |

Place all in a blender and blend until combined. Serves 2-3.

Clockwise: *Light 'n easy drinks. Bloody Jane (top), golden fizz, avocado smoothie, grapefruit mint cooler, orange flip and strawberry sundae.*

Overleaf: *Varner-Hogg Plantation near West Columbia*

BLUE RIBBON COOKING

Blessed with a bountiful array of native ingredients, Texans have the pick of the crop when it comes to preserving food.

Texans have always known relishes, condiments , chow-chows, jellies and preserves add spice and zest to any meal. In the early days, it wasn't unusual for a family to put up a thousand jars of fruit and vegetables a year. Spread out as they were, far from civilization, families depended on what they stored during the growing season to get them through lean periods.

You name it, and Texans have preserved, pickled, marinated or dried it — beef, fruits, vegetables, chilies and cactus, to name a few. As often as not, the ingredients for preserving are home-grown because the state boasts a long growing season. Harvesting starts in the Lower Rio Grande Valley, then moves up to the Winter Garden area and on to the High Plains as the year progresses. While fall and winter offer such crops as spinach, broccoli, cauliflower, sweet potatoes and peppers, spring and summer bring a profusion of native strawberries from Poteet, peaches from the Hill Country and melons from the Pecos area.

Even today, you can look in the pantry of any Texas farm home and find rows of preserved fruits, glistening like jewels in clear syrups (sometimes flavored with liqueurs) and jar after jar of pickled jalapeno peppers, salsas, corn and beets.

Not to be forgotten in the Blue Ribbon cooking of Texas are the candies for which the state is famous. Creamy pralines, often made with buttermilk, are one of the most popular treats. Recipes for this delicacy and other Texas specialties such as fudge show off another state favorite, pecans, which are harvested from backyard trees and native stock which grow in profusion along the rivers of the state.

Harlequin pepper relish (page 167)

Microwave fudge

1 lb powdered sugar, unsifted
½ cup cocoa
½ cup butter or margarine
¼ cup milk
½ cup chopped nuts
1 teaspoon vanilla

Combine sugar and cocoa in an ungreased 9-inch square glass dish. Cut up butter in 4-5 pieces and drop onto the sugar mixture. Pour in milk. Do not stir. Microwave on high 2-3 minutes or until mixture is bubbly. Remove from oven and stir. Thoroughly stir in nuts and vanilla so nuts are evenly distributed. Spread fudge evenly in dish. Refrigerate 1 hour. Cut in squares. Makes 2 dozen.

Chocolate rum cherries

¾ cup candied cherries
½ cup rum
1⅓ cups semi-sweet chocolate chips

Place cherries in a screw-top jar and pour in the rum. Stand overnight, shaking occasionally to distribute rum through the cherries. Next day, drain the cherries carefully and dry on paper towels. Melt the chocolate in a double boiler over hot water. Dip cherries into the chocolate and place on a piece of wax paper until set. Store in candy boxes or jars. Makes about 2½ dozen.

Apricot slices

There are lots of good things in these.

¾ cup chopped dried apricots
½ cup water
½ cup finely chopped walnuts or almonds
2 teaspoons lemon juice
1 teaspoon grated lemon rind
1 tablespoon wheat germ
1 cup instant non-fat dry milk
½ cup chopped golden raisins
½ cup flaked coconut
Extra flaked coconut

Place apricots and water in a small saucepan, simmer 10 minutes, allow to cool. Mix well with remaining ingredients, then divide mixture into three. Shape each portion into a 1-inch roll, wrap in plastic wrap, and chill overnight. To serve, cut in slices and roll in extra coconut if desired. Makes about 2½ dozen.

Cognac bonbons

1½ cups vanilla wafer crumbs
½ cup powdered sugar
½ cup finely chopped pecans
¼ cup water
3 tablespoons instant tea powder
3 tablespoons sugar
3 tablespoons Cognac
3-4 dozen hazelnuts
Lightly toasted flaked coconut

In a medium bowl, combine vanilla wafer crumbs, powdered sugar and pecans. Set aside.

In a small saucepan, combine water, instant tea powder and sugar and cook over low heat until sugar is dissolved. Add Cognac and cook rapidly for 1 minute. Reserve 3 tablespoons tea syrup for dipping. Add remaining syrup to dry ingredients. Blend thoroughly.

Form mixture around individual hazelnuts and shape into 1-inch balls. Dip each into reserved tea syrup then roll in lightly toasted coconut. Chill thoroughly. Makes 3-4 dozen.

Note: Keep these in a covered container; they tend to dry out if exposed to air too long.

Orange date creams

30 large dates, pitted
1 small egg white
3 teaspoons grated orange rind
1 teaspoon orange flower water
About 2 cups sifted powdered sugar
Candied orange rind, walnut pieces, glace cherries etc. to decorate

Flatten each date out a little with your finger to make a cavity for the filling. Beat egg white lightly and mix in the orange rind and orange flower water. Stir in enough powdered sugar to give a firm consistency. (You may need more than 2 cups sugar.)

Make little balls of the powdered sugar mixture and stuff dates. Decorate each one with candied rind, nuts, cherries, etc. and chill until serving time. Makes 30.

Note: You may use lemon juice instead of orange flower water.

Rum truffles

1 cup cake crumbs
3 squares (3 oz) semi-sweet chocolate, melted
3 tablespoons sieved apricot jam
2 tablespoons rum
Chocolate sprinkles or crushed nuts

Mix all ingredients together thoroughly except chocolate sprinkles. Shape into small balls, then roll in sprinkles or crushed nuts. Chill until serving time. Makes about 15 small balls.

Candied orange rind

(photograph right)

3 large thick-skinned oranges
Cold water
1½ cups light corn syrup
Sugar

Peel oranges and cut rind into long narrow strips. Cover rind with cold water and boil 30 minutes, or until tender. Drain. Cover with cold water and heat to boiling. Repeat this process three times, draining well the last time. Pour corn syrup over rind and cook very slowly until rind is translucent. Remove each piece and let excess syrup drain off. Roll in sugar and allow to dry. Makes about 1 lb.

Buttermilk pralines

(photograph opposite, right)

| 3 cups sugar |
| 1 cup buttermilk |
| 1 teaspoon baking soda |
| ½ cup light corn syrup |
| 3 cups pecans, coarsely chopped or halved |
| 3 tablespoons butter |
| ½ teaspoon vanilla |

Combine sugar, buttermilk, baking soda and corn syrup in a large saucepan and bring to the soft ball stage (234°-238° on a candy thermometer). Just before removing from heat, add pecans. Remove from heat, add butter and vanilla. Beat until mixture loses its gloss and holds its shape. Drop on wax paper in mounds. Makes about 5 dozen.

Hard caramels

(photograph opposite, left)

| ½ cup butter |
| 1 cup brown sugar, firmly packed |
| 1 cup sweetened condensed milk |
| ¼ cup corn syrup |

Melt butter in a saucepan, and add sugar, condensed milk, and corn syrup. Stir until the sugar is melted. Cook over low heat, stirring all the time, until the mixture is dark brown and leaves the sides of the pan. Pour into a greased aluminum foil tray and allow to set. Mark into squares before the mixture is quite cold. When cold, cut into squares and wrap individually in cellophane or plastic wrap. Makes 3 dozen.

Bourbon balls

(photograph opposite, center)

| 2½ cups vanilla wafer crumbs |
| 2 tablespoons cocoa |
| 1 cup powdered sugar |
| 1 cup finely chopped nuts |
| 3 tablespoons light corn syrup |
| ¼ cup Bourbon |
| Extra powdered sugar |

Combine all ingredients except extra powdered sugar. Roll into balls, then roll in extra powdered sugar. Makes 4 dozen.

Note: Rum or brandy may be substituted for Bourbon.

Christmas fudge

2 cups brazil nuts

2 cups walnuts

2 cups pecans

1 cup candied cherries

1 cup candied pineapple

3 cups sugar

1½ cups evaporated milk

1 cup light corn syrup

1 teaspoon salt

2 teaspoons vanilla

Chop nuts and fruits , put in a bowl and set aside. Combine sugar, milk, syrup and salt in a large saucepan, cook over low heat stirring constantly, until soft ball stage is reached (234°-238° on a candy thermometer). Remove from heat, add vanilla. Beat until thick and mixture begins to hold shape. Add nuts and fruit and spread on a buttered cookie sheet. Chill and cut in desired shapes. Makes 4 lb.

Note: To crack Brazil nuts more easily, freeze first. To slice, drop nuts into boiling water in saucepan. Remove from heat, let stand about 5 minutes, then slice.

Creamy New Orleans pralines

1 cup sugar

2 cups dark brown sugar, firmly packed

1 cup whipping cream

2 cups pecan pieces

¼ cup butter

1 tablespoon vanilla

Pinch salt

Combine sugars and cream in a large saucepan. Cook slowly, stirring constantly, at least 15 minutes, and bring to the soft ball stage (234°-238° on a candy thermometer). Add pecans and cook a little longer, stirring constantly. Remove from heat. Add butter, vanilla and salt. Beat until mixture looks sugary around edges of pan. To speed the process, put saucepan in cold water. Place wax paper on wooden or metal surface. Drop candy from spoon onto paper. Makes 3 dozen.

Note: If pralines run and do not set when dropped on paper, they have not been cooked long enough. Scoop up candy, cook a little longer, beat and try again. Cool before removing from paper.

Chocolate truffles

12 squares (12 oz) semi-sweet chocolate

1 cup whipping cream

6 tablespoons unsalted butter, very soft

Cocoa, a good imported one

Melt chocolate in a double boiler. Heat cream to boiling point. Add to chocolate and blend thoroughly. Add butter in small pieces, stirring well after each addition. Chill mixture until it begins to hold its own shape. Place in a pastry bag and pipe out in mounds on a parchment-lined baking tray, or use 2 spoons to drop mounds on the tray. (Truffles are not regular in shape.) Chill until truffles can be handled lightly. Roll in cocoa. Store in an airtight container in refrigerator. Makes 4 dozen.

Note: These are at their absolute best if eaten within 48 hours of making. The texture of the truffles alters when stored for a longer time.

Liqueur oranges

Serve with ice cream for dessert.

8 small, sweet oranges

1 cup water

½ cup sugar

4 cloves

Grated rind and juice of 1 medium lemon

½ cup Grand Marnier, Cointreau, or brandy

Peel rind from the oranges and cut into very thin strips. Remove all white pith from oranges and cut through the membranes to separate into segments.

Place strips of rind in a saucepan with water, sugar, cloves, rind and juice of lemon. Bring to a boil and simmer 5 minutes, or until syrupy.

Pour syrup over the orange segments and stir in liqueur. Ladle into a jar or bowl, cover and cool. Chill before serving. This keeps well in the refrigerator. Serves 10-12 with ice cream.

Lemon butter

3 medium-size lemons
½ cup butter, cut in small pieces
1½ cups sugar
4 eggs, beaten

Grate rind from the lemons (being careful not to get any white pith) and squeeze the juice.

Strain the juice, and place with rind, butter and sugar in a bowl set over simmering water. Stir until sugar dissolves.

Pour a little hot lemon mixture onto beaten eggs and mix well. Tip this back into the bowl and continue stirring until mixture coats the back of a spoon. Pour into hot, sterilized jars and seal. When cool, store in refrigerator. Makes about 3½ (8 oz) jars.

Note: Lemon butter is versatile. It makes a lovely filling for cakes or small tarts, and is delicious on hot buttered toast or biscuits. Orange butter is made the same way, but add a dash of lemon juice to sharpen the flavor.

Plum-Madeira jam

2 lb ripe plums
1 cup water
3 cups sugar
1½ teaspoons cinnamon
½ cup Madeira wine

Wash plums, halve and remove stones. Place water and 1½ cups of the sugar in a heavy saucepan and stir until sugar dissolves. Boil 5 minutes without stirring. Add plums, return to a boil and cook for 20 minutes, or until plums are soft and pulpy. Add rest of sugar and cinnamon, stir until mixture returns to a boil then cook without stirring for another 25 minutes (or until jam jells). Stir in Madeira, cool slightly and spoon into hot, clean jars. Put on caps, screw bands firmly tight. Process in a boiling water bath 10 minutes. Makes 5 (8oz) jars.

Quick fig preserves

For lighter preserves, figs may be peeled.
3 cups mashed figs, about 20 medium
1 (6 serving-size) package apricot, strawberry or other favorite flavor gelatin
3 cups sugar
2 tablespoons lemon juice

Thoroughly mix figs, gelatin, sugar and lemon juice in large, heavy saucepan. Bring to a boil over medium heat and continue boiling 3 minutes, stirring occasionally. Pour quickly into hot, sterilized jars, wipe tops with a clean cloth, run a knife blade around edge to release any air bubbles and seal at once. When cool, store in refrigerator. Makes about 5 (8 oz) jars. For extended storage, freeze or process in boiling water bath for 5 minutes.

Sue's toffee

2 cups butter
2 cups sugar
1 (12 oz) bag semi-sweet chocolate chips
Finely chopped walnuts or pecans

Melt butter and sugar together, stir often until the hard crack stage is reached (290°-300° on a candy thermometer). Pour in a greased jelly roll pan. When set, but still hot, pour chocolate chips over and spread thinly on toffee as they melt. Sprinkle with chopped walnuts. Let harden overnight before cracking into pieces. Makes about 2 lb.

Jill's ketchup

(photograph page 166)

A sweet and spicy ketchup that goes with just about everything.

4 lb tomatoes, peeled and chopped
¾ lb cooking apples, peeled, cored and chopped
1 cup cider vinegar
1½ cups sugar
¼ teaspoon each ground cloves and ginger
1 tablespoon salt
Pinch cayenne pepper

Place all ingredients in a large heavy saucepan. Bring to a boil, stirring to dissolve sugar. Lower heat and simmer for 1¼ hours, covered. Puree mixture in batches in a blender or food processor fitted with the steel blade (or press through a sieve).

Return to saucepan, bring to a boil and simmer uncovered for 30 minutes or until a sauce consistency. Pour into hot, sterilized jars and seal tightly. Store in the refrigerator. Makes about 3 pints.

Dill pickles

3-4 heads green dill
3-4 cloves garlic
1 gallon cucumbers
6 cups water
2 cups white vinegar
½ cup pickling salt

Place a washed head of dill and a clove of garlic in 3-4 clean quart jars. Pack in cleaned cucumbers tightly. Combine water, vinegar and salt and bring to a boil, pour in jars leaving ¼-inch headspace. Put on caps and screw bands firmly tight. Process in a boiling water bath 15 minutes. Makes 3-4 quarts.

Dilled pickled okra

Okra, enough to fill 4 pint-size jars
5 heads green dill
5 hot peppers
3 cups water
3 cups white vinegar
¼ cup salt

Wash, drain and prick okra. Pack into clean pint jars. Place a head of dill and a pepper in each jar. Boil water, vinegar and salt together. Fill jars with boiling hot brine. Put on caps, screw bands firmly tight. Process in boiling water bath 5 minutes. Makes 5 pints.

Fig pickles

4 quarts firm-ripe figs
5 cups sugar
2 quarts water
3 cups white vinegar
1 tablespoon whole allspice
2 sticks cinnamon

Peel figs. (If unpeeled are preferred, pour boiling water over figs and let stand until cool, drain.) Add 3 cups sugar to water and cook until sugar dissolves. Add figs and cook slowly 30 minutes. Add remaining 2 cups sugar and vinegar. Tie spices in a cheesecloth bag, add to figs. Cook gently until figs are clear. Cover and let stand 12-24 hours in a cool place. Remove spice bag. Heat figs to simmering point, pack hot into hot jars, leaving ¼-inch headspace. Put on caps and screw bands firmly tight. Process 15 minutes in a boiling water bath. Makes about 8 pints.

Watermelon pickles

Take 5 lb watermelon rind, cut off and discard green rind and inner pink portion. Cut into 1-inch squares. Soak overnight in salt water (4 tablespoons salt to 1 quart water). Drain, cover with fresh water and simmer until rind can be pierced. Drain watermelon.

Make a syrup of 9 cups sugar, 4 cups cider vinegar, 2 cinnamon sticks and 1 tablespoon cloves (tie spices in cheesecloth bag). Heat syrup to boiling point, cover and steep 10-15 minutes. Add watermelon and cook until transparent.

Pack into hot jars, leaving ½-inch headspace. Put on caps, screw bands firmly tight. Process in boiling water bath 5 minutes. Makes about 6 pints.

Fresh fridge pickles

3 cups sugar
2 cups cider vinegar
⅓ cup salt
1 teaspoon celery seed
3 quarts sliced cucumbers (8-10)
2-3 small onions, sliced
1 green pepper, sliced
1 red pepper, sliced (optional)

Bring sugar, vinegar, salt and celery seed to a boil and allow to cool. Combine cucumbers, onions and peppers.

When liquid is cool, pour over cucumber mixture. Marinate in refrigerator at least 24 hours. Store in covered jars in the refrigerator. Makes 5 pints.

Pickled jalapeno peppers

15 whole jalapeno peppers
¾ cup vinegar
1 cup olive oil
1 clove garlic
⅛ teaspoon salt

Wash peppers and cut stems short. Heat vinegar, oil and garlic to a boil. Pack peppers tightly in clean, hot jars. Add salt and pour boiling hot mixture over peppers, leaving 1-inch headspace. Put on caps and screw bands firmly tight. Process in boiling water bath 10 minutes. Makes 1 pint.

Jill's ketchup (page 165)

Harlequin pepper relish

(photograph page 158)

If you can't find peppers in three different colors, the relish will still taste great — but won't look quite as dashing.

2 medium red peppers
2 medium green peppers
2 medium yellow peppers
2 medium white onions
¾ cup cider vinegar
1 cup water
¾ cup sugar
1 tablespoon salt
½ teaspoon freshly grated nutmeg

Remove seeds and ribs from peppers and cut flesh into small dice. Chop onions very finely. Place in a saucepan with cold water to cover and bring to a boil. Cook 30 seconds, then drain.

Combine vinegar, 1 cup water, sugar, salt and nutmeg in a saucepan and boil 10 minutes. Add drained vegetables and cook 5 minutes. Spoon into hot, clean jars. Put on caps, screw bands firmly tight and process in a boiling water bath for 10 minutes. Makes about 3 pints.

Corn relish

16-20 ears young, tender corn
1¼ cups chopped onion
1 cup chopped green pepper
1 cup chopped sweet red pepper
1 cup chopped celery
2⅔ cups white vinegar
2 cups water
1½ cups sugar
1½ tablespoons mustard seed
1 tablespoon salt
1 teaspoon celery seed
½ teaspoon turmeric

Peel husks and silk from corn. Boil corn 5 minutes, then quickly dip in cold water. Cut kernels from cobs. There should be 10 cups of cut corn. Combine corn with remaining ingredients in a large kettle. Simmer uncovered 20 minutes.

Pack into hot jars leaving ½-inch headspace. Put on caps, screw bands on firmly tight. Process in boiling water bath 15 minutes. Makes 6-7 pints.

Pear relish

1 gallon peeled ground pears (hard Keiffer pears are excellent)
8 cups ground onions
8 green peppers, chopped
2 hot red peppers, chopped
2 quarts white vinegar
2½ teaspoons salt
3 tablespoons dry mustard
6 teaspoons allspice
2 teaspoons cinnamon
2 teaspoons turmeric
4 cups sugar

Mix all ingredients in order given and bring to a boil in a large kettle. Simmer 15 minutes. Pack into hot, clean jars leaving ½-inch headspace. Put on caps, screw bands firmly tight. Process in boiling water bath, 5 minutes. Makes 10 pints.

Sweet red pepper relish

10-12 red peppers, seeded
1 tablespoon salt
2 cups white vinegar
3 cups white sugar

Grind peppers, soak in water to cover with salt at least 1 hour, drain. Place ground peppers, vinegar and sugar in a large saucepan and bring to a boil. Simmer uncovered for 2 hours or until thick. Pour into sterilized jars leaving ¼-inch headspace. Can be frozen or processed for 10 minutes in a boiling water bath. Makes about 6 (8 oz) jars.

Overleaf: Sun sets on the Texas heartlands

SWEET EATS

Everyone has a special fondness for desserts whatever the time of day or the occasion. Generally, the sweeter and richer the dessert, the better it is, so far as Texans are concerned.

Most popular Texas desserts are dominated by sugar and flour, perhaps because the pioneers kept huge supplies of those items on hand. Other seasonal fruits and berries were added for additional flavor and variety.

The German and Czech influence on Texas cuisine is nowhere more apparent than in desserts. For their part, the Mexicans contributed sugary-sweet candies and chocolate.

A favorite Texas dessert is pecan pie, made with native pecans that grow in 152 counties in the state. The pecan was named the state tree in 1906 after Governor James Hogg requested one be planted at his grave.

One of the most popular old Texas desserts is buttermilk pie. Despite any preconceived ideas you might have about buttermilk, this pie is worth a try. Originally this Texas classic was prepared when the pantry was bare and no fruits were in season.

Whatever dessert is your pleasure, the best ones are those that are happy endings to memorable meals. Just remember the secret of any good dessert — it should complement, not overpower, the meal.

Ice cream meringue cups (page 184)

Devil's mousse

One of the easiest recipes we know for chocolate mousse.

4 squares (4 oz) semi-sweet chocolate
1 tablespoon sugar
1 teaspoon vanilla
3 eggs, separated
¾ cup whipping cream, lightly whipped

Break chocolate into small pieces and place in the top of a double boiler or a small bowl set over simmering water. Add sugar, vanilla and egg yolks to chocolate, beat constantly until chocolate is melted and mixture thick. Leave to cool. Stir in cream, then fold in stiffly beaten egg whites. Spoon into mousse pots or pretty individual dishes and chill until set. Serves 5-6.

Note: The grated rind of an orange makes a pleasant change if added to the chocolate with the sugar and egg yolks.

Chocolate no-bake cake

A wonderfully easy recipe. Serve as a dessert with coffee.

½ lb vanilla wafers, crushed
½ cup chopped pecans or walnuts
1 cup (4 oz) chopped dried apricots
½ cup brown sugar
Juice and grated rind of 1 orange
1 tablespoon cocoa
½ cup shortening, melted
3 squares (3 oz) semi-sweet chocolate, melted
Extra grated chocolate and pecan or walnut halves to decorate

Combine cookie crumbs, nuts, apricots, sugar, orange juice and rind and cocoa in a large bowl. Pour shortening over and mix very thoroughly.

Grease a 8-inch round cake pan, then line base with a circle of aluminum foil and grease again. Place mixture in the pan, press down firmly using a flat-based glass. Chill for at least 1 hour.

Run a spatula around the edge of pan, turn out onto a sheet of wax paper.

Break chocolate into pieces and melt in a bowl set over simmering water. Spread chocolate over top and sides of cake and decorate with extra chocolate and pecan or walnut halves. Cut in thin wedges, and serve with coffee. Makes 24 wedges.

Pineapple Marsala

(photograph page 174)

2 large, ripe pineapples
1 lb black or green grapes, halved and seeded
2 large, ripe pears, peeled and cut into cubes
3 tablespoons lemon juice
3 tablespoons superfine sugar
¼ cup Marsala wine
12-16 walnut halves

Cut pineapples in half lengthways through green tops. Scoop out fruit with a sharp knife, remove core, and cut fruit in bite-size cubes. Toss with grapes, pears, lemon juice, sugar and Marsala. Cover and chill for 30 minutes. Fill back into pineapple shells and decorate with walnut halves. Serves 6-8.

The ultimate rice pudding

3 cups milk
¼-½ cup sugar
2 cups cooked rice
2-3 tablespoons butter
1 teaspoon vanilla

Combine milk, sugar, rice and butter in a saucepan and simmer until thick, 20-30 minutes. Remove from heat and stir in vanilla. Serves 4, or 2 rice pudding freaks.

Note: If you prefer, use only half the prescribed amount of sugar (¼ instead of ½ cup) and substitute half and half for milk. In case a rice pudding binge leads you to dieting, try the recipe with ¼ cup sugar or granulated sugar substitute and skim milk or skim evaporated milk. It's still super. It makes the best rice pudding for the least effort of any we've tried.

Dewberry cobbler

4 tablespoons butter or margarine

¾ cup sugar

¾ cup flour

2 teaspoons baking powder

Pinch salt

¾ cup milk

2-4 cups dewberries or blackberries, sweetened to taste

Preheat oven to 350°. Place butter in a 6-cup casserole and melt (not brown) in oven. Mix sugar, flour, baking powder and salt. Add milk to dry ingredients and blend thoroughly. Pour into casserole over butter. Add fruit. Do not stir. Bake about 1 hour or until cooked. Cover casserole with foil if top browns quickly. Serve with cream or ice cream. Serves 6.

Note: A (1 lb 5 oz) can of cherry or apple fruit filling can be substituted for berries.

Chocolate souffle with foamy brandy sauce

(photograph left)

An unusual souffle, made with whipped cream.

4 squares (4 oz) semi-sweet chocolate chopped

1 cup whipping cream, whipped with 3 tablespoons sugar

1 tablespoon brandy

3 egg yolks, beaten

4 egg whites

Powdered sugar and grated chocolate to decorate

For sauce:

¼ cup sugar

Pinch salt

1 tablespoon cornstarch

1 egg, beaten

3 tablespoons brandy

1 cup milk

1 cup whipping cream, whipped

Make sauce first. Combine sugar, salt, cornstarch, beaten egg and brandy in a bowl. Heat milk to boiling point, and whisk into cornstarch mixture. Return to saucepan and continue whisking over low heat until thickened. Cool, then chill. Just before serving, fold custard and whipped cream together.

To make souffle, place chopped chocolate, whipped cream and brandy in a bowl set over simmering water. Stir until chocolate melts. Remove from heat and cool for 1 minute. Add beaten egg yolks a little at a time, beating well after each addition. Beat egg whites until they hold soft peaks, carefully fold in.

Butter 4 individual souffle dishes and sprinkle with sugar. Divide the souffle mixture among them, filling each dish about ⅔rd full. Place in a preheated 375° oven and bake for 10 minutes or until well puffed and firm on top. Dredge with powdered sugar and sprinkle with grated chocolate. Serve at once with chilled sauce. Serves 4.

Queen of puddings

(photograph page 183)

A crumb custard is topped with jam, and then a "crown" of snowy meringue.

2 cups milk

2 tablespoons butter

2 teaspoons grated lemon rind

½ cup superfine sugar

1½ cups soft white breadcrumbs

3 eggs

3 tablespoons raspberry or other berry jam

Heat milk just to boiling point and stir in butter, lemon rind, and 2 tablespoons of the sugar. Pour this over the breadcrumbs and allow to stand 15 minutes.

Separate the eggs, beat yolks, and stir into breadcrumb mixture. Spoon into a greased 4-5 cup casserole or individual ovenproof dishes, bake in a preheated 350° oven for 15-30 minutes, or until set.

Remove from oven and spread jam over top of pudding. Whip egg whites until they hold firm peaks, beat in the remaining sugar little by little to form a stiff, glossy meringue.

Spread the meringue over pudding, swirling it into peaks on top. Return to oven for 10 minutes, or until tipped with gold. Serve warm or cold, plain or with cream. Serves 4-6.

Lemon delicious pudding

A wonderful dessert, sponge on top and a lemon custard sauce underneath.

2 tablespoons butter or margarine

¾ cup sugar

3 eggs

1 cup milk

2 tablespoons flour

⅓ cup lemon juice

Grated rind 1 lemon

Beat butter until soft, add sugar and combine thoroughly. Separate eggs and add yolks one at a time. Add milk, flour, lemon juice and rind. Beat to mix well. (Mixture will look curdled.) Beat egg whites until stiff and fold into batter. Pour into a 1½-quart baking dish and set in a pan of hot water that comes half way up sides of dish. Bake in a preheated 350° oven for 40-45 minutes (cover with foil if it browns quickly). Serve warm with whipped cream. Serves 4-6.

Apple Charlotte

There's a tart-sweet stewed apple filling layered between buttery, crisp crumbs. Brown sugar and cinnamon add the classic finishing touch.

4 large, tart apples (e.g. Granny Smith)
½ cup sugar
Grated rind and juice of 1 large lemon
6 tablespoons butter, softened
3 cups soft white breadcrumbs
½ cup brown sugar
2 teaspoons cinnamon

Peel and core apples and cut into thin slices. Place in a saucepan with sugar, lemon juice and rind. Stir over moderate heat until sugar dissolves, then cover tightly, lower heat and simmer until apples are tender. Allow to cool.

Grease a 9-inch pie plate generously with butter, press 1 cup of breadcrumbs around sides and base. Spoon in half the apples. Cover with another cup of crumbs and dot with small pieces of butter. Add remaining apple and top with remaining crumbs. Mix brown sugar and cinnamon together, sprinkle over crumbs, and dot with rest of butter.

Place in a preheated 350° oven and bake 40 minutes, or until crumbs on top and the dessert base are crisp and golden. Serve warm or cold, with cream or custard. Serves 6-8.

Rum sauce

½ cup unsalted butter
1 cup sugar
½ cup whipping cream
2 tablespoons rum
1 teaspoon vanilla
Pinch nutmeg

Combine butter, sugar and cream in a small saucepan, heat slowly and stir until sugar is dissolved. Add remaining ingredients and serve warm over ice cream, apple pie or crepes. Makes about 2 cups.

Note: Make ahead of time and keep warm in a double boiler.

Pineapple Marsala (page 172)

Bread pudding

(photograph page 178)

Some people remove the crusts from the bread, but we like the crispy edges!

4 slices homemade style bread
Butter for spreading
½ cup seedless raisins
2 tablespoons candied orange or lemon peel
2 eggs
1 cup milk
½ cup whipping cream
3 tablespoons sugar
Pinch salt
1 teaspoon vanilla
Freshly grated nutmeg
A little extra sugar

Butter the bread fairly generously, and cut into small squares.

Arrange half the bread in a buttered, 4-cup casserole or pie dish, and sprinkle with fruit and peel. Cover with remaining bread.

Beat eggs with the milk, cream, sugar, salt and vanilla and pour into the dish. Allow to soak for 30 minutes. Sprinkle with nutmeg and a little sugar and bake in a preheated 350° oven for 40 minutes, or until golden-brown and set. Serve warm, either by itself or with whiskey sauce or cream or both. Serves 4-6.

Note: Try substituting chopped pecans for candied orange or lemon peel.

Whiskey sauce

1½ cups milk
3 egg yolks, beaten
½ cup sugar
1 teaspoon vanilla
1 tablespoon cornstarch
¼ cup water
3 tablespoons whiskey

Scald milk. Combine egg yolks, sugar and vanilla in a small bowl. Pour a little of the hot milk over and mix thoroughly. Pour back into the saucepan with milk and stirring constantly, bring to simmering point. Mix cornstarch with water until smooth, add to pan. Continue to stir sauce until thickened, cook a further 1-2 minutes. Remove from heat. When cool, add whiskey. Makes about 2½ cups.

Hard sauce

Delicious served with plum pudding, warm fruit cake or mincemeat pie.

½ cup unsalted butter
1½ cups powdered sugar, sifted
3-4 tablespoons brandy or rum

Cream butter until white and fluffy, gradually beat in powdered sugar. Add brandy or rum little by little to suit your taste, beating well between each addition. Pile into a serving dish, cover, and chill until firm. Serves 8.

Brandy sauce

Serve with plum pudding, fig pudding or mincemeat pie.

1 cup milk
1 tablespoon sugar
Pinch salt
1 small piece cinnamon stick
1 tablespoon cornstarch mixed to a paste with a little extra milk
2-3 tablespoons brandy

Place milk, sugar, salt and cinnamon in a small saucepan and bring slowly to a boil, stirring.

Pour some of the hot milk onto the cornstarch paste, stirring until smooth. Return to the saucepan and simmer, stirring, until sauce is smooth and thickened. Remove from heat, take out cinnamon stick, stir in brandy to suit your taste. Serve hot. Makes 1¼ cups.

Custard sauce

1½ cups milk
2 eggs
Pinch salt
2 tablespoons sugar
2 teaspoons cornstarch
½ teaspoon vanilla

Heat 1 cup of the milk to just below boiling point. Meanwhile, beat eggs with remaining milk, salt, sugar and cornstarch.

Tip hot milk onto the eggs, beat thoroughly. Return to saucepan and continue beating with a hand-held rotary beater over very low heat until custard is thickened and increased in volume.

Remove from heat and beat in vanilla. Pour into a bowl, cover top with a circle of dampened wax paper (to prevent a skin forming) and allow to cool. Beat again before serving. Makes about 2 cups.

Note: The custard may also be served hot, or warm. Excellent with stewed or fresh fruits and fruit pies.

Pecan crepes

Crepes:
1 cup flour
Pinch salt
1 egg
1 egg yolk
1¼ cups milk
2 tablespoons cooking oil or melted unsalted butter
Unsalted butter or oil for cooking
Filling:
1 cup pecans
½ cup unsalted butter
⅓ cup sugar
Powdered sugar and warm fruit sauce to serve

To prepare crepes, sieve flour and salt into a mixing bowl. Make a well in center and drop in egg and egg yolk. Blend together gradually adding milk by degrees. Beat well until batter is smooth. Add oil or melted butter. Strain and allow to stand at least 30 minutes. Heat crepe pan and add a small piece of unsalted butter or oil. When hot, pour excess off. Add sufficient batter to cover base of pan thinly. Cook until crepe is "bubbly" on upper surface. Loosen edge of crepe with a palette knife and turn. Place finished crepes on a plate, separating each with a piece of wax paper.

Spread pecans in a single layer on a cookie sheet, roast them in a preheated 375° oven for about 5 minutes. Watch them, they burn easily. Cool and grind with a rotary hand grinder.

Cream butter and sugar together until light, fold in ground pecans. Spread some filling on each crepe and roll up. Place in a greased serving dish. Put crepes in a preheated 400° oven for about 5-6 minutes until heated through. Dust with powdered sugar. Serve with a warm fruit sauce of your choice (dried apricot, plum, strawberry, blueberry, etc.). Serves 6-8.

Strawberry layer butter cake

1 cup margarine
1 lb powdered sugar
4 eggs, separated
2 teaspoons vanilla
3 cups sifted cake flour or 2½ cups all-purpose flour
2 teaspoons baking powder
Pinch salt
1 cup milk
Sweetened whipped cream and fresh strawberries

Have ingredients at room temperature. Cream margarine and sugar until fluffy. Add egg yolks and vanilla. Beat until smooth. Add sifted flour, baking powder and salt alternately with milk. Fold in stiffly beaten egg whites. Spread evenly in 2 (9-inch) round cake pans which have been greased, then lined with greased wax paper. Bake in a preheated 350° oven about 25 minutes. Cool in pans 10 minutes. Turn out on a wire rack to cool completely. Remove wax paper. Fill and top with sweetened whipped cream and fresh strawberries. Serves 6-8.

Apricot liqueur cake

(photograph right)

1 layer butter cake, (use Strawberry layer butter cake recipe, ½ quantity)
1 (16 oz) can apricot halves
3 tablespoons apricot jam
¼ cup apricot brandy

Place cake on a baking sheet. Drain the apricots, and reduce syrup to half its volume by boiling rapidly in a small saucepan. Stir in jam, strain mixture into a bowl and stir in the apricot brandy.

Spoon half the syrup over the cake. Arrange apricot halves on top, rounded sides up. Spoon rest of syrup over apricots. Place in a preheated 350° oven and bake for 5 minutes, or until cake is heated through. Serve with custard, whipped cream or ice cream. Serves 6.

Apricot souffle

1¼ cups dried apricots
2 cups water
2 pieces lemon rind
1¼ cups milk
3 eggs
½ cup sugar
1 envelope unflavored gelatin
Juice of ½ lemon and water to make ¼ cup
⅔ cup whipping cream
Pinch salt
Extra ⅔ cup water
Extra ½ cup sugar
Chopped pecans and whipped cream to decorate

Soak dried apricots in the water overnight. Stew gently in soaking liquid with lemon rind. When tender, puree in a blender or food processor, cool.

Prepare a 4-cup souffle dish by tying a collar of doubled aluminum foil or wax paper around outside of dish to extend about 2-inches above the rim.

Scald milk. Cream egg yolks with sugar, pour on the milk, blend, return to pan. Stirring constantly, thicken over moderate heat without boiling, strain and cool. Dissolve gelatin in combined lemon juice and water, add to custard. Measure ½ cup of apricot puree. Lightly whip cream and add apricot puree. Whip egg whites with pinch of salt in a separate bowl until stiff. Cool custard and when on the point of setting, fold in apricot cream and stiffly beaten egg whites. Pour at once into prepared souffle dish and chill.

Make a syrup with extra water and sugar. Thin remaining apricot puree with sugar syrup, cool and chill. Pour into jug.

To serve, remove collar from dish, decorate dessert with chopped pecans and whipped cream, pass sauce separately. Serves 6.

Food editor's favorite pastry pie crust

2 cups flour
1 teaspoon salt
¾ cup shortening
½ cup ice water

Mix flour and salt. Cut in shortening with pastry blender and add ice water. Blend until dough cleans bowl and is no longer sticky. Divide equally. Roll out each crust on floured board, 1-inch larger than 9-inch pan. Line pan with the pie crust.

To bake unfilled, prick bottom of crust with fork tines and bake in a preheated 450° oven for 10-12 minutes.

Baked or unbaked crusts freeze well. Makes 2 (9-inch) crusts.

Buttermilk pecan pie

(photograph page 180)

This recipe was reprinted from the Corpus Christi Junior League cookbook, "Fiesta". Buttermilk pecan pie was a family recipe often prepared by a career U.S. Navy chef for such dignitaries as the late President Harry S. Truman. Through the years of his military career, the chef refused to share his recipe. Finally, when he retired he allowed it to be published in a Navy newspaper.

½ cup butter
2 cups sugar
2 teaspoons vanilla
3 eggs
3 tablespoons flour
¼ teaspoon salt
1 cup buttermilk
½ cup chopped pecans
1 (9-inch) unbaked pastry pie crust

Cream butter and sugar until light and fluffy, adding sugar gradually. Blend in vanilla. Add eggs, one at a time. Combine flour and salt, add a small amount at a time. Add buttermilk. Sprinkle pecans in bottom of unbaked pie crust, pour filling over. Bake pie in a preheated 300° oven for 1½ hours. Best served at room temperature. Serves 6-8.

Bread pudding (page 175)

Pumpkin praline pie

¾ cup brown sugar, firmly packed
1 tablespoon flour
½ teaspoon salt
2½ teaspoons pumpkin pie spice or 1½ teaspoons cinnamon and ½ teaspoon each allspice, cloves and ginger
1 (16 oz) can pumpkin
1⅓ cups evaporated milk
1 egg, slightly beaten
1 (9-inch) unbaked pastry pie crust

Praline topping:

½ cup chopped pecans or walnuts
1 tablespoon shortening
2 tablespoons brown sugar
1½ teaspoons grated orange rind
1 tablespoon flour

Mix sugar, flour, salt and pumpkin pie spice and blend well. Stir in pumpkin, then add milk and egg, stir until smooth. Pour into unbaked pie crust. Bake in a preheated 375° oven for 30 minutes.

Meanwhile, mix praline topping ingredients until mixture is crumbly. Add praline topping to top of pie in a ring about 2-inches in from edge. Bake an additional 15 minutes or until knife inserted in middle of pie comes out clean. When cool, serve with mound of whipped cream in center of praline ring. Serves 6-8.

Banana cream pie

(photograph page 180)

2 cups milk
½ cup light corn syrup
4 tablespoons cornstarch
½ cup sugar
¼ teaspoon salt
3 egg yolks
1 teaspoon vanilla
1 (9-inch) baked pastry pie crust
2 medium bananas

Scald 1¾ cups of the milk and syrup in top of double boiler. Mix cornstarch and remaining milk. Add sugar, salt and egg yolks to cornstarch. Gradually stir cornstarch mixture into milk in top of double boiler and cook until thick, about 7 minutes.

Remove from heat and stir in vanilla. Cool. Cover pie crust with sliced bananas. Spoon filling over.

To serve, top with whipped cream or make a meringue from remaining egg whites and 5 tablespoons sugar. Mound on top of pie filling and bake in a preheated 350° oven for 10 minutes to color meringue. Serves 6-8.

Note: This is our standard cream pie recipe and the basis for many delicious variations. For coconut cream pie, omit bananas and stir ¾ cup flaked coconut into pie filling. Make meringue of egg whites and sugar and sprinkle with more coconut before baking if desired. Bake as banana cream pie.

Clockwise: *Texas cream pie* (top left; recipe below), *banana cream pie* (page 179), *buttermilk pecan pie* (page 179) *and chocolate angel pie* (below)

Texas cream pie

(photograph above)

¾ cup sugar

½ teaspoon salt

⅓ cup flour

3 tablespoons cocoa

1¾ cups milk

2 eggs, separated

1 tablespoon margarine

1 teaspoon vanilla

1 (9-inch) baked pastry pie crust

Whipped cream and chocolate curls to decorate

Mix sugar, salt, flour and cocoa. Add milk, beaten egg yolks and margarine. Cook over medium heat, stirring constantly until thickened. Add vanilla. Beat egg whites until stiff, but not dry, and fold into custard mixture. Pour into baked pie crust. Cool. Top with whipped cream and chocolate curls. Serves 6-8.

Lemon chess pie

Chess pie is a Southern tradition, but when you want to splurge or impress company, it's the thing to serve.
Omit the lemon juice and cornmeal in this recipe and you have another delicious version.

½ cup butter or margarine

2 cups sugar

6 eggs

½ cup lemon juice

2 tablespoons cornmeal

1 (9-inch) unbaked pastry pie crust

Cream butter and sugar together. Beat in eggs, lemon juice and cornmeal. Pour into unbaked pie crust. Bake in a preheated 400° oven for 15 minutes, reduce heat to 350° and continue baking for an additional 30 minutes or until pie is cooked and lightly browned. Serves 6-8.

Chocolate angel pie

(photograph above)

2 egg whites, at room temperature

⅛ teaspoon salt

⅛ teaspoon cream of tartar

½ cup sugar

½ cup coarsely chopped walnuts

½ teaspoon vanilla

Chocolate cream filling:

1 (4 oz) package German's sweet chocolate

3 tablespoons water

1 teaspoon vanilla

1 cup whipping cream, whipped

Beat egg whites with salt and cream of tartar until foamy. Add the sugar gradually, beating until very stiff peaks hold. Fold in the nuts and vanilla. Spread in a greased 8-inch pie pan. Build the sides up ½-inch above the pan. Bake in a preheated 300° oven for 50-55 minutes.

Meanwhile, melt chocolate in water over low heat, stirring constantly. Cool until thickened. Add the vanilla and fold mixture into the whipped cream. Pile into cooled meringue shell. Chill 2 hours. Serve with a dollop of whipped cream or chocolate sauce if desired. Serves 6-8.

Note: 1 (8 oz) carton frozen whipped topping may be substituted for cream.

Pecan tassies

Crust:

1 (3 oz) package cream cheese, softened

½ cup butter or margarine

1 cup flour

Pecan filling:

1 egg

¾ cup brown sugar, firmly packed

1 tablespoon butter or margarine, softened

1 teaspoon vanilla

¼ teaspoon salt

¾ cup chopped pecans

Cream cheese and margarine together, blend in flour. Roll into a ball. Wrap and chill 1 hour or overnight. Divide pastry into 2 dozen 1-inch balls. Place in 1¾-inch muffin cups and with fingers, press pastry on base and sides of cups to line each evenly.

To make pecan filling, beat egg, add sugar and mix well. Add butter, vanilla, salt and chopped pecans. Put 1 tablespoon of mixture in each pastry-

lined muffin cup. Bake in a preheated 325° oven for 25 minutes. Cool, remove from cups. Makes 2 dozen.

Note: These freeze well.

Coffee angel pie

This requires a double boiler and a quick, steady hand pouring the sugar syrup into the egg white, but the recipe is really easy. The results, we know you'll agree, are absolutely divine. Serve when you want to impress company.

Chocolate cookie crumb crust:

1⅓ cups chocolate cookie wafer crumbs, about 20 cookies

2 tablespoons sugar

¼ teaspoon cinnamon

5 tablespoons melted butter

½ cup finely chopped blanched almonds

1 quart coffee ice cream

Topping:

⅔ cup sugar

⅓ cup water

2 egg whites

½ cup whipping cream

2 teaspoons cocoa

⅛ teaspoon salt

¼ cup chopped blanched almonds, toasted

Chocolate curls to decorate

Mix crumbs, sugar and cinnamon in a small bowl. Stir in butter and almonds. Press crumb mixture firmly and evenly against bottom and sides of a 9-inch pie pan, building up crumb mixture slightly around the rim. Chill in freezer. Spoon softened coffee ice cream into crust and return to freezer.

Combine sugar and water in a 1-quart saucepan. Bring to a boil and cook rapidly until syrup spins a thread (about 7 minutes or 232° on candy thermometer). While syrup is cooking, beat egg whites until stiff, but not dry. While beating at high speed, gradually pour syrup over egg whites in thin, steady stream. Continue beating until mixture holds shape. Chill.

Combine cream, cocoa and salt in a chilled bowl and whip until stiff. Carefully fold whipped cream and toasted almonds into chilled meringue, only until blended. Mound onto ice cream filling. Decorate with chocolate curls. Return to freezer for several hours until firm. Serves 8.

Our favorite cheesecake pie

This is our favorite because it produces the best results with the least effort and ingredients.

2 (8 oz) packages cream cheese, at room temperature

3 eggs

1 (14 oz) can sweetened condensed milk

1 (10-inch) graham cracker crust, bought or homemade

Topping:

1 cup sour cream

3 tablespoons sugar

½ cup well drained crushed pineapple

Beat cheese, blend in eggs and add condensed milk. Pour into crust. Bake in a preheated 300° oven for 25 minutes. Meanwhile, combine topping ingredients.

Remove cheesecake from oven and very carefully spread on topping. Return to oven for an additional 10 minutes. Cool, then chill for several hours. Serves 6-8.

Miniature cheesecakes

1 (3 oz) package cream cheese

½ cup butter or margarine

1 cup flour

Filling:

12 oz cream cheese

4 tablespoons sugar

2 eggs

2 teaspoons vanilla

Sour cream

Raspberry or cherry jam or drained crushed pineapple

Have ingredients at room temperature. Cream the cheese and butter together until smooth. Blend in flour. Divide into 24 small balls and put in 24 small muffin cups. Press pastry on base and sides with the fingers to line each cup evenly.

Blend all filling ingredients, except sour cream and jam, until smooth. Spoon into pastry-lined muffin cups and bake in a preheated 350° oven for 20 minutes. Cool. Spread with a little sour cream and top with a dab of raspberry or cherry jam or drained, crushed pineapple. Makes 2 dozen.

Avocado ice cream

Delicately flavored, prettily colored, and so easy to make!

1 (1 quart) carton vanilla ice cream

2 medium, ripe avocados

3 tablespoons honey

3 tablespoons lemon juice

Chopped avocados to decorate (optional)

Allow ice cream to soften at room temperature. Peel and seed the avocados and mash the flesh with honey and lemon juice. Combine quickly but thoroughly with ice cream, return to freezer until firm, about 3 hours.

Serve in scoops or squares, and if desired decorate with avocado. Serves 6-8.

Homemade vanilla ice cream

2 cups milk or half and half

1 teaspoon vanilla (or 2-inch piece of vanilla bean)

6 egg yolks, beaten

1 cup sugar

½ teaspoon salt

2 cups whipping cream

Scald milk in saucepan. If using vanilla bean, split lengthways and add to milk. Beat egg yolks in another saucepan, add sugar and salt, mix well. Stir in half the hot milk. Mix well. Add remaining milk. Stirring continuously, cook over very low heat until custard coats the back of the spoon. Don't allow it to boil as custard will curdle. When thickened, remove from heat and set immediately in pan of cold water. Stir until cool.

If vanilla bean is not used, add vanilla flavoring and whipping cream. If bean is used, remove, wash, dry and save for further use. Strain custard into bowl and chill, overnight if possible. Pour into half-gallon or larger hand-cranked or electric freezer. Freeze according to manufacturer's directions. Remove paddle. Seal lid by gently coating edge with melted butter. Cover freezer well and let ice cream ripen for a minimum of 2 hours. Serves 12-16.

Coffee liqueur cheesecake

An absolutely superb cheesecake!

For crust:

½ lb graham crackers

½ cup butter

For filling:

3 (8 oz) packages cream cheese, softened

⅔ cup superfine sugar

1 (8 oz) carton sour cream

4 eggs

1 egg white

1 teaspoon vanilla

2 tablespoons cornstarch

3 tablespoons coffee liqueur

Whipped cream and strawberries or grated chocolate to decorate

Crush the crackers finely. Melt butter and mix with crumbs. Spread over bottom and sides of a 9-inch spring form pan and press firmly. Refrigerate while making the filling. Beat cream cheese and sugar together until smooth, then beat in sour cream, eggs, extra egg white, vanilla and cornstarch. Pour half of the mixture into the crumb crust. Add coffee liqueur to remaining mixture and spoon into crust.

Place cheesecake on a baking sheet and bake in a preheated 300° oven for 1 hour. Turn heat off and allow cheesecake to cool in oven with the door closed. Serve topped with whipped cream and strawberries or grated chocolate. Serves 10-12.

Coconut ice cream

(photograph above)

½ cup flaked coconut

3 egg yolks

3 tablespoons superfine sugar

¾ cup whipping cream

2 tablespoons coconut

Toast coconut in a dry frying pan over medium heat, stirring constantly, until light brown. Combine egg yolks and sugar, beat until fluffy. Whip cream until stiff. Combine egg mixture with cream, liqueur and nearly all the coconut. Mix thoroughly, then pour into a 3½-cup mold and freeze 4-5 hours. To unmold ice cream, dip mold in hot water briefly and invert onto a serving dish. Sprinkle with remaining toasted coconut. Serves 6.

Queen of puddings (page 173)

Jade fruits with rum ice cream

(photograph above)

2 crisp eating apples, such as Granny Smith
3 tablespoons lemon juice
4 ripe kiwi fruit
3 tablespoons sugar
1 (1 pint) carton vanilla ice cream
3 tablespoons rum

Peel apples, cut into matchstick-size strips (julienne) and sprinkle with lemon juice. Peel and slice kiwi fruit, combine with apples and sprinkle with sugar. Chill until serving time.

Meanwhile, place ice cream in a bowl, allow to soften slightly at room temperature, quickly stir rum through. Freeze until firm.

Serve fruit in pretty bowls, topped with scoops of ice cream. Serves 4.

Ice cream meringue cups

(photograph page 170)

Ice cream and delectable almond-topped meringue in crisp pastry shells.

For pastry:

1¼ cups flour
Pinch salt
½ cup butter, firm but not hard
3 tablespoons ground almonds
1 tablespoon sugar
1 egg yolk
2-3 tablespoons ice water

For filling and topping:

3 eggs whites
⅓ cup superfine sugar
10 scoops very firm vanilla ice cream
2 tablespoons toasted slivered almonds

Sift flour and salt into a bowl, rub in butter lightly with fingertips. Add ground almonds and sugar, mix together. Blend egg yolk and water, add to ingredients in bowl, cutting in with a knife. Form pastry into ball. Wrap in plastic wrap and chill for 30 minutes. Divide pastry into 10 pieces. Using floured thumbs, press pastry against sides and base of 10 tartlet pans. Bake in a preheated 400° oven for 10 minutes or until golden. Allow to cool in pans. Preheat oven to 500°. Beat egg whites until peaks firm, then beat in sugar a little at a time to form a stiff, glossy meringue. Place a scoop of ice cream in each almond cup, then cover completely with meringue, making sure it touches edges of pastry all round. Sprinkle with almonds.

Bake in oven for 2-3 minutes, or until meringue is lightly tinted. Serve immediately. Serves 10.

Peachy buttermilk ice cream

A refreshing end to any meal — and it's made in no time.

1½ lb fresh peaches (about 5 medium), pitted and sliced

1 cup sugar

2 cups buttermilk

2 tablespoons lime or lemon juice

Puree peaches in blender or food processor. You should have 3 cups. Add sugar, buttermilk and lime juice and blend until smooth. Pour into hand-cranked or electric freezer. Freeze according to manufacturer's directions. Remove paddle. Seal. Cover freezer and allow ice cream to ripen. Serves 12-16.

Pumpkin flan

Something a little different from the usual pumpkin pie.

Caramel:

⅔ cup sugar

⅓ cup water

Pumpkin custard:

2 eggs, lightly beaten

1 cup evaporated milk

1 (16 oz) can pumpkin

¾ cup sugar

1 teaspoon salt

½ teaspoon ginger

1 teaspoon cinnamon

¼ teaspoon nutmeg

2 tablespoons melted butter

Prepare caramel by heating sugar and water together in a small pan over low heat until sugar is completely dissolved. Bring to a boil and without stirring, boil until golden brown (once it starts to turn color, it burns easily, so watch carefully). Pour caramel into a 9-inch ceramic or ovenproof glass pie plate. Twist around to coat base and sides.

Combine custard ingredients and pour over caramel. Place pie plate in a large baking dish containing 1-inch of warm water. Cook in a preheated 350° oven for 30-40 minutes or until knife comes out clean. Cool, chill and unmold to serve. Serve with whipped cream. Serves 6.

Overleaf: Cheerleaders' exhuberant performance at a Dallas football game.

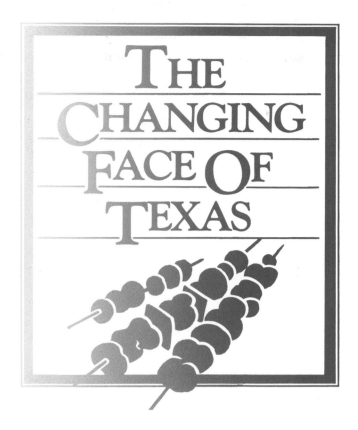

THE CHANGING FACE OF TEXAS

Texans take great pride in the fact their state is a melting pot of cultures. First there were the Indians, French and Mexican settlers, and finally pioneers from throughout the United States and Europe. In recent years, immigrants from Asian countries have been welcomed to Texas.

From this wealth of cultures came the foods for which Texas is famous. Whether everyday or special occasion, historians agree, cooking styles are one of the most important and interesting parts of any culture.

While the main influence on Texas' eating habits is Mexican, and to a lesser degree German and Southern, other international cuisines are appearing. Where it was nearly impossible to find Greek souvlaki, beef teriyaki and Italian zabaglione a few years ago, those international favorites are now available nearly everywhere.

Think of a food or ingredient and you can buy it in Texas, from filo dough to Italian mushrooms. Huge supermarkets and small shops alike offer such previously unknown specialities as kiwi fruit, orange roughy, basil, puff pastry, couscous, fettuccine and egg roll wrappers. And no self-respecting Texas market would be without Mexican cheese, cilantro and fresh poblano peppers.

Dining out is no longer a matter of choosing from steaks, German or Mexican food. If you are in the mood for Oriental cuisine, choose between Thai, Szechwan, Cantonese, Japanese, Vietnamese, Korean or Filipino. If Italian food is your speciality, select from northern, southern or Bolognese-style cooking.

In Texas cities, the cuisine of the world is within reach. Texas cooks, being inventive as they are, are now experimenting with these foreign favorites and adding them to their flour-dusted recipe boxes. In the process of broadening their repertoire, they are incorporating that Texas touch and creating what will eventually become the new Texas classics.

Little rum and raisin tarts (page 203)

Layered terrine

This attractive terrine reveals its layers of meat dotted with juniper berries, white chicken breast and green spinach when sliced, and makes a superb first course for a special meal or a delicious main course with salads.

3 lb finely ground top round steak

1½ lb finely ground pork

1½ lb finely ground veal

1 teaspoon ground coriander

2 teaspoons ground allspice

2 teaspoons thyme

1½ teaspoons salt

1 teaspoon pepper

1 tablespoon juniper berries

8 eggs

1 cup dry vermouth

½ cup brandy

2 bunches spinach — green leaves only — cooked and drained

4 cloves garlic, crushed

3 whole chicken breasts, deboned, skinned and flattened with a meat mallet

6 slices lean bacon

3 bay leaves

Combine ground meats with coriander, allspice, thyme, salt, pepper, juniper berries, 6 of the eggs, vermouth and brandy. Press half of the mixture into the base of a 5-quart deep ovenproof casserole. Chop the cooked and well drained spinach, add crushed garlic and remaining 2 eggs and spread over ground meat layer. Arrange chicken breasts over spinach layer, then top with remaining layer of ground meat. Place slices of bacon over the top, then the bay leaves, and cover with a lid. Stand casserole in a pan of cold water and bake in a preheated 225° oven for 4 hours. Remove casserole from pan of water, allow to cool, refrigerate for at least 6 hours before serving. Serves 10-12.

Note: Check food import shops or specialty stores for juniper berries.

Chicken-sherry soup
(photograph above)

A superb, delicate, creamy soup.

1 lb chicken pieces

5 cups water

1 small onion stuck with 2 cloves

6 peppercorns

Salt

½ cup whipping cream

2 egg yolks, beaten

3 tablespoons medium sherry

Finely chopped parsley to garnish

Place chicken pieces, water, onion, peppercorns and salt to taste in a saucepan and bring to a boil. Lower heat, cover and simmer for 45-60 minutes. Strain broth and reserve. Pick meat from chicken bones, cut into small cubes.

Return broth to saucepan with chicken meat and bring to a boil. Whisk together cream, egg yolks and sherry. Remove saucepan from heat and whisk in cream mixture. Serve at once in heated bowls and sprinkle with chopped parsley. Serves 4-6.

Dutch pea and ham soup

1 lb green or yellow split peas

1 ham bone

10 cups water

1 large onion, sliced

2 cloves garlic, crushed

1 large carrot, chopped

2 ribs celery, sliced

White pepper to taste

Wash peas and soak overnight in cold water. Next day, drain, and place in a large pan with ham bone, 10 cups water, and remaining ingredients. Bring to a boil, lower heat then cover and simmer 3 hours, stirring occasionally to stop peas sticking to the bottom of the saucepan.

Remove bone from soup, take off the meat, and cut into small pieces. If you want a smooth texture, puree soup in a food processor or blender. If you like a coarse texture, leave it as it is. Return meat to the soup, reheat, and ladle into heated bowls. If desired, float a few croutons (small pieces of fried bread) in each bowl. Serves 8.

Salad superb (page 194)

Vichyssoise

Served chilled, it makes a first course for a dinner party. Served hot with crusty bread and a tossed salad, it's a satisfying lunch.

4 tablespoons butter
2 leeks, washed and trimmed and sliced into rings
1 medium onion, chopped
4 cups chicken broth
1 large potato, peeled and sliced
1 tablespoon chopped parsley
Salt and white pepper
1 cup whipping cream
Finely chopped chives to garnish

Melt butter in a heavy saucepan. Add leeks and onion and fry very gently with the lid on for 10 minutes. Do not brown. Add chicken broth, potato and parsley, bring to a boil, and simmer covered for 30 minutes. Remove from heat and cool. Puree soup in a blender or push through a sieve. Reheat and adjust seasoning with salt and pepper. Cool, then chill thoroughly. Just before serving, stir in cream. Serve chilled, in individual soup bowls, sprinkled with finely chopped chives, mint, parsley or mixed herbs. Serves 4-6.

Note: Vichyssoise can be served hot or cold depending upon the season. Make it the day before for chilling in the refrigerator.

Chestnut soup

Unsweetened cooked chestnuts bought in vacuum-packed jars can be substituted for fresh chestnuts.

1 lb fresh chestnuts
2 tablespoons olive oil
2 medium carrots, coarsely chopped
2 leeks, cleaned and chopped
2 ribs celery, chopped
1 large onion, chopped
6 cups chicken stock or broth
8 sprigs parsley
3 whole cloves
½ teaspoon salt
½ cup coffee cream
3 tablespoons brandy
Salt and freshly ground pepper
Finely chopped parsley to garnish

Make a small slit in the bottom of each chestnut with a sharp knife. Cover chestnuts with boiling water, and simmer 30-40 minutes, until soft. Drain, peel off the skins when cool enough to handle. Heat oil in a heavy saucepan and brown the carrots, leeks, celery and onion for 5 minutes. Add the chestnuts, chicken stock, parsley, cloves and salt and simmer until vegetables are very soft. Remove cloves. Rub the soup through a fine sieve, or puree in a blender or food processor, return to pan. Add the cream and brandy. Adjust the seasoning, and heat just to boiling point. Serve in warmed soup bowls and garnish with chopped parsley. Serves 6.

Paradise salad

1 (4-5 lb) duck, roasted (see below)
1 lb green beans, trimmed and cut in 2-inch lengths
2 red peppers, cut in narrow strips
1 mango, peeled and cut in small pieces
½ cup macadamia or cashew nuts
14 canned lychees, cut in half
3 tablespoons lemon juice
½-¾ cup walnut or olive oil (or a mixture)
Salt and freshly ground pepper
3 tablespoons chopped parsley

To roast duck: Wipe duck with a damp cloth and sprinkle inside and out with salt and pepper. Prick skin on the thighs and breast with a skewer to allow fat to drain during cooking. Truss bird, place on a rack in a roasting pan and roast for 2 hours or until tender in a preheated 350° oven. Remove fat from pan as it accumulates. Take duck from the oven and discard trussing strings. Return to oven for 10 minutes. Take out and allow to cool. Cut duck into neat joints.

The salad: Drop beans into boiling water and simmer uncovered for 4 minutes after they return to a boil. Drain, and run quickly under cold water. Set aside to cool and drain thoroughly. Drop red pepper strips into boiling water and when water returns to boil, drain and run under cold water. Set aside to cool and drain thoroughly. Combine beans, peppers, mango, nuts and other ingredients in a bowl and toss and blend well. Arrange pieces of duck on a serving plate and garnish with the salad. Serves 4-5.

Note: This salad is best prepared as soon as possible before serving, and should be eaten at room temperature, not chilled.

Salad nicoise

(photograph right)

There are several versions of this robust salad, but essential ingredients are olives and anchovies, with a garlic-flavored dressing.

1 Romaine lettuce
2 medium tomatoes, sliced
½ small green pepper, sliced
1 onion, sliced and separated into rings
8-10 black olives
1 (2oz) can anchovy filets, drained
2 hard-boiled eggs, sliced
For dressing:
2 tablespoons wine vinegar
6 tablespoons olive oil
1 fat clove garlic, crushed
Salt and freshly ground pepper

Line a salad bowl with lettuce leaves, arrange salad ingredients over the top. Combine dressing ingredients by shaking in a screwtop jar, and spoon over salad when ready to serve. Serves 4-6.

Yakitori

Chicken pieces and green onions are marinated, then grilled, in this classic Japanese dish. It is usually served as a first course or snack.

1 (2½ lb) chicken
10 large green onions
¾ cup light soy sauce
¼ cup sugar
⅓ cup dry sherry
Cayenne pepper

Disjoint chicken, remove meat from bones and cut into 1-inch pieces. Cut green onions into 1-inch sections. Arrange pieces of chicken on skewers, with 2 or 3 pieces of green onion between. Warm together soy sauce, sugar and sherry, pour over skewered chicken and green onions and leave for 10-15 minutes.

Grill slowly until tender, turning skewers and brushing frequently with the sauce. Serve sprinkled lightly with cayenne pepper. Serves 4.

Chicken with mint

Serve this popular Vietnamese dish as an appetizer.

2 chicken drumsticks and thighs, steamed until tender
1 small onion
White vinegar to cover
⅓ cup finely chopped mint leaves
¼ teaspoon salt
Freshly ground black pepper to taste

Remove chicken meat from bones and discard bones. Slice chicken into shreds, put aside. Slice the onion into paper-thin rings, place onion in a bowl and cover with vinegar. Stand for 10-15 minutes.

Place shredded chicken in a bowl and mix thoroughly with chopped mint, salt and pepper, stirring until salt has dissolved. Strain vinegar from onions and rinse onions quickly in cold water. Add onions to the chicken mixture, stir, and serve. Serves 4.

Potatoes Anna

A French way of turning sliced potatoes into a crisp, delicious potato cake.

2 lb medium-size potatoes
¾ cup butter
Salt and freshly ground black pepper

Peel potatoes and slice them as thinly as possible. Thickly butter a 9-inch heavy iron skillet, line the sides and bottom with potato slices placed close together and firmly attached to the butter. Sprinkle lightly with salt and pepper and dot with butter. Cover with another layer of potatoes, and salt, pepper and butter, and so on until potatoes are used up. Cover with buttered paper. Cook in a preheated 375° oven for 45 minutes or until tender when pierced with a pointed knife. Run a knife around the potatoes and invert onto a heated plate. Let stand a few minutes to settle. The inside should be soft and the crust crisp and golden. Cut into wedges and serve with meat, fish or poultry. Serves 6.

Curry puffs

2 tablespoons cooking oil

2 cloves garlic, crushed

3 teaspoons curry powder

2 medium onions, chopped

1 lb lean ground beef, chicken or pork

1 large potato, grated

1 cup beef or chicken bouillon made from cubes, or 1 cup canned unsweetened coconut milk

Salt

1 (1 lb 1 oz) package frozen puff pastry

1 egg, beaten

Heat oil in a heavy pan. Add garlic and curry powder and blend. Add the onions and ground meat, stir over moderate heat until meat changes color, about 5 minutes. Add the potato and mix together, stir in bouillon and salt to taste. Cover, reduce heat, and simmer 10-15 minutes or until mixture thickens, but is still moist. Set aside and allow to cool.

Roll out pastry thinly on a floured surface and cut into 3-inch squares. Place a portion of curried meat in the center of each square of pastry, fold over corner to corner to form triangles, sealing the edges with beaten egg. Brush tops of triangles with beaten egg and bake in a preheated 375° oven for 15-20 minutes, or until pastry is puffed and browned. Makes 20-30 puffs.

Note: Chopped seedless raisins can be sprinkled into the curried meat mixture to give a sweeter flavor if desired.

Salad superb

(photograph page 191)

*When you want to impress a luncheon guest, serve this sumptuous salad.
It's expensive — but worth it!*

Squeeze of lemon juice

½ ripe avocado, peeled and cut into wedges

1 Romaine lettuce, or ½ firm head of lettuce

4 cooked asparagus spears, cut into short lengths

½ chicken breast, cooked and cut into julienne pieces

¼ lb cooked, peeled shrimp

Salt and freshly ground white pepper

2 oz sliced smoked salmon

2 oz black caviar

¼ cup mayonnaise

3 tablespoons sour cream

Celery leaves to garnish

Squeeze a little lemon juice over the avocado. Make a bed of lettuce leaves on a serving plate, arrange avocado, asparagus, chicken and shrimp over it. Season with salt and pepper. Arrange salmon slices overlapping on top, forming a cup shape, and spoon caviar into the middle.

Combine mayonnaise and sour cream. Spoon some over the salad, and serve remainder separately. Garnish salad with celery leaves. Serves 2.

Italian eggplant parmigiana

1 large eggplant

Salt and pepper to taste

1-1½ cups fine dry breadcrumbs

2-3 eggs, lightly beaten

Cooking oil, preferably olive oil

1½ cups tomato sauce, heated

8 oz sliced Mozzarella cheese

1 teaspoon basil

¼ cup grated Parmesan cheese

Wash eggplant and cut crossways into rounds ¼-inch thick. Do not peel. Season with salt and pepper. Dip into breadcrumbs, dip into egg and then again into breadcrumbs. (Depending on size of the eggplant, more breadcrumbs and egg may be necessary.) Refrigerate 30 minutes. Heat about ⅛-inch of oil in a skillet. Fry eggplant slices until tender and golden on both sides. Add more oil when necessary. Drain on paper towels. Line a buttered shallow baking dish with some of the sauce. Arrange a layer of eggplant slices over the sauce. Cover with a layer of Mozzarella slices, more sauce and a sprinkling of basil and Parmesan. Repeat layers until the dish is full. Bake in a preheated 350° oven for 25-30 minutes. Serves 6.

Pesto Genovese

This famous Italian green sauce is eaten with pasta or gnocchi. It is a dish for the summer, when fresh basil is available, and it cannot be made with dried basil.

3 cloves garlic, chopped

1 cup firmly packed fresh basil leaves

3 tablespoons pine nuts

½ cup grated Parmesan cheese

1 cup (approximately) olive oil

Freshly ground black pepper

In a blender or food processor fitted with a steel blade process together garlic, basil, pine nuts and cheese. With machine running, gradually add the oil. Only add enough oil to make a smooth, thick sauce. Stir in freshly ground pepper.

Note: This amount of sauce makes enough for 1 lb pasta.

Chinese pancake rolls (page 196)

Chinese pancake rolls
(photograph page 195)

Light, tender pancakes wrapped around a spicy pork filling are just right for almost any occasion — a first course, a main course with rice and vegetables, a super luncheon snack.

| 2 eggs |
| ¾ cup flour |
| 1 cup milk |
| ½ teaspoon salt |
| 3 tablespoons melted butter |

For filling:

| ½ lb finely ground pork |
| 2 tablespoons cooking oil |
| 2 tablespoons soy sauce |
| Salt and freshly ground pepper |
| 1 teaspoon sugar |
| 1 tablespoon dry sherry |
| Pinch Chinese 5 spice powder |
| 3 cups finely shredded white cabbage |
| ½ cup finely chopped green onions |

To brush rolls:

| 1 tablespoon cooking oil mixed with 2 teaspoons soy sauce |

Beat eggs, then mix in flour, half a cup of the milk, and salt. Beat for 2 minutes, stir in melted butter, then gradually beat in remaining milk.

Heat a greased crepe pan or small frying pan, and pour in enough batter to form a thin layer over bottom of the pan — about 1½ tablespoons. Cook pancakes on the underside only until golden. (The top should be set by this time, and not "runny".)

Stack pancakes with sheets of wax paper between them. When all are cooked, place a heaped tablespoon of filling in the center of each, tuck in the ends, and roll up.

Arrange rolls in a greased baking dish and brush tops with oil-soy mixture. Bake in a preheated 400° oven for 6-8 minutes, or until piping hot. Serves 6.

Filling: Fry ground pork in hot oil until brown, stirring to get rid of any lumps. Add remaining ingredients and continue cooking until cabbage is tender but still firm. Allow to cool, and taste for seasoning before filling pancakes.

Note: For a variation, try chopped shrimp or finely chopped ham instead of pork — or try a mixture of all three.

Zucchini special

This is a particularly delicious way to prepare zucchini. Serve it hot as a vegetable with meat, poultry or fish, or cold as a salad, alone or in company with others on a buffet.

| 2 lb zucchini, coarsely grated on a hand grater or in a food processor |
| Salt |
| 4 tablespoons cooking oil |
| ½ teaspoon sugar |
| 1 tablespoon lemon juice |
| 1 tablespoon each chopped fresh parsley and basil, marjoram or thyme |
| Freshly ground black pepper |
| Extra chopped parsley and herbs |

Put grated zucchini in a strainer over a bowl and sprinkle with salt. Leave for 1 hour or longer to allow moisture to drain off. Squeeze excess moisture out before cooking and pat with paper towels so zucchini is as dry as possible.

Heat oil in a heavy pan and cook zucchini with the sugar over moderate heat, stirring until tender, but not too soft. This will only take a minute or two. Add lemon juice and raise heat a little. Sprinkle with herbs and toss well. Spoon into a serving dish, grind black pepper over, and sprinkle with extra parsley and herbs. Serves 4-6

Noodles with fennel and shrimp

This is one of our favorite recipes — as pretty as it's delicious.

| 1 lb green or white fettucine (ribbon noodles) or better still, a mixture of both colors |
| 1 bulb fennel, trimmed |
| 2 cloves garlic, crushed |
| Salt and freshly ground pepper |
| 16 large raw shrimp in shells |
| 6 tablespoons butter |
| ½ cup freshly grated Parmesan cheese |
| ½ cup finely chopped parsley |

Bring a large saucepan of lightly salted water to a boil. Add fettucine, the whole bulb of fennel, and garlic.

Cook rapidly for 8 minutes, or until fettucine is tender but still firm. Drain.

Place fettucine in a heated bowl. Cut fennel into thin slices and mix through the fettucine. Season with salt and freshly ground pepper. Meanwhile, peel and devein the shrimp. Heat butter in a heavy frying pan and cook shrimp over medium heat until they turn pink, about 4 minutes.

Arrange shrimp over the fettucine and fennel, and pour the buttery pan juices over. Sprinkle with cheese and parsley and serve at once. Serves 4.

Plum sauce

Many Chinese dishes are served with plum sauce for dipping. Here's a short-cut way to make your own.

| 2 tablespoons butter |
| 4 green onions, finely chopped |
| 1 clove garlic, crushed |
| 1 teaspoon finely chopped fresh ginger |
| ¾ cup plum jam |
| 1 tablespoon soy sauce |
| 1 tablespoon brown sugar |
| Salt and freshly ground pepper |

Heat butter in a saucepan and gently fry green onions, garlic and ginger until very soft, about 6 minutes. Stir in remaining ingredients, seasoning to taste with salt and pepper. (You may also like to add a little extra vinegar or sugar, depending on the sweetness of the jam.) Simmer for 3 minutes, then push through a fine sieve. Serve hot or cold. This sauce keeps well in a screwtop jar in the refrigerator.

Surfer's buttery scallops

Quick cooking keeps scallops tender and juicy. This dish is literally tossed together in minutes. If you have a chafing dish, you might like to cook it at the table.

| 1 lb bay scallops |
| ½ teaspoon salt |
| ½ teaspoon curry powder |
| 1 small onion, grated |
| 1 clove garlic, crushed |
| 6 tablespoons butter |
| 3 tablespoons fresh lime or lemon juice |
| 3 tablespoons finely chopped parsley |
| Lime or lemon wedges to garnish |

Pat scallops dry with paper towels. Combine salt, curry powder, onion and garlic, sprinkle over scallops, and toss lightly. Cover and allow to stand 15 minutes. Heat butter in a heavy frying pan, add scallops, and toss over moderately high heat for 3 minutes, or until scallops are just tender.

Sprinkle lemon juice and parsley over and stir gently to combine. Serve at once, garnished with lime or lemon wedges. Good with rice. Serves 4.

Crisp-skin ginger fish

Double frying gives fish a really crunchy surface. It's a method the Chinese have perfected, and not too difficult to manage at home.

| 4 medium-size whole trout |
| 2 teaspoons finely chopped fresh ginger |
| 1 tablespoon salt |
| ¼ teaspoon Chinese 5-spice powder |
| Flour |
| Cooking oil |
| 1½ tablespoons light sesame oil |
| Finely shredded green onions to garnish |

Make sure fish are thoroughly cleaned and scaled. Make 3 diagonal slashes through the skin on each side of fish.

Mix together ginger, salt and 5-spice powder and brush over inside and outside of fish. Cover, and leave for several hours.

Dip fish on both sides in flour, gently shake off excess. Leave another 15 minutes to dry out.

Heat enough oil in a deep fryer or heavy saucepan to cover fish completely. Lower fish into hot oil in a frying basket, fry until golden and crisp, about 4 minutes. Remove and drain on paper towels. (You will probably need to cook fish in 2 batches.)

Reheat oil, fry again for 3 minutes, or until brown and very crisp. Drain well, arrange on a hot platter, sprinkle with sesame oil and shredded green onions. Serve with rice. Serves 4.

Note: Light sesame oil is available at Oriental food stores. If you can't find it, use ordinary oil flavored with a little extra grated ginger.

Cinnamon chops with prunes

| 4 tablespoons butter |
| 6 pork loin chops |
| Salt and freshly ground pepper |
| 2 medium onions, thinly sliced |
| ¾ cup red wine |
| ⅔ cup water |
| 12 soft prunes, pitted |
| 1 cinnamon stick about 1½-inches long |
| 3 strips lemon rind |

Heat butter in a large frying pan and brown chops on both sides. Remove chops from pan, sprinkle with salt and pepper and set aside. Add onion slices to pan and cook gently until softened. Replace chops and add wine, water, prunes, cinnamon stick and lemon rind. Bring to a boil, reduce heat and cover with a tight fitting lid. Simmer 45 minutes, or until chops are tender. Remove cinnamon stick before serving. Serves 6.

Pork sates with peanut sauce

| 1 lb boneless lean pork |
| 2 macadamia nuts, grated |
| 1 teaspoon trassi (fish sauce) |
| 3 tablespoons sweet soy sauce |
| 3 tablespoons cooking oil |
| 1 clove garlic, crushed |

Cut pork into ½-inch cubes. Mix with remaining ingredients, cover, and marinate for 2 hours. Thread meat onto small bamboo skewers (soaked in water to prevent charring) and grill on both sides until brown and cooked through. Serve with peanut sauce. Serves 4.

Note: Trassi and sweet soy sauce are available at Oriental food stores. If you can't get trassi locally, use 1 teaspoon anchovy paste instead. If you can't get sweet soy sauce, use ordinary soy and add 2 teaspoons sugar to the marinade.

Peanut sauce

| ¾ cup water |
| 6 tablespoons peanut butter |
| 1 clove garlic, crushed |
| ¾ teaspoon salt |
| 2 teaspoons brown sugar |
| 1 tablespoon sweet soy sauce |
| 1 tablespoon tamarind juice or lemon juice |
| ½ teaspoon sambal ulek or pinch chili powder |

Mix water and peanut butter in a small saucepan and bring to a boil. Remove from heat and stir in remaining ingredients. Taste, and add extra salt, sugar or lemon juice to suit your own preference. Serve warm, as a dip for sates, or over freshly cooked vegetables.

Party beef curry

(photograph right)

An easily-prepared curry that cooks in the oven, leaving you free to do other things.

| 1½ lb round steak |
| 3 tablespoons cooking oil or clarified butter |
| 2 large onions, finely chopped |
| 2 cloves garlic, chopped |
| 2 teaspoons finely chopped fresh ginger |
| 1½ tablespoons curry powder |
| 1 teaspoon salt |
| 1 large tomato, peeled and chopped |
| 1½ cups beef stock or bouillon |

Trim any fat from steak, and cut meat into 1-inch cubes. Heat oil, brown the meat on all sides over fairly high heat, then transfer to a casserole. Add onions, garlic and ginger to the same pan and cook 2-3 minutes. Stir in curry powder and cook another minute or two. Add salt, chopped tomato and stock and bring to a boil, stirring. Taste for seasoning and pour over meat. Cover the casserole and cook in a preheated 350° oven for 1½ hours, or until very tender. Serves 4-6.

Indonesian meatballs and rice

(photograph page 200)

These subtly-flavored little meatballs are served with rice as a main course. As an appetizer, you can spear them on toothpicks and serve with mild chili sauce for dipping.

| 4 tablespoons butter |
| 1 small onion, finely chopped |
| 1 teaspoon ground cumin |
| 1 teaspoon ground coriander |
| ½ teaspoon ground allspice |
| ½ teaspoon ground ginger |
| 2 teaspoons cornstarch |
| 1 egg, beaten |
| Salt and freshly ground pepper |
| 1 lb ground beef or pork |
| **For rice:** |
| 4 tablespoons butter |
| 3 small peppers (if possible, green, red, yellow) cut into small cubes |
| 4 cups cooked rice (1½ cups uncooked) |
| 1 (11 oz) can mandarin segments, drained |
| Salt and freshly ground pepper |

Heat 2 tablespoons of the butter in a frying pan and fry onion until soft. Add spices and cook for a minute, stirring. Allow to cool, mix with cornstarch, egg, salt and pepper and ground beef. Shape into walnut-size balls, and fry in remaining 2 tablespoons of butter until brown all over and cooked through, about 6 minutes. Serve in a ring of savory rice. Serves 4.

Rice: Heat butter, and toss peppers over moderate heat until starting to soften. Add rice, and stir until piping hot. Fold in mandarins, and season with salt and pepper.

Arni souvlakia

A traditional Greek dish of lamb kebabs flavored with lemon and oregano and served with steamed rice and Greek salad.

| 1 shoulder of lamb, boned |
| Salt and freshly ground pepper |
| 4 tablespoons olive oil |
| 3 tablespoons lemon juice |
| 2 tablespoons chopped fresh oregano or 2 teaspoons dried |

Remove excess fat from lamb. Cut meat into 1-inch cubes and put into a bowl. Sprinkle with salt and pepper, then add oil, lemon juice and oregano. Stir and set aside for 30 minutes or more.

Thread pieces of meat onto skewers and grill until tender, brushing with the herb mixture. Serves 4-5.

Note: Greek salad is a mixture of tomato slices, onion rings, thick slices of cucumber, black olives and cubes of salty Feta cheese. It is tossed with a dressing of olive oil and lemon juice seasoned with salt and black pepper, and served by itself or on a bed of tender lettuce leaves.

Chicken Piraeus

A lovely chicken dish from Greece, flavored with cinnamon, wine and orange juice.

| 1 (3½-4 lb) chicken, quartered |
| Salt and freshly ground pepper |
| 2 teaspoons cinnamon |
| 3 tablespoons lemon juice |
| 4 tablespoons olive oil |
| ¾ cup orange juice |
| ¾ cup chicken broth |
| 1 lb zucchini, unpeeled and cut into sticks |
| Extra 2 tablespoons olive oil |
| 1 clove garlic, crushed |
| 3 oranges, peeled and sliced |

Rub pieces of chicken with salt, pepper, cinnamon and lemon juice. Cover and allow to stand for 30 minutes.

Heat oil in a large, deep frying pan and brown pieces of chicken on all sides. Add orange juice and broth to the pan, cover, and simmer until chicken is almost tender, about 35 minutes.

Meanwhile, fry zucchini quickly in extra oil until golden brown. Season with salt, pepper and garlic and add to chicken with orange slices. Simmer another 5 minutes, or until chicken is quite tender.

Remove chicken, zucchini and orange to a heated platter. Reduce liquid in pan to sauce consistency by rapid boiling. Taste for seasoning, spoon over chicken, and serve piping hot with rice. Serves 4.

Vietnamese curry

1 tablespoon dried lemon grass

1½ tablespoons curry powder

Freshly ground black pepper

1 teaspoon sugar

1 tablespoon salt

1 large chicken cut into 10 pieces,
with breast cut into 4.

½ cup cooking oil

3 small sweet potatoes or
3 potatoes,
peeled and cut into 2-inch cubes

4 cloves garlic, chopped

1 large onion, cut in wedges and
separated into "petals"

3 bay leaves

2 cups water

1 large carrot cut into ½-inch slices

2 cups canned unsweetened
coconut milk

Extra 1 cup water

Soak lemon grass in water for 2 hours,
drain, and chop finely. Combine curry
powder, pepper, sugar and salt and rub
into the chicken pieces. Leave to absorb
flavors for 1 hour.

Heat oil and fry potatoes over high
heat until well browned but not cooked,
about 5 minutes. Set aside. Pour off most
of the oil, leaving 2 tablespoons. Fry garlic a few seconds, add onion, bay leaves
and lemon grass, toss for a minute.

Add chicken, stir-frying until meat is
slightly seared. Add 2 cups water and
carrot. Cover and bring to a boil, turn
down heat and simmer 5 minutes. Take
off lid and stir, cook covered another 10
minutes. Remove lid and add browned
potatoes, coconut milk and extra water.
Simmer covered for another 15 minutes
or until chicken and vegetables are tender.
Serve with noodles or rice. Serves 8.

Stuffed chicken breasts in Marsala

*This is a very special dish for a
dinner party — a little bit fiddly to
prepare, but that's no drawback to
the cook who likes to serve
something different.*

8 half chicken breasts, boneless

Flour seasoned with salt and pepper

8 thin slices ham

8 thin slices Swiss cheese

8 cooked asparagus spears

6 tablespoons butter

½ cup Marsala wine

¼ cup chicken stock or broth

Finely chopped green onions
to garnish

Place chicken breasts between sheets of
plastic wrap and flatten with a rolling

pin. Dip in seasoned flour and shake off excess. Place a slice of ham on each chicken breast, then a slice of cheese. Place an asparagus spear in the middle. Roll chicken up neatly, tucking in the ends, and tie in place with string.

Heat butter in a large, heavy frying pan and slowly brown the chicken rolls on all sides. This will take 8-10 minutes altogether. Remove rolls and keep warm. Add Marsala and stock to pan. Bring to a boil, stirring to get up the brown bits from the bottom, and simmer until reduced a little. Taste for seasoning.

Untie string from rolls, arrange on a heated platter, and spoon sauce over. Sprinkle with finely chopped green onions to serve. Serves 6-8.

Tandoori murg

Serve this Indian chicken on a bed of salad made up of sliced onion, tomato, cucumber and radish rings. Garnish chicken with fresh limes and coriander. Crisp fried poppadums and rice are appropriate accompaniments.

| 2 (3 lb) chickens, cut into serving pieces |
| 1 teaspoon saffron threads or turmeric |
| ½ teaspoon red food coloring |
| 3 teaspoons salt |
| 1½ teaspoons coriander seeds |
| 1 teaspoon cumin seeds |
| 2 teaspoons finely chopped fresh ginger |
| 2 cloves garlic, crushed |
| ¼ cup lemon juice |
| 1 (8 oz) carton plain yogurt |

Place chicken pieces in a large bowl. Combine remaining ingredients and pour over chicken, turning pieces until well coated. Cover and refrigerate for at least 12 hours. Place chicken on a rack in a large baking dish, and spoon any remaining marinade over. Bake in a preheated 350° oven for 45 minutes-1 hour or until tender. Baste often with juices that collect in pan. (If necessary add a little water to the pan to prevent scorching.) Serves 8.

Indonesian meatballs and rice (page 198)

Chinese braised duck

| 1 (4 lb) duck |
| Neck and giblets from duck |
| 3 tablespoons medium sherry |
| 3 tablespoons soy sauce |
| 1 teaspoon sugar |
| 1 teaspoon salt |
| Freshly ground pepper |
| 3 tablespoons cooking oil |
| 1 clove garlic, crushed |
| 2 cups duck stock |
| ¾ cup sliced celery |
| ¼ lb mushrooms, cut in thick slices |
| 6 green onions, cut into short sections, including green tops |
| 3 tablespoons cornstarch mixed to a paste with a little water |
| Extra green onions to garnish |

Remove excess fat from duck and wipe inside with a damp cloth. Make stock with giblets and neck simmered in 2 cups of water for 30 minutes. Combine sherry, soy sauce, sugar, salt and pepper.

Brown duck all over in oil, in a large, deep pan. Pour oil from pan, add sherry mixture and garlic to duck and cook for 2 minutes. Add stock, cover pan and cook gently 1¼ hours. Add the celery, mushrooms and green onions. Replace lid and continue cooking gently for 30 minutes or until very tender.

Remove duck, cut into pieces, put on a serving platter and keep hot. Add cornstarch mixture to liquid in pan. Stir until boiling, simmer a minute or two and pour over duck. Garnish with extra green onions, shredded and scattered over duck. Serves 4.

Zabaglione

| 6 egg yolks, at room temperature |
| 6 tablespoons superfine sugar |
| Juice ½ medium-size lemon |
| ¾ cup Marsala or sweet white wine |
| Crushed toasted nuts to decorate |

Put egg yolks into a mixing bowl with the sugar and beat until combined. Place bowl over a saucepan of simmering water, without letting water touch the bowl, and beat until thick.

Gradually add lemon juice, beating constantly, then beat in the wine. Continue beating until mixture is thick and creamy. Pour into individual glass or crystal dishes, sprinkle with crushed toasted hazelnuts or almonds. Serve warm, with a plate of small cookies. Serves 4-6

Baklava

(photograph page 202)

This is one of the best known Middle Eastern pastries and a great Greek favorite.

| 1 cup melted, unsalted butter |
| 1 (1 lb) package filo pastry |
| 2 cups pistachio nuts or walnuts, coarsely chopped |
| 1 cup almonds, coarsely chopped |
| 3 tablespoons sugar |
| **For syrup:** |
| 1 cup sugar |
| ½ cup water |
| 1 tablespoon lemon juice |
| 3 tablespoons honey |
| 2-inch cinnamon stick |
| 3 whole cloves |
| Thin strip lemon rind |

Make the syrup first: Place all ingredients in a saucepan, stir over medium heat until sugar dissolves. Simmer until thick enough to coat a spoon. Strain, cool, and chill for 30 minutes.

Take an oblong cake pan, approximately 13 x 9 x 2-inches, and grease bottom and sides with a pastry brush dipped in melted butter. Fit half the pastry sheets one at a time in the pan, brushing each one with melted butter and overlapping or folding the sides to fit where needed. Mix chopped nuts and sugar together and spread evenly over pastry in the pan. Cover with the remaining sheets, brushing each sheet with butter and also the top layer.

With a sharp knife, cut through top layers of filo diagonally, to make diamond shapes. Bake baklava for 30 minutes in a preheated 350° oven then raise heat to 400° and bake another 15 minutes or until puffed and golden brown.

Remove from oven and spoon cold syrup over the hot pastry. Allow to cool. When cold and ready to serve, cut into diamond-shaped pieces, following the outlines on pastry.

Baklava (page 201)

Little rum and raisin tarts

(photograph page 188)

For pastry:

1⅔ cups flour

½ teaspoon salt

1 tablespoon sugar (optional)

½ cup plus 1 tablespoon
unsalted butter, cold

1 egg yolk

2 tablespoons ice water

For filling:

8 oz Ricotta cheese

3 tablespoons dark rum

1 tablespoon whipping cream

1 tablespoon powdered sugar

½ cup chopped seedless raisins

Whipped cream to decorate

Put dry ingredients into food processor or a bowl. Cut in butter until fine. Add egg yolk and water and process only until pastry comes together in a ball. If mixing by hand, mix egg and water in with a spoon and knead slightly to thoroughly mix pastry. Chill pastry in wax paper for 30 minutes.

Place pastry between two sheets of lightly floured plastic wrap or wax paper and roll out thinly. Using a floured cutter, or the rim of a glass, cut into circles to fit greased tartlet pans about 3-inches in diameter. Prick all over with a fork and bake in a preheated 350° oven for 10-12 minutes, or until lightly browned and crisp.

Remove from oven, allow to cool for a minute or two in the pans, then gently remove to a wire rack to finish cooling. When ready to serve, add a generous spoonful of filling and top with whipped cream. Makes about 18 tarts.

For filling: Beat cheese until creamy, then beat in rum, cream and sugar. Fold in raisins and chill until ready to fill tarts.

Mulled wine

*A good hot drink for your
winter parties.*

½ cup sugar

1½ cups water

Grated rind ½ lemon

6 whole cloves

1 cinnamon stick, about 1½-inches

1 (25 fl oz) bottle Texas red wine

¾ cup brandy

Freshly grated nutmeg

Put sugar, water, lemon rind, cloves and cinnamon in a saucepan, bring to a boil, stir until sugar has dissolved.

Reduce heat and simmer gently for 10 minutes, strain. Stir in the wine and brandy and gently reheat, but do not boil. Pour into heated mugs and serve topped with a sprinkling of nutmeg. Serves 6.

Strawberry punch

*Perfect for special events such as
weddings, christenings,
anniversaries and important parties.*

1 quart strawberries, sliced

½ cup Grand Marnier liqueur

2 (25 fl oz) bottles rose wine, chilled

1 (25 fl oz) bottle champagne

Orange and lemon slices to decorate

Combine strawberries and Grand Marnier and steep for 2-3 hours. Place in a punch bowl with chilled rose. Just before serving, add chilled champagne and float orange and lemon slices on top. Serves 12.

Rose punch

*A pink and beautiful party
punch flavored with strawberries,
spice and peaches.*

½ cup Texas rose wine

½ cup sugar

Pinch each nutmeg, cinnamon and
ground cloves

½ cup fresh orange juice

1 pint strawberries

2 fresh ripe peaches

2 (25 fl oz) bottles Texas sparkling
white wine, chilled

Put rose wine into a saucepan with sugar and spices and gently heat, stirring until sugar has dissolved. Stir in orange juice, and allow to cool.

Wash and hull strawberries (halve them if large) and peel and dice peaches. Add these to the rose mixture and chill thoroughly. To serve, pour over ice cubes in a punch bowl and add the sparkling wine. Makes about 15 punch-size servings.

The dramatic canyon country of The Panhandle.

ELIZABETH GERMAINE

Elizabeth Germaine is a cookery consultant, cookbook editor and author.

She was born in Australia but has lived with her husband and two daughters in the United States for many years.

Elizabeth trained at Invergowrie Homecraft Hostel in Melbourne, Australia, and completed an advanced course in French and Italian cooking at Cordon Bleu in London. She returned to Australia and, over the next few years, had a variety of jobs, all food related. Elizabeth ran a restaurant at a ski resort for two years and was Household Manager at Women's College, Sydney University, for three years.

As Cookbook Editor for the Paul Hamlyn Publishing Company (Australia), Elizabeth wrote four cookbooks. She also wrote cookery articles for a nationally distributed monthly women's magazine.

ANN CRISWELL

Ann Criswell is a third generation Texan and has been food editor of the Houston Chronicle since the inception of the food section in 1966.

Having lived in three areas of the State, she has become fascinated with the diversity of Texas food and the various influences of Texas under six flags — Spanish and Indian, French, Mexican, Southern, Western and American — and, to a lesser extent, German, Chinese, Greek, and Scandinavian. The influx of Vietnamese and other Asian peoples, and the reborn Texas wine industry, continue to change the face of Texas cooking.

Ann has written freelance food articles, authored two cookbooks, and edited several others. Her interest in wines has led to several wine tours through Europe and California. She has judged Texas wine competitions and cooking contests such as the National Beef Cook-Off, National Chicken Cooking Contest, and America's Bake-Off. She is a member of the Newspaper Food Editors and Writers Association, the Houston Culinary Guild and Chaine des Rotisseurs.

Picture Credits
The publishers wish to thank **Texas Highways** for permission to reproduce the photographs which appear on the following pages:
2-3, 6-7, 10, 12, 16-17, 25, 29, 30, 31, 35, 36, 38-9, 40-1, 43, 45, 49, 52, 58-9, 66, 69, 75, 78, 80, 82, 86-7, 93, 94, 99, 100-101, 104, 106, 109, 117, 119, 126, 127, 130, 133, 136, 137, 138-9, 140-1, 146, 149, 150-1, 156, 160, 164, 173, 175, 179, 181, 192, 194, 196, 198.
Photographs have also been supplied by the following:
Marc Bennett. Endsheets, 8-9.
Bill Ellzey. 14-15, 20-21, 88, 98, 122-3, 168-9, 185, 204-205.
Image Bank. 111
Woodfin Camp & Associates. 18-19, 84-5, 186-7.

Index

Page numbers in *italics* refer to photographs of recipes.